Minds, Markets, and Money

Minds, Markets, and Money

PSYCHOLOGICAL FOUNDATIONS
OF ECONOMIC BEHAVIOR

Shlomo Maital

Basic Books, Inc., Publishers   New York

Library of Congress Cataloging in Publication Data

Maital, Shlomo.
  Minds, markets, and money.

  Includes bibliographical references and index.
  1. Economics—Psychological aspects.   I.   Title.
HB74.P8M34   330'.01'9   81–68410
ISBN 0–465–04623–1   AACR2

To My Mother and Father,

Sally and Morris Malt

CONTENTS

ACKNOWLEDGMENTS

THE gestation period for elephants is two years. Books often take longer, even pint-size books like this one. Only the support of my family, friends, and colleagues enabled me to complete it.

My wife Sharone, a school psychologist, supplied sources and ideas and helped me shape them into print. When the book and the piles of materials from which it sprang intruded on time and space rightfully hers, she offered words of praise and encouragement rather than complaint. She is as much my coauthor of this work as she is of our son Ronen and our daughter Temira, who surrendered their father to his typewriter for an unconscionably long time. Instead of griping, they cheered for each completed chapter and urged me on to the next. Without their love, I would have been forever stranded on chapter 1.

My editor and publisher, Martin Kessler, had a far clearer concept of this book, from the outset, than I did. Despite my best efforts, he kept me from straying from it. If there is a Max Perkins in nonfiction, it is Martin. I am also grateful to Kathleen C. Antrim and Maureen Bischoff for superlative copy editing.

Among those whose ideas I begged, borrowed, and stole are Julian Simon, Noah Meltz, Jay Schmiedeskamp, Randy Filer, Steve Plaut, Uwe Reinhardt, Harvey Leibenstein, Jerome Stein, and Benjamin Bental. My thoughts for this book took shape during a three-year stay at the Woodrow Wilson School of Public and International Affairs, Princeton University, for which I am indebted to Donald Stokes and Charles Berry. While at Princeton, I taught three groups of Sloan Fellows in Economic Journalism. The questions these journalists asked were far better than my answers and stimulated much of this book. I especially want to

ACKNOWLEDGMENTS

mention Linda Ellis, Harry Gould, Craig Stock, Mike Norman, Brian O'Reilly, David Treadwell, Clara Hemphill, and Ken Berents. I also want to thank J. C. O., who taught me the nobility of people and of the words that describe them.

I am deeply grateful to three countries. Canada, country of my birth, welcomed my father and mother from Bessarabia, fairly rewarded their hard work, and helped educate me. The United States generously provided resources to support my doctoral studies at Princeton University. And above all, Israel, my adopted country, taught me courage, strength, laughter, and love.

Technion, *Haifa, Israel, July 1981*

PART I

Economic Man as Child

1

WHAT IS IT WORTH?
WHAT MUST I GIVE UP?

ECONOMISTS are like police officers and armies. They are most successful when their services are needed least. By that criterion economics has not been doing too well lately. More than at any time since the Great Depression, economic news seizes space and attention on the front pages of newspapers and on television screens. Domestic policy matches or overshadows foreign policy in election campaigns. And ordinary people spend much more time thinking about their own financial well-being and the country's— along with, of course, the experts—than they did, for example, in the 1960s. The results of this preoccupation have been anxiety, concern, and more than a little confusion.

If Americans have trouble making sense of what they read, hear, and see about the economy, they are in good company. So do the experts. In the last decade the economic world has been literally turned upside down. Markets behave perversely. Prices jump erratically. Causal arrows reverse direction. Eternal truths become falsehoods. And forecasters run for cover and hope for better days.

Here are just a few examples:[1]

- Once, high interest rates were *de*flationary. By making consumer borrowing more expensive and investment funds harder to get, the Federal Reserve System would tug interest rates up to cool the economy; or it would drag interest rates down to stimulate it. If anything, the reverse is true today. Higher interest rates now contribute to inflation, at least in the short run.
- Conventional economic wisdom once believed that higher taxes slowed inflation by soaking up purchasing power and cutting demand. The American people now believe that higher taxes cause inflation. So do sizable groups of economists.
- A whisper of higher inflation used to send the Dow-Jones stock average up, when common stock served as a hedge against uncommon inflation. Inflation now drives stock prices down.
- More money used to mean *lower,* not higher, interest rates. Now, when *New York Times* reporters write that the money supply rose by more than expected during a given period, they often add that as a result interest rates *rose* (and bond prices fell).[2]
- When prices rise, it means people agree to pay more for something than they paid for it before. This happens when there are fewer goods available at existing prices than people want to buy (excess *demand* for goods). When men and women are out of work, it means that people would be unlikely to buy the goods and service that the jobless could produce if they were employed. This is consistent with the idea that there are more goods available than people want to buy (excess *supply* of goods). At present we have both high inflation and high unemployment—that is, market situations that imply both excess demand for goods and excess supply of them. The past decade, moreover, has seen inflation and unemployment rise together, a phenomenon known as stagflation. In the 1950s and 1960s inflation and unemployment moved in opposite directions. Why do they seem to march in step now?

Conventional economics can explain each of the preceding topsy-turvy propositions, if they are taken separately. As a whole, however, they and other puzzling phenomena demand more than patchwork alibis. New perspectives are needed.

Despite the above, let me emphasize that this is *not* primarily a book about what is wrong with economics. Economists do indeed have much to be modest about, as Henry Wallich, a member of the Federal Reserve Board of Governors, recently said. Many pens have been put to paper to point out why. Many axes have been wielded to round off the awkward corners of economics. In this literature some much-needed gaps have been filled.

It *is* a book about what can be *right* about economics if it strikes out in a new direction. That direction is psychology, the science of behavior. Economics tries to understand markets; markets are comprised of people. It stands to reason that improving our basic insight into people can deepen our understanding of markets. The rest of this book develops this idea. I will try to show how the concepts and methods of psychology beautifully complement and strengthen those of economics.

That psychology underlies markets, and thus economics, is an obvious truth. *How* psychology affects economic behavior is, however, as subtle and complex as human nature itself. Comte once said, "It is for the heart to suggest our problems; it is for the intellect to solve them."[3] If our intellect is to solve our economic problems, it must first look into the ways of the heart. There, I shall argue, is often where the problem lies.

People and Prices

The Battle of Waterloo shaped the course of history for decades or even centuries. The financial coup Nathan Mayer Rothschild effected immediately following the battle had much less sweeping consequences. But it does introduce and illustrate nicely the interplay of heart and intellect. Besides, it is a good story.[4]

Tuesday, June 20, 1815—the mood at the London Stock Exchange was somber. Here and there, deals were struck and consols (government bonds) changed hands at 30 percent below their par value. But everyone's thoughts lay elsewhere, across the Channel in Belgium. Napoleon, the wily scourge of Europe, had returned from Elba and had massed one hundred thousand men. Two armies totaling twice that number faced him—the Anglo-Dutch forces led by the Duke of Wellington and Marshal Blucher's Prussians. In London rumors flew that Marshal Ney's cavalry had defeated Blucher at Ligny. Could Wellington alone stem the tide?

That morning Nathan Rothschild, leaning against his accustomed pillar, took up his usual post on the exchange floor. His arrival drew great interest. The third son of Mayer Amschel Rothschild, founder of the banking dynasty, Nathan Rothschild had left his home in Frankfurt at the turn of the century to make his own fortune in England. With typical decisiveness he came to his decision on a Tuesday, and left on Thursday.

Soon after Rothschild's arrival in London, Napoleon invaded Germany. Convinced of England's fundamental soundness, Rothschild bought large amounts of the Duke of Wellington's bills. This seemed like folly to many as Napoleon swept through Europe and only the choppy waves of the Channel appeared to keep him off English soil. But Rothschild had faith. He had not grown wealthy by chance. His loans were backed by an extensive information-gathering network. He had an army of private messengers. He even had a costly system of getting mail from the Continent by carrier pigeon.

So when Nathan Mayer Rothschild appeared on the London Stock Exchange floor, all eyes were on him. Was Wellington's Dutch-Belgian division fleeing in disarray? Did Europe belong to Napoleon? If anyone knew for sure, Rothschild did.

And he did know. He knew that the previous Sunday, June 18, Marshal Ney had thrown a dozen cavalry charges at Wellington's well-positioned troops, set in tight British squares on the reverse sides of hillsides safe from Napoleon's cannon. The line held. That evening Prussian reinforcements arrived and threw the French back. Even Napoleon's Imperial Guard crumbled. Wellington had won. Some ninety thousand men were dead or wounded. Rothschild's speedy pigeons had brought him word. Government couriers had not yet arrived.

The economics of consol prices on June 20, 1815, with news of Napoleon's defeat impending, was straightforward. When word arrived, bond prices would rise. If you knew the news before others, you would buy consols when they were cheap. Later, you would sell them when they were dear. Wasn't that the prescription for financial success—buy low, sell high? An upward shift in demand for consols (when word of victory arrived) would shoot bond prices up. Anyone anticipating that rise could reap large profits.

Of course, Rothschild did not buy. He sold—small amounts, but in the eyes of those watching him, highly significant. The price of consols plummeted. Moments before word arrived, Rothschild bought up large amounts of bonds at a fraction of their previous price. He had knowledge even more valuable than that of money markets, capital funds, and the cotton trade. He saw into people's minds. In the complex teleology of markets and the forces of supply and demand, human nature is the ultimate cause.

Other investors met their Waterloo that day. Nathan Rothschild did not. His original £2,500 grubstake brought from Frankfurt grew 2,500 times within five years, thanks to Wellington, Waterloo, psychology—and a curious human asymmetry. As A. C. Pigou once noted, it is illegal or immoral for a *seller* to conceal information but laudable for a *buyer* to do so.[5]

Nathan Rothschild's financial killing was quite extraordinary. Psychology figures not only in such relatively rare events, but also in the ordinary humdrum economics of everyday living.

To anyone who has scanned the financial pages, bought a used car, supported a family, or worried about making ends meet, it must be obvious that the material components of our well-being— the focus of economics—interact closely with our thoughts and feelings—the focus of psychology. In knowing this, those who *live* economics (and that includes nearly everyone who breathes) are far ahead of those who mainly think and write about it.

222,000,000 Economists

At last count, there were sixty-thousand economists in the United States, one-fifth of them employed by universities. There are more than twice as many psychologists.[6] Apparently the fisc is less worrisome than the psyche, or at least easier to neglect.

A strong case can be made that everyone is an economist—about 222,000,000 of us, when we were counted in April 1980. The term *economics* comes from two Greek roots—*oikos,* meaning house, and *nomos,* manager. In Greek *oikonomikos* means skilled in the management of a household.[7] Heads of 80 million American households know well, without consulting the *Oxford English Dictionary,* how much art and science are involved in building income and managing spending.

One of the deepest thinkers of our age Albert Einstein believed that "the whole of science is nothing more than a refinement of everyday thinking."[8] Highly capable of stratospherically abstract thought, Einstein showed, in his special and general theories of relativity, how ordinary entities such as mass, energy, space, and time are related. Einstein and Alfred Marshall never met. If they had, they would have agreed at least on this issue. To Marshall "economic science is but the working of common sense aided by appliances of organized analysis and general reasoning."[9]

In one sense we are all physicians or physicists or chemists or botanists. We observe our own bodily functions and natural phenomena daily. We watch tides, see the stars, check the weather, and smile at the sunset or moonrise. All these acts are by nature observations. We do not cause tides or storms or moonbeams, nor do we choose them. We do, however, choose jobs, houses, cars, common stocks, cities, socks, and soaps. So we are all economists, actively, in a sense that we are not physicists.

I often tell my first-year students that before they crack a book, they already have advanced degrees in economics. Much of what

8

they learn involves labeling already familiar ideas and placing them in neat categories. If the word *economics* signifies something deep and perplexing to ordinary people, a meaning developed over the past 100 years, it is because we academic economists have inordinate skills at mystification.

The same reasoning that turns all of us into practicing economists, who use good sense, makes some of us economists into obfuscators, who use bad science.

> If physicists cannot understand the world of matter [a letter to the *New York Times* reads], it is because that world is not of their own creation. Money is a human creation, and there is a science which is supposed to produce understanding of how it works. But . . . economists seem to be less able to understand their subject than physicists understand theirs.[10]

Money is indeed a human creation. So are the thoughts and motives of those who use it. Fools and wise men alike part with their money; how they do so is what in part distinguishes between them. It is this aspect of economics that is badly underdeveloped.

If disciplines could lay claim to conjunctives, economics would have sole ownership of *or*. Every economic choice is one of two types—this or that, and now or later. A shopper in a supermarket faces some 5,000 items on the shelf; on an average shopping trip, about 50 or 100 of them are chosen. This is choice requiring selection of items from a large array at a given point in time—this or that.

Some of life's toughest decisions are now or later—spending now or saving in order to spend later, studying now in order to earn more later, leaving a job and a secure income to go into business and build more wealth for the future. Both this-or-that and now-or-later choices beg for what I call two-question logic: a way of making choices that typifies economic thinking. What follows is a brief discourse on how two-question logic works and why it is inseparable from psychology.

Economics on One Foot

The Talmud tells of a man who approached two prominent scholars, Hillel and Shammai, with a purposely provocative request. He asked to be taught the entire body of Jewish ethical instruction while he stood on one foot. Shammai curtly dismissed him. But Hillel agreed. He fulfilled the man's request with one sentence.*

Today, those who want to learn the entire body of economic knowledge while perched on one foot are assigned an 800-page text —as an introduction! (In life introductions are brief; in the classroom, massive).

There is, however, a Hillelian response. Economics, the logic of choice, commands us to ask two questions before making any choice:

- What is it worth to me?
- What do I have to give up to get it?

Choose whatever is worth more than it costs. Reject whatever is not. Books covering rows and rows of shelves expand on this simple theme. The calculus of benefits and costs applies equally to buying a tube of toothpaste and to the construction of the multibillion-dollar MX missile system. In one way or another, everyone has in fact used this logic. Economics explains how it might be used ideally, by incredibly smart, fast-thinking calculators. Psychology, the study of behavior, dissects how humans, frail of will and laden with inertia, make choices in reality. When hung on the framework of everyday living, economics and psychology combine to become both common sense and commonplace. This is true science, as Einstein told us. Like many basic ideas, the principle is simplicity incarnate, while its application in society can be despairingly complex.

*What is repugnant to you, do not do unto others; all the rest is commentary. (Talmud: *Gemara Shabbat,* p. 31.)

What Is It Worth? What Must I Give Up?

This two-question logic of choice presumes that whatever is being chosen has both value and cost. If something is worthless, by definition it is not a candidate for our choice. If something is costless, in the sense that nothing need be sacrificed to get it, and it has worth, no sleep need be lost in deciding.

Economics begins when what is available to satisfy our wants falls short of satisfying them. This is presumably as permanent and enduring a state of affairs for individuals as it is for society as a whole. Psychology enters the picture when we ponder the gap between our physical needs and our growing wants.

Food, shelter, and clothing are among our most basic needs. In May 1979 an American couple with one small child spent an average of $55.90 a week on food.[11] A nutrition expert once calculated the minimum-cost nutritious and palatable diet for a family of three. His menu consisted of fresh milk (about 15 quarts), margarine (about 1 pound), fresh carrots (1½ pounds), fresh potatoes (21 pounds), picnic ham and cured butts (2½ pounds), and white enriched flour (16½ pounds). The total weekly cost, at 1979 prices, came to about $23.00.[12] Yet few families, if any, would believe that more than half their food budget represents self-indulgence or "psychological" needs. The last $32.90, for most of us, satisfies as real a need as the first $23.00.

For most of recorded history, people managed to produce just enough to subsist. The problem of choice was overshadowed by the exigencies of survival. For more than half the world's population, this remains true. For the other half, technology and capital have generated an economic surplus—the means to produce more than we need for subsistence.

By choice or by accident, much of the economic surplus in modern industrial societies seems to have gone into collective consumption of public goods such as education and defense. A surprisingly large part of the average family's budget still seems to go to the basics.

The great Prussian statistician Engel carefully recorded the spending patterns of working men in Saxony in 1857. It is interesting to compare that budget with the one of an American urban family.[13] (See table 1.1).

A large chunk of what was once spent on food now goes to housing. Overall, then as now, only 8 percent of family income is left for other than basic needs. This does not, of course, mean we live no better than in 1857. The quality and variety of our consumption has grown tremendously. But it may help explain why our standard of living exceeds that of a Prussian prince, yet we struggle to make ends meet and feel like paupers, not kings.

William Baumol relates this story. Just before writing "Scarcity and Choice: The Economic Problem," the third chapter of his and Alan Blinder's introductory economics textbook, he was dining in a Chinese restaurant. The saying in his fortune cookie read, "Our necessities are few but our wants are endless."[14] It was used to lead off the chapter. The blurred line between wants and needs, and the infinite expansibility of wants, explain both why the need for making economic choices will never fade and why understanding those choices compels us to turn to psychology.

Table 1.1

Family Budgets in Saxony, 1857, and the United States, 1977

Budget Items	Saxony (%)	United States (%)
Food, Clothing, Transportation	73	43
Lodging, Light, Fuel	17	44
Health Care	2	5
Basics	92	92
Other	8	8
Total	100	100

SOURCES: Saxony—from Alfred Marshall (1890), p. 97n; transportation is not separately mentioned. United States—revised "basket" computed by Bureau of Labor Statistics in December 1977 for purposes of computing the consumer price index.

Paying Less Mind to Matter

Systematic thinking about anything demands that in moving from a series of facts to a conclusion, we must follow a set of rules. The rules are what comprise logic. Economics, the logic of choice, provides a simple and appealing framework for organizing our thinking about day-to-day decisions.

Logic is helpful in leading us to the right conclusions from a set of propositions. But it is not in itself sufficient. Logic tells us nothing about where to find those propositions or whether they are relevant or true.

Economics has had a long love affair with mathematics. The abstract power of mathematics—the logic of numbers, forms, and arrangements—has been enormously important in advancing economics, the logic of choice. It has made possible both good theory and good applications. Mathematics has helped make the fundamental slogan of modern economics—everything depends on everything else—both rigorous and operational.

Within the economics profession, there have at times been bitter opponents to the mathematical emphasis. Paul Samuelson once had to rewrite and diagram the concepts in a path-breaking article that some readers felt was needlessly technical.[15] But it is inconceivable that in the future the rigor and clarity offered by mathematics should be discarded.

New times, however, require new tools. Bertrand Russell once defined mathematics as the subject in which we never know what we are talking about nor whether what we are saying is true.[16] At times, the circularity of deductive mathematical logic in economics almost becomes self-parody. We learn about husbands who "would read in bed at night only if the value of reading exceeded the value (to him) of the loss in sleep suffered by his wife"; about persons who marry "when the utility expected from the marriage exceeds the utility expected from remaining single"; about couples who sepa-

13

rate when "the utility expected from remaining married falls below the utility expected from divorcing and possibly remarrying."[17]

Even Paul Samuelson, who invented a good part of modern economics, has assented that

> the consumer's market behavior is explained in terms of preferences, which are in turn defined only by behavior. The result can very easily be circular, and in many formulations undoubtedly is. Often nothing more is stated than the conclusion that people behave as they behave, a theorem which has no empirical implications, since it contains no hypothesis and is consistent with all conceivable behavior, while refutable by none.[18]

The problem is *not* the mathematical nature of modern economic theory. The problem is that the theory's fundamental assumptions and propositions about people are thin straws indeed, too thin for making decent bricks of science. To grasp adequately how people think and act, we must enlist another discipline: the science of behavior, psychology. Welded together, the logic of choice and the science of behavior can illuminate the human condition in a way that neither economics nor psychology alone can. These two social sciences, economics and psychology, have already established diplomatic relations. It is not implausible that by the end of this century they will have formed a common market and share a common language and currency. By then, perhaps, it will no longer be necessary to praise economics with faint damns.

Ninety years ago, the great Victorian economist Alfred Marshall, whose wise words I shall often quote, published his *Principles of Economics*. On page one, he defines economics as "the study of men as they live and move and think in the ordinary business of life."[19] Marshall had both good sense and good prose. He understood people well. The phrase "human nature" is sprinkled through his textbook like raisins through fruitcake. *Principles* went through eight or nine editions and was the dominant text of its day in economics.

But Marshall had a rival. Leon Walras, in his *Elements of Pure*

Economics set out, by his own admission, to do for economics what Newton had done two centuries earlier for celestial mechanics.[20] Walras adopted Newton's own tools.

Elements is one of the densest, most abstract economics books on the shelf. In spite of this, or perhaps because of it, Walras triumphed over Marshall.

"We curtsy to Marshall," Milton Friedman once said, "but we walk with Walras."[21] There is real irony in this. Marshall was a first-rate mathematician, far superior to Walras, who learned calculus in a school of mine engineering (where he flunked). Marshall saw the economic system as analogous to a biological one. Walras's analog was the planets. The mathematical tools that show how the stars and planets impinge upon one another cannot, by themselves, reveal how human beings impinge upon one another. Those tools have now encountered strongly diminishing returns in their economic applications.

A hoary old joke popular in the mid-nineteenth century goes: What's the matter? Never mind. What is mind? No matter.[22] There is nothing the matter with the mathematics of matter and material choice that paying a little more mind to mind cannot cure.

Enter Psychology

To properly answer questions about value and cost, we clearly need to call on the science of behavior—psychology.

William Baumol once said "value is a relation between persons, expressed as a relation between things."[23] It is human preferences and perceptions that underlie value and cost, not just money, machines, or manpower. Marx used the term "fetishism" (not the kind in sex manuals) to describe conventional economics' obsession with objects rather than with people. He had a point.

Partly by choice modern economics has opted to keep tightly sealed the black box it calls *utility*—economics' buzzword for pleasure or satisfaction. What is utility? How does it vary among persons? How does it change over time? The need for answers to these questions is obviated by the tail-chasing idea of *revealed preference,* described earlier in the words of Paul Samuelson.

Take, for instance, tastes. A leading introductory text asserts that "changes in demand that are due to changes in taste cannot be identified because taste changes cannot often be measured." The authors then reason that "whatever the cause, whenever tastes do change, the quantity demanded will increase for commodities that have come into favor and decrease for those that have become less popular."[24] Period.

One economist who has thought deeply about this issue and ingeniously applied physiological psychology to economic behavior is Tibor Scitovsky. He notes that while economists are content to attribute differences in what people consume to revealed preference, "the psychologist is not content to accept these and stop there; he tries to penetrate beneath the surface to find the causes and explanation of the differences."[25]

Let me make this point in another way. Today's standard working definition of economics originates with Frank Knight. He said that every economic system answers certain basic questions: What to produce, where and how to produce it, who should get the output, and when resources should be used.[26]

Rudyard Kipling wrote about "six honest serving men" who, he wrote, taught him all he knew: what, where, how, who, when, why.[27] Knight's definition covers only five. One serving man is conspicuous in its absence: Why.

As long as people and the economy march along smooth trend lines, perhaps economists can justify overlooking *why.* But in recent years we have been unable to build confident predictions of spending patterns, savings rates, inflation, or productivity growth, or even devise persuasive explanations for why or where our predictions went wrong. If we are to learn how to ask and answer the *why*'s of economic behavior, we must change course and proceed with undue haste toward psychology.

What Is It Worth? What Must I Give Up?

A poll of economics professors at fifty-five American universities —mainly large state schools—showed two out of three answered yes to the question, Is there a sense of lost moorings in economics? Three out of four responded yes when asked if they had increasing doubt about the accuracy of macroeconomic models.[28]

One reason for this professional anomie can be traced to the shift in interest from households and firms (microeconomics) to the economy as an integral whole (macroeconomics)—a shift led by John Maynard Keynes. Natural sciences, such as biology and physics, tend to move toward studying ever-smaller units of observation; in biology these are genes and their molecular composition; in physics, subatomic particles. Economics has moved toward the aggregate, perhaps because during the Great Depression the aggregate economy behaved inexplicably badly.

There are signs of a ground swell trend back to microeconomics or even, in Harvey Leibenstein's phrase, "micro-microeconomics" to search for the basic roots of economics in the behavior of individual consumers, managers, workers, and investors.[29]

Macroeconomics looks increasingly like a six-story building without a first and second floor. Psychology can help with the rebuilding, from the ground up. There are two major areas where psychology can contribute. One is in understanding economic behavior of people in groups. The other is in methodology—the way economists go about answering their questions.

The answers to "What is it worth?" and "What must I give up?" frequently entail intricate, complex mental processes. A good deal is already known about these processes. Some of this knowledge appears in this book. But there is even more to be discovered. Rich and rewarding research awaits those flexible enough to embrace new approaches.

We must borrow not only the *ideas* of psychology but also its methods. Economists do not as a rule generate their own data, nor do they commonly come into close contact with their subjects. The thick layers of insulation separating the observed from the observer must be torn away. A first step in that direction is more open-mindedness toward standard procedures in psychology. Such procedures—for example, controlled small-group experiments, interviews, questionnaires, and surveys—are now viewed by economists with some suspicion. In many ways psychology's methods, not just its models, are its main message. We economists would do well to listen.

There *is* mind under matter. Before we can find it, however, we must first agree to learn how and where to look.

Is Two-Question Logic Immoral?

"A science which has wealth for its subject matter," Marshall wrote, "is often repugnant at first sight to many students."[30] Some readers will nod in assent. They may find the two-question approach to choice, with or without psychology, too obvious to be helpful or too cold and calculating to be anything but cynical and immoral.

Some things, such as human life, are literally priceless. Other things are so desirable that we should have them even if they cost more than they are worth, it is sometimes said. One of Oscar Wilde's characters in *Lady Windermere's Fan,* asks, "What is a cynic?" The response is, "One who knows the price of everything and the value of nothing."[31] There are those who would transform Wilde's epithet into a definition of *economist.*

For individuals it is apparently still respectable to try to get value for money. Assaults on two-question logic focus mainly on its use for evaluating social programs with such concepts as *cost-benefit ratio* (CBR), which Norman Cousins has called "one of the least attractive terms in the English language." His trenchant assault reflects widely held views.[32]

"In the refrigerated patois of the budgeteers, [CBR] means that any proposed action must produce tangible returns equal to or greater than its expense," Cousins wrote. "The term descends like a death sentence on any proposal that would apply creative imagination to socially essential programs or long-range goals."

There is a kernel of truth in this. Two-question logic, applied to individuals, families, corporations, and governments, means that the tangible and *nontangible* benefits of an action must be greater than its expense (including nontangible costs). It is certainly true that for many social projects, nontangible, psychological benefits tend to be greater than nontangible costs—for instance, the benefits of noise abatement and the costs of baffles on jet engines. Ignoring nontangible costs and benefits is not a flaw in two-question logic itself but is a failing of those who practice and preach it. This is in itself another powerful argument in favor of broadening economics' horizons to include behavioral science.

A tale is told of a Saudi Arabian prince in a Harvard economics class. When taught that income constrains spending, he responded that in his part of the world, this law does not hold. The story is apocryphal, because according to reliable reports, Saudi Arabia needs every one of its $100-billion-a-year oil dollars to fund its ambitious development program.[33] We may feel little sympathy for the strained Saudi coffers, but in one sense, everyone—individual, family, business, government, nation, and sheik—is strapped. No one has unlimited means. Like it or not, the dilemma of choice is with us forever. Choosing among alternate uses of our limited means is inevitable and inescapable. We do not have the freedom not to choose; *not* deciding is itself a decision, often the worst of all.

The question really is not whether to make economic choices, but how best to manage them. Basing choices on costs and benefits need not in itself be cynical or immoral. Take, for example, the painful question health economics poses: Who shall live? If sustaining life in the face of certain illnesses requires costly resources—dialysis, heart-lung machines, or expensive drugs—available only in limited amounts, how do we decide who gets them? There are probably worse ways of answering the ethics-laden question—Who shall live?—than by trying to measure what life is worth and what it costs to sustain it. The alternative is choice by whim, wealth, chance, or sentiment, none of which lay claim to great moral stature.

An interesting debate rages over government health and safety regulations: Occupational Safety and Health Administration (OSHA). Some say they are indispensable. Others claim they impose intolerable cost burdens. Opponents of OSHA like to cite its costs. Supporters emphasize benefits.

Murray Weidenbaum, now Chairman of the Council of Economic Advisers, once estimated the cost of Environmental Protection Agency (EPA) regulations at $22.7 billion for 1978. Ralph Nader estimated the EPA's benefits at $22.2 billion for the same year. These figures may, or may not, be accurate. The point is, putting figures on the table, together with information about how they were derived, is in no way morally inferior to vague appeals to human needs or the dictates of conscience.

Life As a Multiple-Choice Exam

From birth to death, from childhood to maturity—as we study in schools and learn outside of them, make money and spend it, choose a profession, worry about the future or discount it, court risks or avoid them, invite change or shun it, move or retire, learn from old mistakes and invent entirely new ones—life is a long string of multiple-choice questions.

In this exam we ourselves make up both the questions and the answers. Skill and wisdom in framing the questions, and setting out possible responses, are as crucial as checking the right box—if there *is* a right box. The exam is mostly self-graded, with considerable unsolicited help from those around us. No one can say precisely what constitutes doing well, although some elements of success are taken for granted: wealth, fame, power, and contentment. Very few people walk around asking, "How am I doing? How have

I done?" Society has ways of letting us know. We may choose not to compete or to compete fiercely. Whether we do or not, as we journey through life, the need to choose presses upon us. There is no escape. The dilemma of choice is part of the beauty, mystery, and cruelty of living. That we are able to choose is a measure of our individual freedom and progress.

Nobody ever sat up all night cramming for an 8 A.M. quiz in Life 101. Even if it were possible to cram for a 514,212-hour test, the average life expectancy of a twenty-year-old Caucasian American woman, what would you study?[34] There is no evidence that those with long strings of letters after their names manage life choices better (or worse) than the unschooled.

For a start, why not study economics? Not the economics of William Stanley Jevons, framed like a problem from a geometry primer: "Given, a certain population, with various needs and powers of production, in possession of certain lands and other sources of material; Required, the mode of employing their labor which will maximize the utility of their produce."[35] Nor even the economics of Lionel Robbins's famed 1933 essay, which marked the surgical excision of human behavior from economics, even while the term itself was inserted into the standard definition: "the science which studies human behavior as a relationship between ends and scarce means which have alternate uses."[36]

Instead, why not learn about the economics of Alfred Marshall: the study of men as they live and move and think in the everyday business of life; the economics that temper the objective logic of choice with the subjective traits of ordinary people.

I invite the reader to join me, Marshall, and a few psychologists on a leisurely and rather unconventional tour of economic life. We begin in childhood. Long before we reach the time when we need to make economic choices of substance, we begin to acquire the values and knowledge that permanently influence those choices. Part 1, "Economic Man as Child," discusses how children learn such basic concepts as value, price, exchange, work, reward, and money and how they relate future gratification to the present.

When asked for the criteria of a mature person, Sigmund Freud once listed two: *"Lieben und arbeiten."*[37] Love and work capture most of our waking hours as adults. Part 2, "People as Producers," centers upon work and production. Does education make us more productive—better "human capital"—or does it simply distinguish those who are already smart from those who are mediocre? Are personality and productivity related? Are there some personality traits employers pay good money for? When we work alongside others, what determines whether we shirk or work? These are all questions for which both economics and psychology have partial, and at times conflicting, answers.

Work produces goods and services and generates the income to buy them. Our role as consumers is the subject of part 3, "People as Consumers," which deals with debt and borrowing, spending and inflation—areas in which psychology seems to be of decisive importance.

Perhaps the only certain feature of life is its uncertainty. Part 4, "People as Risk Takers," addresses the riddle of why people both seek and avoid risk at the same time. What determines how people invest their savings? What is the relationship between investment patterns and personality? Why do some people gamble and yet insure their lives and possessions for large amounts of money? Who is more willing to take risks? How are the odds of risks perceived? Experiments reveal many interesting differences between people's actual behavior and how conventional economics portrays it.

The concluding section is part 5, "People, on the Whole." Here the economic psychology of public spending, taxes, and tax evasion is examined in detail. When life is subject to rules and penalties for breaking them, why do some people comply and others do not? The final chapter outlines areas where economics and psychology are already joined in near-marriage, and it delineates other areas where economics must divorce itself from outmoded, obsolescent ideas in favor of fresher, behavioral ones.

"Mind over matter" is a phrase that has come to signify the

superiority of human will over the material chains that bind it. It is an idea of hope and faith.

"Minds pervade markets" is the less elevated, but perhaps more practical, message of this book. It, too, is a proposition of hope. But it need not be taken on faith. It harbors the secret of our ultimate gross rational product—how to live together in dignity, in security, and without fear. I hope the evidence this book marshals on its behalf will prove useful, interesting, and persuasive.

2

LEARNING THE WORK OF SOCIETY: HOW CHILDREN ACQUIRE ECONOMIC VALUES

ECONOMIC MAN is an obstetric marvel. From the pages of texts and journals, he springs to life full-blown. His intelligence is boundless, his experience vast, his knowledge sweeping. He errs rarely, if at all. His actions are unerringly guided by two-question logic: cost versus value.

In Herbert A. Simon's words, Economic Man has "a complete and consistent system of preferences that allows him always to choose among the alternatives open to him; he is always completely aware of what these alternatives are; there are no limits on the complexity of the computations he can perform in order to determine which alternatives are best."[1]

Ordinary people usually find Economic Man, when they encounter him, like Thurber's native domestic burgundy—amusing by his presumption. Students of economics, in my experience, are less amused. They tend to gripe about the unreality of their discipline's fundamental concept of man. Their complaints persist, unless and until they sink so much intellectual capital into their discipline that they must switch from depreciating their assets to defending them.

Learning the Work of Society

Economists' responses, predictably, are that *every* science peddles abstractions. Economics is no worse in this regard than nuclear physics or molecular biology. No physicist has ever seen an Economic Man, but then no economist has ever seen a neutrino. Judge us by how well our theories hold water—by *results*—not by how badly our assumptions leak or by how badly our abstractions distort reality. As Robert Solow wrote, all theory depends on assumptions that are not quite true; that is what makes it theory.[2]

Anyway, just how realistic is *psychology's* concept of man? Surely no better. As both an economist, a psychologist, and many other things, Herbert Simon applies his lash equally to social psychology, especially to "tendencies . . . that try to reduce all cognition [knowledge] to affect [pertaining to emotion]."[3] If Economic Man is a superfast, superrational calculator, Psychological Man is a quivering bundle of feelings and nerve ends.

The plea to judge science by results, not assumptions, has been called the *F-twist,* after Milton Friedman, who wrote a forceful essay on the topic. Lately the F-twist has had trouble straightening itself out. Economics has not been doing well in predicting the future, understanding the present, or even interpreting the recent past. I think one of the roots of the problem is not Economic Man's bionic brain, but how he *got* it.

How does the average person develop his economic outlook? Underlying the thousands of economic decisions people make over a lifetime are issues related to childhood. How do children learn about exchange, value, rules, morals, and work? Why do some children grow up to be successful, prosperous parts of the economic system and others become heavy burdens upon it? Are the values children learn and internalize appropriate for the economic conditions they will later encounter? Are children kept children too long?

These are questions that an economist would not normally try to answer, or even ask. But in order to understand economic behavior properly, I believe we must face them. A vast body of knowledge exists on child development. Some of this knowledge can help knit together childhood experience and adult choice. Giving Economic Man a childhood is, I believe, a natural starting point for integrating economics and psychology.

A hundred years ago, when Marshall sat down to write his *Principles,* he cautioned that "whenever [the economist] occupies himself largely with conditions and motives . . . he must forego nearly all aid and support from the observations and thought of others at home and abroad."[4] This was true in his day, perhaps, but it is not in ours. There is much to learn from those who study "conditions and motives." It is time to seek their wisdom.

Every generation builds its own bridge to pass on its culture to those who follow. Sociologists and psychologists are deeply interested in this process, and they have learned a great deal about it. Many of the more important values that travel the generational bridge are economic in nature—attitudes and behavior toward work, spending and saving, risk, and sharing. Did childhood experiences adequately prepare today's adults for their economic journey through life? And are we adequately preparing our children for the economic roles they will play?

Economics must look to psychology for some answers. This chapter summarizes some of them. They are not especially comforting. They suggest that children gain insufficiently broad experience as producers, learn to overemphasize their roles as consumers, and most of all, adopt and adapt the supreme value of self-interest precisely at a time when sacrifice, altruism, and accommodation are in desperate need.

Socialization, for What?

Earlier I defined economics as two-question logic that compares worth and cost. The very definition begs us to pay our dues to the process of *socialization,* which Brim defines in his famous essay as "how man is taught to get the work of society done."[5]

"What is it worth to me?" can translate roughly as, "What do

I think it is worth to others?" Our own values are indeed learned from others. Though this process continues through life, it is particularly important in childhood. "What do I have to give up to get it?" relates to the process of exchange. In every exchange the values of at least one other person are involved. Two-question logic cannot be properly used unless those values are familiar to us.

Children acquire the values and habits of their culture from parents, peers, siblings, schools, and their general surroundings. The economy is part of their culture. Curiously, no special term or word exists for learning economic, as opposed to social, values. To "economize" a child, I suppose, means not to have him or her.

An economist, James Duesenberry, once wittily explained the difference between economics and sociology. "Economics is all about how people make decisions. Sociology is all about why they don't have any decisions to make."[6]

The pointed stake of this aphorism really strikes at economics, which tends to denigrate social constraints on choice. "Others," wrote Albert Bandura, a leading expert on behavior modification, "are the most influential and ubiquitous stimulus for the regulation of human behavior."[7] James W. Baldwin, one of the first social psychologists, said this same thing quite elegantly, referring particularly to children: "We are all members of one another."[8] At every stage, Baldwin reasoned, we are really in part someone else, even in the way we think of ourselves.

Others have, with some exceptions, not figured importantly in economic theory. Ironically, one of the major exceptions is Duesenberry. He developed a plausible and predictively accurate theory of consumption, where consumers are interested not so much in the absolute level of what they spend as in what they spend compared to other people.[9]

The entire economic system is built on the willingness of successive generations to offer their labor in return for pay, exchange their pay in return for goods and services, and trade their savings for some promised future return. Such willingness takes the form of social norms or standards of behavior. The first systematic book on economics, Adam Smith's *Wealth of Nations,* emphasized the importance of one of those norms—accumulating capital—in explaining why some countries are rich and others are poor.

As a student I recall having had one especially memorable, vigorous class with development economist Sir W. Arthur Lewis. Several of us mustered our collective *chutzpah* and pressed him for a one-line, stand-on-one-foot answer to Adam Smith's question, What determines the wealth of nations? He answered, "national energy." A fuller answer is found in Lewis's landmark book, *Theory of Economic Growth:* "Economic growth depends on attitudes to work, to wealth, to thrift, to having children, to invention, to strangers, to adventure, and so on, and all these attitudes flow from deep springs in the human mind."[10]

Sigmund Freud was among the first to reveal many of those springs. He provided a helpful clue. "The psychic development of the individual," he wrote, "is a short repetition of the course of development of the race."[11] In ten-dollar words *ontogeny*—the development of the individual—prefigures *phylogeny*—the development of the tribe or race. By this reasoning it may be that socialization, in all its aspects, can become the glue that joins the two broken halves of economics that should never have been separated: microeconomics (individuals) and macroeconomics (the national economy).

Society teaches its values to children from a very early age, in a great many ways, mostly indirect and oblique ones. A few innovative experiments, however, have been conducted to teach young children economic concepts as part of a formal program of instruction.

Kinder Economy

Beginning as early as preschool and extending through high school, ingenious attempts are underway to bring the central ideas of economics to children as part of their schooling.

"Romper Room," a television program aimed at three-year-olds and watched by 1.5 million children in seven countries, features five-minute segments on supply and demand and scarcity. In one episode hostess Sally Gelbard asked children in the studio to view a television monitor showing a stage backdrop of a forest. She defined a natural resource as "something that grows in our country and that we can use." The children began to think up ways to use wood. With each suggestion, part of the forest backdrop disappeared.[12]

What happens when we've made all our pencils, houses, floors, and toys? Mrs. Gelbard asked. "The trees are gone," one child responded.

An award-winning program in Fort Smith, Arkansas, tries to bring economics to children from kindergarten through high school.[13] Emphasis is on economics as a part of real life.

"The fact is that children live in an economic world," Wallace C. Floyd, director of instruction, noted. "Almost every childhood experience is rich in the elements of economics. At first he does not understand the impossibility of satisfying his unlimited wants. Without some instruction, a child cannot understand that even his nonmaterial wants have certain economic significance. It's the job of education to create this awareness—at an early age."

First graders in Houston, Texas, start their own firms and learn about selling and buying, managing inventories, and paying bills.[14] Children in fourth through sixth grades in Nof Yam, Israel, fifteen minutes north of Tel Aviv, tackle such questions as: What is a consumption basket? What is a budget? What is a smart buy? How does advertising influence us? Where does the country get its resources? "I read about inflation and the cost of living," one sixth-grader said, "and don't understand. But I won't be a child forever."[15]

An experimental project dubbed Kinder Economy teaches nine basic economic concepts to kindergarten children in four metropolitan schools.[16] Five- and six-year-olds learn about scarcity, decision making, production, distribution, specialization, consumption, demand and supply, business organization, and money and barter.

Some of the concepts, in particular, specialization, proved especially hard for the children to grasp. But overall, Kinder Economy graduates showed higher economic literacy than teachers. The children reached a 72.5 percent mastery level, compared with 68.5 percent for teachers, before the teachers took a preparatory workshop, of course.

Marilyn Kourilsky, author of the program, argues that

> students, in every state of the Union, are required to demonstrate knowledge of U.S. government to graduate from high school, but no such requirement (with few exceptions) applies to demonstrating a knowledge of our economic system. . . . Economic naïveté can make a citizen with a thorough understanding of government vote for a candidate who promises to cure inflation, reduce taxes, follow an easy-money policy and balance the budget . . . and [that citizen will] believe that such goals are simultaneously attainable.

A spinoff of the program was increased economic literacy of parents, some of whom found their five- or six-year-olds more knowledgeable in economics than they themselves were.

Invisible Hand—or Clenched Fist?

Despite these interesting experimental programs, only one American in every twelve is ever exposed to formal instruction in economics before graduating from high school. Children become adult producers, consumers, investors, risk takers, and entrepreneurs, mainly through indirect channels of influence.

How sturdy, stable, and well suited to its era is the bridge over which social values travel from one generation to another? As high school valedictorian, I recall orating rather pompously, "the youth of a nation are the trustees of posterity." Those to whom posterity is entrusted are not always aware of how powerfully they are shaped by their ancestry. For most of history, socialization lent stability to society by giving children the same dreams and desires that had served their ancestors. But what happens when socialization passes on values that are obsolete or dysfunctional?

What follows is a rather long digression on the nature of competitive economies. I shall argue that economic systems based on free markets rely upon the fundamental values of competition, initiative, and self-interest. Today's world, though, requires precisely the opposite—cooperation, sacrifice, and altruism. Our generational bridges are badly in need of modification to suit the times. First I will turn to the free-market economic system, its beauties and its flaws.

Birds fly without having advanced degrees in aerodynamics. Minnesota Fats's billiard balls spin, bank, and angle with precision without the man behind the cue knowing the laws of physics. Our economic system is built on large numbers of people, propelled mainly by their own self-interest and guided by exceedingly limited information, making even larger numbers of choices. That the system works at all is surprising. That it has proved so efficient is amazing. There are almost 15 million businesses in the United States —partnerships, corporations, and self-owned firms—employing 90 million people. How exactly does it happen that in Thomas Schelling's example, cow, dairy, barge, mine, and plant somehow mesh together to get a pat of butter wrapped in aluminum foil with an airline insignia on it to the right place at the right time?[17]

The answer lies in a fortuitous coincidence. The logic of choice that brings to firms maximum profits and to individuals maximum utility, also, *under certain circumstances,* makes collective well-being optimal. In other words, what's best for me is best for you and ultimately best for everyone.

In free-labor markets, employers bid for workers. Employers for whom workers are most valuable, that is, most productive, bid most and succeed in hiring those workers. Two-question logic— What is the worker worth? What does the worker cost?—guides labor to its best employment. In free markets, people compete for goods and services. Those to whom goods are worth more offer to pay more. In this way the output of labor finds its way to those who value it most. This is the fundamental theorem of economics: When individuals try to maximize their own welfare, knowing only their own preferences and wealth and the existing prices, the result will meet certain "broad requirements" of optimality.

One of the most famous passages in *Wealth of Nations* describes how an individual who "intends only his own gain" is led "by an invisible hand to promote an end which was no part of his intention. . . . By pursuing his own interest he frequently promotes that of society more effectually than when he really intends to promote it."[18] Self-interest, freely expressed in free markets, guides us like an invisible hand to collective contentment. By the principle of voluntary exchange, whatever changes hands must benefit both buyer and seller, otherwise, there would be no deal.

This is the basic theme around which economics builds endless variations. It is a theme sounded in the first bars of introductory economics and on down through the intricate chords of abstract, mathematical economics. The profession never seems to tire of it. There is, of course, a catch. It lies in the phrase *under certain circumstances*. Those circumstances essentially boil down to the following: Built upon unbridled self-interest, the invisible hand does work, provided individuals do not appreciably affect one another, favorably or unfavorably. Once important interactions occur among economic agents, both the theorem, and the system it purports to describe, begin to limp.

Winston Churchill once said in the House of Commons that the inherent vice of capitalism is the unequal sharing of blessings.[19] It is hard to deny that *unequal sharing* is indeed a shadow cast by the invisible hand. But does the present form of capitalism, and the values it encourages and in turn is encouraged by, really yield blessings? Which hand really prevails in our age: the invisible hand that guides resources to their efficient use or the avaricious hand that appropriates someone else's wealth, income, or living space?

Adam Smith knew both hands well. He saw them both at work in eighteenth-century England, and they are still at work today. Here is what he wrote about capitalists:

> The proposal of any new law or regulation of commerce which comes from (those who live by profit) ought always to be listened to with great precaution. . . . it comes from an order of men, whose interest is never exactly the same with that of the public, who have generally an interest to deceive and even to oppress the public, and who accordingly have, upon many occasions, both deceived and oppressed it.[20]

Increasingly, our behavior does affect those around us. An irascible driver, with one blast of his horn, can disturb several hundred people. Men were not islands in John Donne's day, and they cannot pretend to be so now.

A study by the psychologist Stanley Milgram, described more fully in the last chapter, showed how a Kansas wheat farmer is a close neighbor of a Cambridge, Massachusetts clergyman.[21] Precisely the same forces that bring Wichita and Harvard Square close together open an enormous conceptual gap between Harvard Square, the home of Thomas Schelling and the super-duper pat of butter, and Boston Commons, once an open grassy area where livestock owners grazed their cattle. Almost imperceptibly the invisible hand has become a clenched fist. It now gives way to a different metaphor, the tragedy of the commons. The effect upon us and upon our children is hard to overstate.

Our Common Tragedy

Skyscrapers now tower above the few acres in Boston where villagers once grazed their livestock. The enterprise, spirit, and industry that turned colonial America into modern industrial America, as well as the clash between individual enterprise and collective harmony, find expression on that one spot. A decade ago a biologist, Garrett Hardin, called this clash "The Tragedy of the Commons" in a brilliant speech.[22] It is best explained by the example Hardin gave (which follows), drawn from an 1833 essay on Malthusianism.

The tragedy of the commons develops in this way. Picture a pasture open to all. It is to be expected that each herdsman will try to keep as many cattle as possible on the commons. Such an arrangement may work reasonably satisfactorily for centuries because tribal wars, poaching and disease keep the numbers of both man and beast well below the carrying capacity of the land. Finally, however, comes the day of reckoning, that is, the day when the long-desired goal of social stability becomes a reality. At this point, the inherent logic of the commons remorselessly generates tragedy.

As a rational being, each herdsman seeks to maximize his gain. Explicitly or implicitly, more or less consciously, he asks, "What is the utility to me of adding one more animal to my herd?" This utility has one negative and one positive component.

(1) The positive component is a function of the increment of one animal. Since the herdsman receives all the proceeds from the sale of the additional animal, the positive utility is nearly +1.

(2) The negative component is a function of the additional over-grazing created by one more animal. Since, however, the effects of overgrazing are shared by all the herdsmen, the negative utility for any particular decision-making herdsman is only a fraction of −1.

Adding together the component partial utilities, the rational herds-man concludes that the only sensible course for him to pursue is to add another animal to his herd. And another; and another. . . . But this is the conclusion reached by each and every rational herdsman sharing a commons. Therein is the tragedy. Each man is locked into a system that compels him to increase his herd without limit—in a world that is limited. Ruin is the destination toward which all men rush, each pursuing his own best interest in a society that believes in the freedom of the commons. Freedom in a commons brings ruin to all.

GARRETT HARDIN,
"The Tragedy of the Commons"

Learning the Work of Society

Suppose ten people each own a half-ton bull. All ten bulls graze on common pasture. There is enough rich grass for them to maintain their weight.

Now, suppose an additional bull is added to the herd. Eleven bulls now graze where there were once only ten. Suppose this now means that the pasture can maintain only 9,900 pounds of bull, rather than 10,000 as before. The average weight of the eleven bulls drops from a half ton to 900 pounds (9,900 divided by 11).

If you could, would you graze the eleventh bull? *Collectively,* it doesn't pay. Overgrazing imposes a one-hundred-pound tax. *Individually,* it pays handsomely. Grazing two 900-pound bulls (on common pastureland, remember) is much more profitable than grazing a single 1,000-pound bull, in fact 80 percent more profitable.

To coin a cliché, there is no free lunch, even for grazing bulls. The 800 pounds of bull you gain, if you graze the eleventh one, cost the nine other owners 100 pounds each, because their bulls each slim down to 900 pounds from 1,000. Your gain is less than everyone else's loss. Society loses 100 pounds of bull. Even if overgrazing causes no damage at first, and the aggregate weight of bulls is preserved at five tons, the basic fact remains—each additional bull, say, the nth one, gains for its owner $\frac{5}{n}$ and costs every other owner $\frac{5}{n-1} - \frac{5}{n}$ tons of bull. Here individual incentives are at odds with collective profit. In the absence of some form of legal constraint, collective agreement, or binding moral principle, the same self-interest that once made the commons hum with industry and vigor may now work to destroy the common good.

The problem extends far beyond misuse of depletable resources. It applies to an extremely broad and diverse group of social conflicts. Productivity is an example. Most work is done in groups. Each member of the group is interested in minimizing his toil. If everyone acts this way, nothing gets done. Inflation is another. People try to defend their living standards by buying in advance of price rises. If everyone does this, buy-in-advance spending brings the very result it tries to forestall. Later chapters expand on this theme.

How, then, did human society ever progress? The invisible hand worked beautifully as long as there were not too many visible ones present. Metaphorical pastures were spacious and grassy enough for all. It took most of the first nineteenth centuries of the common era for world population to quadruple and reach 1 billion. The next quadrupling took only a century and has, painfully and irreversibly, thrust us into the region of sharp conflict between individual aims and social cohesion.

American pioneers used to quip that if you could see smoke from your neighbor's chimney, it was too crowded, time to move on. That era, and the economic, social, and moral values consonant with it, we shall never again see. The real tragedy of the commons, a permanent feature of society henceforth, is that there are no ready solutions.

Modern believers in free competition and unfettered markets like to equate economic freedom with political freedom, both logically and historically. In a free society I am free to choose. Increasingly, however, the following dilemma arises: I am free to choose what is mine and also some of what is yours. The dividing line between "mine" and "yours" is often very difficult, or impossible, to draw for common resources. Even if I am altruistic and choose only what is "mine"—for example, to graze just one bull—the chances are others will not follow suit but will be tempted to exploit my high-mindedness.

Suppose well-enforced rules are imposed. Here lies a bitter paradox. In modern society I am free to choose only when I can not. I am constrained to act egoistically and atavistically, unless some restraint on my freedom forbids it, or we all decide to become St. Francis.

Choice is an economic problem. In an ever-shrinking world, where "we are all members of one another," choices are exceedingly interdependent. Oil fields, library books, pay telephones, freeways, parks, swimming pools, backyards, the very air we breathe and water we drink—it is easier to think of a clenched-fist choice than an invisible-hand one. The more interdependent we become, the more important our knowledge of, and feelings toward, other people become. The tragedy of the commons has deep roots in both economics and psychology.

Consider a world comprised entirely of me, the writer, and you, the reader. It is possible that my efforts on my own behalf—working, saving, studying, accumulating capital and putting it to good use—improve my own well-being without harming yours. This is the world of the invisible hand, where egoistic competition generates collective bliss. Each individual climbs on the achievement curve as high as he or she wishes. A society of ambitious, highly motivated individuals can go very far, and the transference from one generation to another of the desire to excel promotes the well-being of that society. The world may well have looked this way in the eighteenth or nineteenth century.

Now suppose that my efforts to improve my own well-being end up damaging yours. The damage may be psychological. In a society of highly competitive persons, it may hurt to see others get ahead. It may also be material, as in the preceding commons example.

I am arguing that in this world competitive values are no longer functional. Cooperation is the key to collective rationality. But national character changes slowly. If the world has indeed transformed itself in this century, the character of its inhabitants may not yet have adapted to this change. And this maladaption, in turn, reflects itself in the various economic roles children learn to play as producers, consumers, and competitors.

Children as Producers

Every economic system fulfills certain basic functions of social organization—production, consumption, distribution, and growth. From time to time economists have altered the aspect of the economic system they think is most interesting and important. Adam Smith was preoccupied with growth. David Ricardo concentrated on distribution. Jevons and Marshall emphasized production and efficiency. As a staunch Victorian moralist, Marshall wrote with great conviction: "The most imperative duty of this generation is to provide for the young such opportunities as will both develop their higher nature and make them efficient producers." Marshall's prescription for making children "efficient producers" was simple: "Long-continued freedom from mechanical toil" and "abundant leisure for school . . . and play."[23]

The adjective *child* when attached to labor has overtones of suffering and exploitation, a lingering residue of the Industrial Revolution. Some of Marx's most vivid passages in *Capital* dwell on this. Marx mentions nine-year-old William Wood, who came to work "every day in the week at 6 A.M. and left off about 9 P.M.," and quotes twelve-year-old J. Murray, "who worked all night last night, till 6 o'clock this morning. I have not been in bed since the night before last."[24] Legislation finally halted such abuses—in America, not until 1938, when new laws were passed, after 1916 and 1919 child-labor laws were found unconstitutional.[25]

However, child-labor laws did not put a complete end to child labor. An International Labor Office study claims there are now more than 50 million children under the age of fifteen at work around the world. Even in the United States during World War II, more than 3 million children aged fourteen through seventeen worked full or part-time.

It has been replacement of unskilled labor with machinery, and affluence, more than legislation, that have worked to erase the importance of children as suppliers of labor. Some educators and psychologists think this has been a mixed blessing. Uri Bronfenbrenner, a psychologist and an expert on child development, cites a study by Elder of adults who were of adolescent age during the Great Depression.

> The labor-intensive economy of deprived households in the '30s, [Elder wrote] often brought older children into the world of adults. These children . . . were needed, and . . . being needed . . . gives rise to a sense of belonging and place, of being committed to something larger than the self. . . . Since [that time] . . . various developments have conspired to isolate the young from challenging situations in which they could make valuable contributions to family and community welfare. . . . In this consumption-oriented society, urban middle-class families have little use for the productive hands of offspring, and the same applies to community institutions.[26]

Today we are richer than ever before. But by not needing our children as producers, have we made them, and ourselves, poorer? Not everyone agrees with this line of argument. Every parent knows how children dislike chores and drudgery. Perhaps, given the increasingly automated and capital-intensive nature of production, children should be prepared for leisure rather than labor. In any event, the way Americans look upon hard work is undergoing rapid change. Ten years ago nearly six people in ten thought hard work always paid off if one had faith in himself and stuck to it. Today only 44 percent think so.[27] As the work ethic fades, the dominant economic role our culture provides may be shifting from producer to consumer.

Children as Consumers

For most of our history humans have lived at the bare subsistence level, producing just enough to make ends meet, with *ends* defined meagerly. If production is the main economic problem, one would expect values favorable to production to be an important part of socialization.

During the Great Depression a revolution occurred in how economists saw the world. Its main architect was John Maynard

Keynes. He urged us to discard the worn assumption that everything produced would be bought and consumed. The downward
plunge of the economy—the U.S. national income fell by more
than half between 1929 and 1933—supplied extra persuasion. In
the United States and Europe there was plenty of productive capacity. But lack of demand left machines rusting and men idle and
desperate. The supply of labor was strong, but the demand for it
—derived from the demand for goods—was not.

In a society where spending and consumption are the major
problems rather than production, values must change. Learning to
spend and learning to *value* spending become important. Work
becomes not an end in itself but a means, a path to income and
spending.*

In 1930, on the eve of the Great Depression, Keynes wrote a
remarkable essay entitled, "Economic Possibilities for Our Grandchildren." In it he noted how the "struggle for survival"—the
economic problem—has always been the "primary, most pressing
problem of the human race"; and he explained how we have been
"expressly evolved by nature—with all our impulses and deepest
instincts" to solve it.

Within a hundred years, Keynes claimed, the economic problem
may be solved—a remarkable prediction, if we recall that he was
writing at the onset of a world depression, with unemployment
already high. He predicted a standard of life "four to eight times
as high"; this is conservative, in fact, as two to three doublings in
a century is accomplished by only 2 percent or so annual growth.
Man's real problem will become wise consumption—"how to use
his freedom from pressing economic cares"—rather than ample
production.

What role will socialization play? "I think with dread," Keynes
wrote, "of the readjustment of the habits and instincts of the ordinary man, bred into him for countless generations, which he may

---

*A recent survey asked Americans what aspect of working they found most
rewarding. Getting paid ran ahead, overall, of sense of achievement or satisfaction,
and for those aged eighteen to twenty-four, it ran far ahead.[28]

be asked to discard within a few decades." The love of money will be recognized as a "somewhat disgusting morbidity." "Purposiveness" will no longer be applauded.

But, not quite yet, Keynes concluded. "Avarice and usury and precaution must be our gods for a little longer still. For only they can lead us out of economic necessity into daylight."[29]

If consumption, not production, is the main job of the economic system, children become important as spenders rather than as workers. Children and teen-agers now make up a rich market, for whose favors retailers battle intensely. Courses in consumerism proliferate in elementary and high schools as well-intentioned educators try to train children to spend wisely.

But meanwhile winds of change have again shifted the economic dunes. The economic possibilities of our children and grandchildren, I believe, rest not on how diligent they are as producers, or how wise and liberal they are as consumers. The problem has shifted perceptibly away from the solutions society teaches its children.

Who's in First?

An efficient economic system, I have argued, was long viewed as one in which a collection of free-spirited people motivated by self-interest competed vigorously with one another for resources and goods. For efficiency certain values and habits are typically regarded as functional, or favorable—frugality (for saving and capital accumulation), industry, and competitiveness. Presumably, then, an efficient system can remain so only by passing on these values to its children. It stands to reason that a competitive economic system needs its members to be competitors. Socialization is highly relevant because the desire to excel, both absolutely and in relation to others, is a value children acquire from their culture.

Not all cultures are competitive or value competitive behavior.

41

Research done among Anglo-American and Mexican-American children by George Knight and Spencer Kagan consistently found the latter to be less competitive, with differences in behavior increasing between ages five to six and seven to nine. Other things being equal, lower-income children also tend to be more cooperative.[30]

In a study by Madsen, children from various cultural backgrounds, including an Israeli kibbutz and a Mexican village, played a game with either cooperative or competitive moves.[31] The children were initially rewarded according to results attained by the whole group. Then rewards were switched to reflect individual achievement. Kibbutz and village children continued to cooperate, while children from other cultures quickly switched to competitive —and in this game, collectively ruinous—behavior.

Kagen and Madsen, in discussing some of their findings, refer to Jean Piaget's work on morality. Four- and five-year-olds, they suggest, tend to cooperate more, either because they fail to distinguish their own goals from those of others or because at their stage of development children are highly egocentric, and thus, paradoxically, are less influenced by what others do or get. As they grow older, children develop intellectually and become able to understand the nature and costs of competition. In some cultures a morality of cooperation develops at this stage. In others, increased ability of children to perceive the benefits of cooperation is offset by competitive drives implanted by social norms. Cultural differences in competitiveness beyond ages seven through nine have been found to remain fairly constant. Emphasis on labeling, tracking, and grades in American schools must surely maintain and foster the competitive ethic.

Curriculum of Caring

If cooperation is essential to our collective well-being and competition inimical to it, what can be done? In an interdependent world, whose pastures are figuratively enclosed and increasingly crowded, altruism—caring for others—becomes more than an intrinsically good value. It becomes a basic ingredient for society to function.

How do children learn selflessness? A surge of research activity occurred in the 1960s that attempted to find the causes for urban violence and unrest. A well-known study by Rosenhan found that the more dedicated, altruistic civil rights workers were raised by "nurturing, altruistic parent-models."[32] Later research showed how parents can foster altruism in their children. (A question rarely addressed is, *should* they? One St. Francis in a mass of egoists is a lamb in a wolf pack, likely to meet the same fate).

Yarrow, Scott, and Waxler showed children two types of distress. One was symbolic, in pictures or dioramas; for example, two children were in a playroom and one had all the toys or all but one child in a group had ice-cream cones. Another type of distress was behavioral. Children were exposed to such incidents as a child in a playpen with all its toys beyond reach or an adult's special vase knocked off a shelf by a child. The children involved in the experiment were subject to influence from parents, of various sorts, to see if they could be "trained" to behave altruistically.

"Altruistic responses with symbolic materials," Yarrow, Scott, and Waxler reported, "were relatively easily acquired; helping real victims was not." True altruism, they found, is instilled by parents who practice and not just preach. "The parent who conveys his values to the child didactically as tidy principles and no more, accomplishes only that learning in the child. Generalized altruism would appear to be best learned from parents who not only try to inculcate the principles of altruism, but who also manifest altruism in everyday interactions." Nurturance alone, they assert, is not sufficient for altruism in children.

"There is no compelling evidence," the researchers state, "to indicate that in the rearing of its children, society has given high priority to the inculcation of personal concern for the welfare of others."[33]

If, then, old dogs—adults—can indeed learn new tricks, but much prefer old ones, and if young dogs—children—can also learn new tricks, but in fact learn mainly old ones through socialization, what is the answer? The school system?

Uri Bronfenbrenner has labeled schools "one of the most potent breeding grounds for alienation in American society." He writes,

> In the United States, it is now possible for a person eighteen years of age, female as well as male, to graduate from high school, college, or university without ever having cared for, or even held, a baby; without ever having looked after someone who was old, ill, or lonely; or without ever having comforted, or assisted, another human being who really needed help. Again, the psychological consequences of such a deprivation of human experience are as yet unknown. But the possible social implications are obvious, for—sooner or later, and usually sooner —all of us suffer illness, loneliness, and the need for help, comfort, or companionship. No society can long sustain itself unless its members have learned the sensitivities, motivations, and skills involved in assisting and caring for other human beings.[34]

He calls for what he terms "a curriculum of caring," aimed not at *learning* about caring (Yarrow, Scott, and Waxler showed how futile that was) but at *engaging* in it. Children would be asked to take responsibility for spending time with, and caring for, others. By altering their roles, we can wield powerful influence on children's values, he contended.

Caring and Politics

Every human being is, from birth, simultaneously a member of three different types of organizations: society, economy, and polity. Just as economy and society are closely interrelated, so are economy and polity. Once, this relationship was officially recognized: Economics was known as political economy. One of the ironies of modern economics is that the adjective was dropped precisely at the time the public sector was mushrooming, and with it was dropped the importance to economics of the political process.*

How well do children understand politics? Does their grasp of social relationships and economic principles exceed or fall short of their knowledge of political relationships? Joseph Adelson, a leading researcher of this topic, has compiled evidence showing that children grasp the political facts of life much later than they learn about money, for example, or even about sex.[35] Abstract concepts of justice, freedom, and equality are exceedingly vague in the minds of children or adolescents. Only around age sixteen, it appears, do mature conceptions of political thinking, based on formal reasoning, emerge. It is not that children are ignorant of the facts, Adelson observes. Rather, they do not comprehend the nature of political custom and convention.

This suggests to me that the largely competitive and individualistic values of economics are learned and internalized by children long before the cooperative, democratic, and collectivist values of politics. In time this priority may come to dominate children's value systems. Perhaps, then, a part of the curriculum of caring should be a formal or informal curriculum of politics—a curriculum on how the political system tries to resolve differences among individuals and groups.

*The polity, among its other functions, is the instrument for collective decisions regarding resources deemed *public* in nature. I have argued that virtually all resources are, in a broad sense, public. The smooth functioning of the political process, therefore, will take on growing importance in the future.

Adults as Children

So far I have focused on the social development of children and how it affects the life cycle and the economic system in general. But causal arrows run in both directions. The economic system itself shapes the personality of our children, not exclusively, as Marx would have us believe, but significantly.

A major feature of modern industrial economies is the preeminence of knowledge. An entire history of the human race could be written by tracing shifts in power from one factor of production (labor, land, capital) to another. For centuries land was vital, and those who owned it owned other peoples' lives as well. With the Industrial Revolution power shifted to physical capital. With the development of sophisticated markets for transferring resources from those who had them to those who could use them—capital markets—financial capital ascended. Today, as John Kenneth Galbraith and Daniel Bell contend, in the new, or post industrial state the knowledge, skill, information, and intelligence needed to run complex organizations are uppermost.

Growth of such knowledge is exponential and rapid. To master even a small part of it long years of study are needed, and a major part of the life cycle is now devoted to acquiring knowledge rather than to applying it. The result is what some view as an artificial, and harmful, prolongation of childhood, and a deferral of responsibility and economic maturity long beyond attainment of biological maturity.

The Coleman Report stated this view most forcefully.[36] The report notes that schools and colleges have become the general social environment for youth. Where once parents and other adults were the main instruments of socialization, schools and peer groups have now taken over. If biological maturity occurs at age fourteen, social maturity—including responsibility for the well-being of others—may begin at age twenty-four or later. More than any other period in the life cycle, the decade from fourteen to twenty-four is a period in which biological, psychological, and economic maturity do not jibe.

Not everyone sees the prolonged childhood inherent in modern society as an evil. Oscar Lewis notes that one of the characteristics of poverty is the absence of a conventional childhood as a "specially prolonged and protected stage of the life cycle."[37] But for poor and rich alike, the social structure has added years onto the age at which young people first become producers.

During the past century, David Elkind pointed out, the age at which children attained physical maturity—menarche and puberty—fell sharply. Each generation saw taller, heavier, stronger children who developed physically at earlier and earlier ages. This trend has now leveled off. In contrast, children are now developing *socially* at much earlier ages, owing perhaps to television, child-rearing practices, and peer-group pressure. Yet even as children become biologically and socially prepared for responsibilities at earlier ages, the social structure puts off, to later and later ages, placing those responsibilities upon them. The result: adults who remain, in effect, children.[38]

What happens when the three key axes around which our life cycle revolves—biological, social, and economic maturity—drift far apart?

Two sociologists, Carl Danziger and Matthew Greenwald, claim in fact that a new stage of life has arisen, falling between adolescence and adulthood.[39] They call it *transadulthood* and place it from the age of college entrance to the late twenties or early thirties. It is a stage of minimal responsibilities, of experimentation with life-styles, and with maximal personal freedom. According to Danziger and Greenwald, those in this stage seek to defer the responsibilities of adulthood or shun them entirely.

With people spending from a sixth to a quarter of their lives in school, much of that well beyond the time they are children, schools assume new roles. They become institutions for deferring entry of large numbers of young people into the labor force. They have contributed to a shift in the locus of social influence on children, from the one-time chief instrument, parents, to friends and acquaintances. This is a trend some psychologists see as destructive. "The more adults withdraw from children," one researcher wrote, "the more they expose them to peer influence. And the more children interact in the absence of adults . . . the more likely they are to engage in fights and quarrels over property and privileges."[40]

Generations ago, Marshall had no doubt about the main purpose of schooling. "The schoolmaster must learn that his main duty is not to impart knowledge," Marshall wrote, "for a few shillings will buy more printed knowledge than a man's brain can hold. It is to educate character, faculties and activities; so that the children even of those parents who are not thoughtful themselves may have a better chance of being trained up to become thoughtful parents of the next generation. *To this end public money must flow freely"* (italics mine).[41]

Conclusion: Socialization and Watermelons

Market behavior for watermelons is said to follow a pattern. A high price in one season draws extensive plantings the next. When this extra supply hits the market, it drives watermelon prices down. Low prices cause growers to cut back acreage the next season. Curtailed supply then drives the price back up, and so on. Price cycles of this sort are common in agriculture.

As supply trails behind (or overshoots) demand for watermelons, so do values trail behind the economic conditions that made those values appropriate and useful. In Marshall's words: "Each generation seems to be chiefly occupied with working out the thoughts of the preceding one; while the full importance of its own thoughts is not yet seen."[42]

For many generations the work of society was teaching children the society of work. The age of mass production heralded the era of mass consumption. But the values of frugality and thrift, driven deep into our culture through many layers of history, died hard and changed very slowly. Keynes's message to the world was broadly social: Ordinary man's "habits and instincts" would not supply sufficient private demand to generate full employment in the short run, hence government had to fill the gap.

Now that the values of spending and mass consumption have burrowed through a generation or two, they may again be out of phase with the new realities of economic life. Just as in the watermelon market, where demand and supply march out of step, so in society penury and profligacy are poorly synchronized with the conditions they suit. But unlike the watermelon market, the problem of socialization is not merely a cyclical one. It is not simply that production and consumption take uncoordinated turns at the top of the values ladder. A new candidate has appeared—distribution—and it demands its own set of habits and instincts.

A major change in the way we think about production and consumption, and one another, and in the way our children learn these values, must take place if we are to continue to exist on our ever more crowded planet.

This century has brought us new ways of perceiving time and space, through the mind of Albert Einstein. The scientific revolution he wrought could not escape notice; it announced its arrival with explosive force. A quiet revolution has been taking place in our knowledge of the time and space dimensions of child development. Its revolutionaries were Freud, Piaget, and many others. Piaget showed us how, and when, the space perceived by children expands to embrace more than their own egos. Piaget and other thinkers have transformed our understanding of how children come to be what they are. And through this transformation, our conception of *adults* has also changed.

Not much of this revolution in psychology has trickled through to economics. Eventually it will. As a nation, an ever-large proportion of our economic difficulties has a psychological source. As individuals, we march along the milestones of our economic lives carrying mental baggage dating back to childhood. Prying open those bags is both enlightening and helpful. It may help us learn how to equip our children as they set out on their own journeys through life and how best to navigate ourselves.

Man reproduces himself biologically. His culture regenerates itself socially and psychologically. How well it does so has vital implications for the economy. Economic Man, therefore, badly needs a childhood.

Postscript: Children Are Scarce

What children are like, and how they got that way, is a difficult, complex subject laden with paradoxes and contradictory findings. How *many* children there are is much simpler. The number of children turns out to have lasting social and economic importance. So before moving on to discuss one especially important part of childhood and maturation—the process of learning patience—I close this chapter with a brief analysis of changes in the number of children.

Suppose a blindfolded social scientist is allowed to ask just one question of someone. Which single question would likely elicit the most information about that person?

How about, "How old are you?" A person's age provides several crucial pieces of data. It reveals the part of history he or she has lived through. It tells us the current life-cycle stage. It also helps us find—with the help of a handy *Statistical Abstract*—the size of that person's cohort. (A cohort is a group of people born in the same period of time, usually a calendar year.) How many pairs of elbows exist to bang against ours is one of a handful of key childhood variables that powerfully affects the life cycle. (Some other candidates: Whether your parents were rich or poor, and, decreasingly, whether you were born a boy or girl.)

Learning the Work of Society

People of 1942 vintage (such as myself) have different life experiences from people of 1947 vintage (my wife, for instance). In elementary school and high school I was in small classes. My wife's classrooms bulged. Entering college, I found, was not hard. My wife faced stiff competition. Graduate school offered, for me, fairly abundant financial aid. For my wife's cohort, fellowships were spread more thinly. With the passage of time, as the age specificity of life-cycle stages becomes blurred, this effect softens. But it never disappears. The crop of babies in 1942 was minimal. There was a bumper harvest of babies in 1947. The year of birth has, and will have, lasting effect on myself and my wife, and on members of our respective cohorts.

Childbearing in America has in fact followed a steep rollercoaster pattern since the start of the Great Depression. The dips and climbs of fertility have been sharper than in most other Western countries, and each zig or zag of the curve has ripple effects that are felt for generations.

Depression and war drove fertility steadily downward from 1930 through 1945. In 1946 war-postponed babies began arriving and drove fertility up 20 percent in a single year. The birth rate climbed to its peak in 1957, when more than one in every ten women of childbearing age actually gave birth. By 1977, fertility had fallen by 50 percent.[43]

Taking the long view, the baby boom was a short aberration in a two-hundred-year aging trend. In 1840 half the American population was under age eighteen. One person in forty was sixty-five or older. Today the median age is thirty, and about one person in nine is sixty-five or older.

But even if short-lived, the bulge of babies in the 1950s has had a powerful impact. Like a deer passing through a python, it has muscled its way through elementary schools, high schools, colleges, job markets, and housing and durable-goods markets. Unlike the deer, the baby boom is trailed by its own echo, a self-made boomlet of children of baby-boom children. Their effect has already begun in this decade. And even the echo of the echo will not be negligible.

The 1946–1960 cohorts are now between about 22 and 36 years of age. They reflect a period when the number of children grew 3 percent yearly (compared with a 1 percent decline annually during the depression). In the past two years the part of spendable income set aside as savings fell to about four cents on the dollar. Some analysts attribute this to the predominance of people in low-saving ages—people of the baby boom. As the 1946–1960 cohorts enter the job market, swelling the supply of labor relative to the demand, wages have been influenced, and, it is claimed, have risen more slowly than they might have otherwise. Capital investment has been lagging recently. One explanation is that employers are substituting plentiful (hence cheap) labor for expensive machinery and equipment.[44] The baby boom even impinges on the energy problem. Harvard economist Dale Jorgenson has suggested that baby-boom labor arrived just in time for employers to substitute human muscle for expensive fossil fuel.[45]

Current low levels of fertility, making children "scarce" relative to previous decades, are somewhat disguised by the large number of women of childbearing age. In other words, the larger number of women aged 22 to 36 (prime childbearing years) partly offsets the lower average fertility per woman. To neutralize this "bulge" effect, the Bureau of the Census made an interesting calculation.[46] Suppose fertility were at replacement levels—a little more than two children per couple, with the *little more* offsetting mortality. This is not much below present patterns. If enough time were to pass to let the baby boom and its echoes fade away, what would the age structure be? Computations show that by 2050, only one person in five would be fifteen or younger, compared with one in three in 1960. How scarce or plentiful children are has had, and will continue to have, great impact on both our society and economy.

As they grow older, children's horizons widen in time as well as in space. Time expands to encompass more than the immediate moment. As it does so, children acquire the ability to perceive future events and bring them into perspective with present ones. This transition—the shift from the *pleasure principle* to the *reality principle,* in Freud's terms—has an inestimable impact on later life. The following chapter delves into economic and psychological aspects of children's perceptions of the present and the future.

3

FROM PLEASURE TO REALITY: LEARNING TO WAIT BEGINS IN CHILDHOOD

AT AGE four-and-a-half, John Maynard Keynes was asked what is meant by interest. "If I let you have a halfpenny and you kept it for a very long time, you would have to give me back that halfpenny and another too," Keynes answered. "That's interest."[1]

The pervasive preference for a certain and immediate dollar, or halfpenny, over a delayed future one—*time preference* in economists' jargon—is an apparently permanent fixture in human society. Despite biblical injunctions and Roman, Islamic, and canonical laws banning usury, interest rates have left unmistakable footprints throughout recorded history.[2] Why? It is a "riddle," wrote Irving Fisher, author of a definitive work on interest rates, "which for 2,000 years economists have been trying to solve."[3]

So have psychologists, if not for two millennia, then at least for all of this century. They call time preference "unwillingness to defer gratification." Their theoretical and experimental research shows it to be an important aspect of personality that varies with age, differs among persons, and is partly learned from others. On this subject, psychology provides a fresh and illuminating point of view that complements, and at times contradicts, that of economics, as this chapter aspires to show.

Now or Later?

From the trivial to the sublime, from distant history to yesterday's newspapers, from election-year politics to Madison Avenue, present-future choices pop up incessantly, uniting seemingly dissimilar phenomena. Here are four examples:

- In the "18-cent election" Canadians turned out of office a Conservative prime minister who had asked them to pay higher gasoline prices and thus forgo "short-term gain for long-term gain."[4]
- In 1929 a Soviet leader—enamored with future-oriented capital goods—found a way to overcome his people's hunger for consumer goods. He didn't produce them.
- Although savings bank windows resemble appliance stores, and interest rates top 14 percent, personal saving as a fraction of disposable income plummets to a thirty-year low; in fact, apart from contractual pension deductions, households spent more than they earned in 1979.[5]
- Cracker Jack boxes no longer contain put-together toys; in their place are glitter stickers, instant tatoos, and sponge toys that pop into shape in water. The prize buyer explains, "their toys have to have instant gratification."[6]

A common theme embraces Joe Clark and Joe Stalin, prizes for candied popcorn, and thirty-month deposits—*now-or-later choice.* For both individuals and society as a whole, the necessity of choosing between present and future gratification is inescapable. In particular, many microeconomic decisions center on giving up something now to get something later. Schooling, work, savings, even having children—all are instances of forgoing income, leisure, or consumption for some future gain.

Separated by an ocean, but close in time and in thought, Irving Fisher—America's greatest economist of all time, who specialized in interest-rate theory—and Sigmund Freud both thought and wrote about now-or-later choice at the turn of this century. Freud wrote a major essay published in 1911, entitled "Formulations on the Two Principles of Mental Functioning."[7] The two principles Freud refers to are the *pleasure principle,* which governs behavior in infants, and the *reality principle,* which characterizes mature behavior. There are few demands more insistent than a hungry baby's call for immediate gratification at 5:00 A.M. As children mature, Freud reasoned, there occurs "the supercession of the pleasure principle by the reality principle," where "what was presented in the mind was no longer what was agreeable but what was real, even if it happened to be disagreeable." This transition is a vital step toward maturation. In Freud's theories, it is related to the ability to think, where thought is defined as "experimental action." Children realize that a large but deferred reward may be better for them than a small immediate one. As examples of the reality principle Freud cites religion ("renunciation of pleasure in this life by means of the promise of compensation in a future existence"), science, education, art, and even Yellowstone Park (conservation of land and resources for the benefit of future generations) which he may have visited during his 1909 American tour.

As far as I know, Freud and Fisher never met. But their paths may have crossed. European tours in 1894 and in 1911 took Fisher to Vienna, where he met with Austrian School economists. He published an article entitled "The Impatience Theory of Interest" in an Italian journal. It appeared the same year as Freud's "Formulations."[8]

"Impatience is a fundamental attribute of human nature," Fisher asserted. He tried to explain why a future dollar is less valuable to people than a present dollar. Dating from Freud, psychologists who study "unwillingness to defer gratification" have tried to explain why future dollars have any value at all to people —the impatience expressed in infants' demands for instant gratification. In now-or-later choice economists and psychologists share the same turf, without knowing it.

Interest as the Price of Impatience

Economists relate future values to present ones with the help of interest rates. Interest is a sort of price. It is the premium that *now* dollars bring in comparison with *later* dollars, simply because *now* dollars are available immediately. In this sense, interest is the price of impatience *or* the reward for patience.

How large a rate of interest is required to elicit patience? This example should help illustrate the kind of reasoning that underlies now-or-later choice: Suppose you are offered a $50 money prize, payable at once, or alternately, $100 payable in five years. Which would you choose? In making up your mind, perhaps some or all of the following considerations would be evaluated.

What can be bought today for $50 will likely cost more than $100 in five years. When prices rise 2 per cent a year, erosion of money's purchasing power is not predominant in present-future choice. But when prices are rising 15 or 20 percent a year, interest rates primarily reflect compensation for dwindling purchasing power of money, and they are dominated by inflation and inflation expectations.

I may not be alive in five years to collect the money. Actual mortality cannot be a major factor in determining interest rates. For a white, prime-age male, the probability of dying in a five-year period is less than 1 percent; it is half that for females.[9] *Perceived* mortality, though, may be much higher; overweighting of small probabilities is discussed in chapter 8.

The payer may welch. Psychological studies show interpersonal trust is an important determinant of ability to wait, a point I discuss at length later on.

I need the $50 to meet a pressing debt. The poor are experts at deferring gratification, it has been said; they practice it all the time.

Yet to those who have little, $50 now is worth much more than it is to those who have much and are thus able and willing to wait.

If I invested $50 now at 15 percent interest, and reinvested the interest each time it was paid, I would have $100 in five years. That is a good return, well worth waiting for. Using a little algebra, the equation is: $50 \times (1.15)^5 \approx $100.

The $100 to be received in five years has a present value of $50, assuming a 15 percent rate of interest: $50 \approx $100 \div (1.15)^5$. If my own subjective rate of interest is smaller than 15 percent—that is, if the reward I require for waiting is less than 15 percent—it pays for me to take the $100 and pocket the generous (for me) premium for patience.

In addition to inflation, uncertainty, need, and profit, there are many other relevant considerations. Each person brings his or her own personality, experience, and circumstances to now-or-later choices. Psychologists suggest there are likely as many different subjective interest rates as there are people. In this, they differ from economists.

Economic logic suggests that borrowing and lending should work to even out differences in subjective interest rates among people. Suppose banks lend to worthy candidates at 15 percent and pay similar rates to borrowers. Those for whom $1.00 now is worth *more* than $1.15 in a year from now will borrow. They will keep on borrowing—economic reasoning suggests—until they have so many *now* dollars that their internal interest rate just matches 15 percent. Those who think $1.00 now is worth *less* than $1.15 in a year from now will save and deposit their savings. They should continue to do so until they have so few *now* dollars that their subjective interest rates rise to equal what the bank pays. In this way the workings of the marketplace even out interpersonal differences in impatience.

Even those who believe in free markets regard this "evening out" process as only partial. Milton Friedman reports subjective interest rates "drastically out of line with market interest rates," and explains that most wealth consists of either assets that cannot easily be bought and sold or assets whose buying and selling price differ widely, such as *human capital* (education).[10] Moreover, many people cannot borrow at all, choose not to borrow, or can get funds only from loan sharks. For these reasons we should expect to find wide differences in subjective interest rates among people of differing circumstances. A large study by Kurz, Spiegelman, and West bears this out.[11] It reveals interest rates ranging from about 22 percent for educated, high-income family heads to 60 percent for less-educated, low-income family heads. Apparently a time-preference rate is psychological baggage each of us carries through life, which varies with age and circumstances, differs widely from one person to another, and has enormous influence on our life-cycle decisions. Ability to wait is, according to recent empirical findings from psychology, learned in childhood, is part of the process of socialization and can be permanently altered.

TABLE 3.1

*Subjective Interest Rates, by Education and Earnings of Family Head**

Earnings of Family Head	Years of Education		
	8 (%)	12 (%)	16 (%)
$2,000	60	47	34
$5,000	57	44	31
$10,000	53	40	27
$15,000	48	35	22

NOTE: Reprinted by permission from M. Kurz, R. G. Spiegelman, and R.W. West, "The Experimental Horizon and the Role of Time Preference for the Seattle-Denver Income Maintenance Experiments," *Memorandum 21* (Stanford: Stanford Research Institute, November 1973).
*For a Caucasian family head, thirty-six years old, with $5,000 in assets, two children, owning own house.

Learning to Wait

Stanford psychologist Walter Mischel, the author of many ingenious studies about self-imposed delay of gratification, has pointed
out the "enormously complex chains of deferred gratification patterns . . . necessary for people to achieve the delayed rewards and
distant outcomes" far in the future that society dangles before us.[12]
Typically he gives children booklets with some immediate reward
shown on the left-hand page and a larger, delayed reward shown
on the facing right-hand page. They are asked to examine the
choice pairs, pick one, record their choice, turn the page, and
proceed to the next pair. As an incentive to decide carefully and
realistically, they are told that they will receive one of the items
they select.

Some of the prizes—two *Mad* magazines now or three later, a
hit-tune record now or three later—may seem small and unimportant. But the subjects themselves find the prizes attractive. The
essence of the method is to create inner conflict so that the difference between immediate and delayed rewards is large enough to
induce some children to wait, yet not so large that the immediate
choice is no longer tempting.[13]

Mischel and R. Metzner found that among children, preference
for delayed rewards increases with age.[14] The crucial *switchover*
point, at which ability to wait develops most rapidly, is at ages nine
and ten (grades 3, 4, and 5). By adolescence, time preference seems
quite firmly shaped, although it is still subject to influence and
modification.

Jean Piaget has tried to explain the link between age and impatience. He found that at around age seven, children develop the
ability to shift their attention away from the immediate prizes in
front of them and consider the *largeness* of delayed rewards. His
theory resembles Freud's idea of thought as experimental action.[15]

Accuracy of time perspective also has something to do with
impatience. Among older children Mischel found that those who

picked immediate rewards had less accurate judgment of time.[16] In Western culture we are wedded to our watches. This is not necessarily true in other cultures. Aborigines, for example, allow a very fluid concept of time. In choosing between small immediate rewards or larger but delayed ones, they were found to pick randomly, regardless of their age, intelligence, or experience of success.[17]

In some of his earlier experimental work, Mischel thought that focusing a child's attention on the larger, delayed reward would help him or her await it instead of opting for the smaller, immediately available one. Instead he discovered that "attention to the rewards significantly and dramatically *decreased* delay of gratification. The children waited longest when *no* rewards faced them during the delay period; they waited significantly less long when they faced the delayed reward, or the immediate reward, or both rewards."[18] This led to Mischel's *two-part theory*. *Choosing* deferred rewards, Mischel thought, is influenced by different factors than the ability to actually *await* the deferred reward. He suggested that the choice between immediate and delayed rewards is influenced mainly by past experience and trust in other people. Sustaining the delay choice by waiting the prescribed period of time for it depends on activities that reduce the unpleasantness of the waiting. Skill at thinking about other things or engaging in some distracting action is important. The more successful people are at making the waiting time pleasant or at least pass quickly, the better they are at fulfilling decisions to wait. The earliest instance of this is Jacob's behavior; he worked seven years for each of his wives, Leah and Rachel, but, according to the Bible, found the time passed like "a single day."

Mischel's subjects invented elaborate techniques to distract themselves while waiting for delayed rewards they had chosen. Some of them covered their eyes with their hands, put their heads on their arms, talked quietly to themselves, sang ("This is such a pretty day, hurray"), played games with their hands and feet, or —a method familiar to droning college professors—went to sleep.

The "get thee behind me, Satan" technique may, however, have a fatal flaw. Total forgetfulness of the delayed reward makes waiting seem pointless and leads to its termination. Those most successful at deferring gratification seem able to alternately divert themselves and recall the desired goal.

Patience and Trust

As part of his research, Mischel went to the West Indian islands of Granada and Trinidad to study the relationship between delay of gratification and culture. Anthropologists had observed that the hardy independent Granadans were less present-oriented (though poorer) than the Trinidadians. The inhabitants of Trinidad had been under colonial rule for many years, had been largely landless until their island became independent, and were accustomed to subservience in business, government, and the professions. In contrast the typical Granadan clung to his own land from generation to generation and eked out a bare living on it. He was familiar with long-term payoffs arising from the forebearance of hard work in tilling the land, and was "far less suspicious and skeptical in his relations to strangers as well as to his own peers." In Trinidad people apparently had had less favorable experiences in actually receiving promised rewards. They were less trusting and less confident in their ability to influence or control events.

Mischel studied several groups of black and East Indian Trinidadian children aged eight to nine and eleven to fourteen, and black Granadan children aged eight to nine. He chose children from lower- and lower-middle-class backgrounds. Younger children were offered a 2¢ candy bar at once or a 10¢ candy bar in one week. Older children were offered 10¢ or 25¢ candy bars. The older children were asked to respond to two statements with yes or no answers: "I would rather get ten dollars right now than have to wait a whole month and get thirty dollars then"; and "I would rather wait to get a much larger gift much later than get a much smaller one now."

As expected, Granadans chose delayed rewards more heavily than Trinidadians. But among younger black children whose fathers were absent, there was no detectable difference in delay choices between the two groups. Might the greater impatience of the Trinidadians be due in part to the higher incidence of father absence? Mischel suggested that the presence of a father helped transmit cultural values such as forebearance and saving to children, and that father absence may have increased children's uncertainty about the future.[19] His result brings to mind the orphan Pip, Dickens's hero of *Great Expectations,* whose first impression of his parents "were unreasonably derived from their tombstones." Pip complains to his friend, "My dear Herbert, I cannot tell you how dependent and uncertain I feel, and how exposed to hundreds of uncertain chances."

For older children aged eleven to fourteen, Mischel found no significant difference in delay choice between those whose fathers were present and those who fathers were absent. He conjectured that as children mature, they participate in a wider environment outside their own immediate family. From age ten or eleven, children move about freely, visit with other relatives, and become fairly independent of the family. Expectations about the keeping of promises, and about the future, are based more on past experiences and on influences much wider than those found in the household itself.

Patience and Parents

An attempt to find direct evidence of a link between parents' time preference and that of their children was made by my wife, Sharone, in her study of 142 eighth-grade school children from four suburban Tel Aviv schools.[20] Preference for delayed reward was measured by a Mischel-type booklet. Parents' time preference was determined in interviews by presenting choice pairs similar to those used by Mischel. Finally children were asked to answer their parents' questionnaires *in the way they thought their parents would answer them.*

Out of a wide array of characteristics, including socioeconomic background, the variable most closely linked to children's *preference* for delayed rewards was *parents'* time preference as perceived by the child. (No significant link was found, though, with actual parental time preference.)

To test Mischel's two-part theory, the children were offered an immediate money reward or a larger reward if they waited two weeks. The experimenter returned to the schools daily to see if those who had opted for the larger reward would actually wait the required interval, or they would give up and ask for the immediate sum. Actually awaiting deferred rewards, she found, was influenced by different factors than delay preference (measured by the questionnaire). Here, ethnic origin, a measure of mistrustfulness, and actual parents' time preference were most closely related to waiting. Another observation was that children of Middle Eastern ethnic origin were likely to express preference for a delayed reward but fail to actually await it. This suggests that early adolescence is a time when the social *norm* of waiting may have been acquired by children, but the ability to *act* according to that norm is still being formed.

Who Gets Ahead?

The logic of now-or-later choice suggests that building the potential to earn income and acquire wealth requires present sacrifice. By studying longer and more effectively, by working harder and longer, by saving, and by planning over long time horizons rather than short ones, future-oriented people get ahead.

Learning to Wait Begins in Childhood

This is a very old idea. It was used by Adam Smith to explain the wealth (or poverty) of nations. John Stuart Mill attributed England's high savings rate during the Industrial Revolution to the frugal Puritan ethic. Later Weber and Tawney built theories of the rise of capitalism around that idea.

Modern psychology provides an additional, very important contribution: Present-future preferences are developed in childhood, depend to a large extent on interpersonal trust, and are learned from parents and friends. Mischel wrote,

> A person's willingness to defer immediate gratification depends to a considerable degree on the outcomes that he expects from his choice. Of particular importance are the individual's expectations that future delayed rewards for which he would have to work and/or wait would actually materialize. . . . Expectations, or feelings of trust depend, in turn, on the person's history of prior promise-keeping and on past reinforcement for waiting behavior and for other forms of planful, goal-directed self-control. [Apart from direct personal experiences] . . . learning experiences through observation of the behavior of social models—such as peers, parents, and teachers—substantially influence [the subject's] choices.[21]

Economics has long lacked a decent, credible theory about who gets ahead. Findings from psychology suggest that we should begin with a fundamental subjective "price"—the value of the future in relation to the present. Those who value the future more highly than others and act on that value will get ahead faster.

There is strong evidence that people differ widely in their present-future preferences. The evidence linking those preferences with income and wealth is, however, weak. In *Inequality*, a research team led by Christopher Jencks reevaluated a massive amount of data on education and income originally compiled in a study directed by James Coleman. Jencks's finding was that "neither family background, cognitive skill, educational attainment, nor occupational status explains much of the variation in men's incomes. . . . When we compare men who are identical in all these respects, we find only 12 to 15 percent less inequality among random individuals." What, then, does matter? "Some men value money more than others," Jencks asserts, "and make unusual sacrifices to get it."[22] Willingness and ability to make unusual sacrifices are simply another way of describing present-future preference.

There are two different dimensions of the *who gets ahead* question that must be understood: Why, in a given group, or cohort, of people do some do better than others; and how does inequality pass from parent to child and from one generation to another? Contrary to common belief, poverty is not generally a permanent condition families sink into and never escape from. A five-year study of a panel of five thousand families showed much vertical movement out of, and into, poverty.[23] But it is hard to dispute the advantages of being born to parents who have already gotten ahead. Long before real estate and stocks and bonds are inherited, *planfulness,* or future orientation, is passed on from parent to child. Fortunately, though affluence is a medium friendly to valuing the future, the ability to defer gratification is not and never was the exclusive property of the upper class.

The Culture of Poverty and the Poverty of Culture

> Like I said, you can't make no plans. I know I can't make no plans for myself until my children grow up and marry. Then I will be old. I have never thought too much about making any plans at all . . . maybe after (my children are able to look out for themselves) I can plan something for myself, but sometimes I don't see no use in trying to make plans because something is always happening to upset you.[24]

The concept of the *culture of poverty* originated with the anthropologist Oscar Lewis. His studies of Mexican and Puerto Rican families identified impatience as a component of their economic distress. In *The Children of Sanchez,* he pointed to a "strong present-time orientation with relatively little ability to defer gratification and plan for the future, a sense of resignation and fatalism based upon the realities of their difficult life situation."[25] This, he felt, characterizes the cultural milieu of those who live in poverty. The passage cited above was spoken by a young mother, with several children and whose husband was absent.

"By the time slum children are six or seven," Lewis continued, "they have usually absorbed the basic values and attitudes of their subculture and are not psychologically geared to take full advantage of the changing conditions or increased opportunities that may occur in their lifetime." In his famous study of streetcorner youngsters in Washington, D.C., Liebow argued that "when Richard squanders a week's pay in two days, it is not because . . . he is present oriented . . . he does so precisely because he is aware of the future and the hopelessness of it all."[26] Some experimental evidence exists too. A. R. Mahrer told 234 schoolboys, aged seven to nine, that they would each receive a reward the following day. For one group, the rewards were faithfully delivered as promised. For a second, only some of the rewards were delivered. For a third, none of the rewards was given. Three days later the children were offered the choice of immediate or larger but deferred rewards. Not surprisingly, much greater choice of delayed rewards was made by boys in the group that actually received the promised prizes.[27]

Recently John Kenneth Galbraith has rediscovered and elegantly restated the economic psychology of hopelessness. His study of poverty in India traces its source to the peasant's rational conviction that since nothing he does can lead to future gain, there is nothing left but to accept present misery.[28]

Though currently unfashionable intellectually, the culture of poverty is alive and unwell. It reflects the poverty of our entire culture, one in which promised opportunities for the disadvantaged do not materialize or are not sufficiently rewarding or believable to call forth forebearance. A generation ago Allison Davis wrote, "It is all or nothing . . . our economic system does not offer any prospect of a regular income to slum people; therefore they lack the relative security which must underlie habits of saving, buying insurance, home buying and so forth."[29] Not much has changed since those words were written. The *culture of poverty* concept has waxed and waned among scholars and legislators. Regrettably the conditions that make *present-* oriented behavior within that culture sensible and rational seem to be as permanent and deep-rooted as ever.

In a 1940 study of black children Allison Davis and John Dollard found, in a series of case studies in Natchez and New Orleans, that the children did not learn forbearance because "the upper caste either does not reward his efforts as it does the white child's or it constantly punishes them."[30] They suggest it is the "prime function of the caste system to withhold these rewards." As a result,

> if a parent wishes to teach a child to save money, he must not only try to prevent him from buying candy or a toy whenever the impulse seizes him, but he must also constantly tell him what more desirable object (a train, a doll, a rifle) he will be able to buy in the distant future with his savings. And this day may not be postponed indefinitely; the child must occasionally be reinforced in his saving by being allowed to take part of his hoard downtown to buy a doll or rifle.

As children grow up, rewards for delay are increasingly those of promised higher status and are more "long run" in nature. But "in the (lower class boy's world) the long range goals do not seem to be there. . . . he does not see other people in his class attaining them, or practicing the behavior required of him, and he feels his parents and teachers are 'crazy' when they demand it of him." In a sense, perhaps they are. It was in this study, published in 1940 as *Children of Bondage,* that the term *deferred gratification pattern* was coined.

In a later study Davis asks why parents from lower social classes do not instill attainment, aspiration, and forbearance norms in their children.

> The incitement to learn (on the part of lower class children) . . . which means in part to renounce direct impulse gratification and build up

more complex habits and skills, is crippled by the scarcity of available rewards. There must be a push behind human beings to make them learn, and this push is most effective when it not only punishes undesired actions but also rewards the constant effort required to build more effective habits.[31]

In life situations where opportunities are limited, options are narrow, prospects are bleak, and promised future rewards are utterly beyond belief, deferring gratification may be the precise opposite of rational behavior.

From time to time society quickly embraces, and just as quickly abandons, compensatory education as a way to attack poverty. There have been many such cycles, going back to John Ruskin. Education is typically seen as a key path to upward mobility for the lower classes. But Jencks's study *Inequality* shows that equalizing education will not equalize much else. And there are always *nature, not nurture* contentions to pander to the permanence of poverty. In 1920 Marshall's successor, A. C. Pigou, quoted a leading geneticist of his day: "Education is to man what manure is to the pea. The educated are in themselves the better for it, but their experience will alter not one jot the irrevocable nature of their offspring." Pigou's response is noteworthy. "The environment of one generation can produce a lasting result, because it can affect the environment of future generations. Environments . . . as well as people have children."[32]

Pigou's response presages both the delay-of-gratification theory of inequality and the implications that spring from it. Environments do indeed have children. Environments can be altered. A key feature that must be altered is the uncertainty and mistrust that makes it difficult or impossible to study, work, save, and plan effectively. Until this is done, expanding the supply of educational opportunities to the disadvantaged—an admirable policy—may be met by disappointingly small demand. We should not respond by cutting the supply. Rather, conditions should be created that foster more demand, a policy that in itself calls for collective patience.

Is There Hope?

What is learned can be taught. If patience is learned by children, then it can be taught to them, better or differently. Walter Mischel and behavior-modification expert Albert Bandura provide a compelling illustration.[33] Some 250 fourth- and fifth-graders were given paired reward choices, and a group of 60 with the lowest delay scores was selected for further study. Some of them were exposed to the following procedure. In their presence an adult was asked to choose immediate or delayed rewards. This *model* selected the delayed rewards, making comments such as,

> The wooden chess figures are of much better quality, more attractive, and will last longer. I'll wait two weeks for the better one. You have probably noticed that I am a person who is willing to forgo having fewer or less valuable things now for the sake of more and bigger benefits later. I usually find that life is more gratifying when I take that carefully into account.

Other children were exposed to *symbolic* models. The children were simply shown the adult's answer book and written philosophy-of-life comments without actually observing the model's choices being made. For still another group, neither a live nor a symbolic model was present. Four weeks later all the children were given the original delay-choice questionnaire.

The effect of *modeling* is shown in figure 3.1. Mischel and Bandura concluded that "both forms of modeling produced highly significant temporary and long-term increases in self-imposed delay of reward." They do note, however, the difficulty in *maintaining* delayed-reward behavior, as shown by the downturn in the curves during prolonged absence of the model. They emphasize "the necessity for supporting newly established self-control behavior, particularly . . . in the case of readily available rewarding resources."

For adolescents, school environment may have an even greater

Learning to Wait Begins in Childhood

FIGURE 3.1

The Effect on Low-Delay Children of Three Experimental Conditions: Exposure to Live and Symbolic "Delay" Models, and no Model Present.

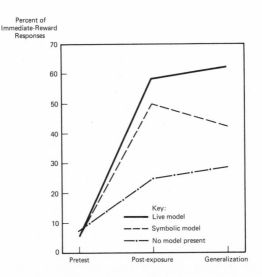

NOTE: Reprinted by permission of publisher from A. Bandura and W. Mischel, "Modification of Self-Imposed Delay of Reward Through Exposure to Live and Symbolic Models," *Journal of Personality and Social Psychology* 2 (1965): 702. Copyright 1965 by the American Psychological Association.

impact than adult models. In the previously mentioned study of Israeli schoolchildren, one of the schools involved had a roughly equal mixture of children from Middle Eastern and European-North American backgrounds, while another had children from Middle Eastern families exclusively. Other things being equal, children from the *mixed* class had significantly higher delayed-reward *preferences* than children from the unmixed one. But the proportion of those from the mixed class who *actually waited* for the delayed reward was no different from the other classes. Apparently patience as a value and as a social norm is a delicate flower; it is learned from others and must be carefully cultivated before behavior consistent with it develops. Such behavior may never develop if the environments the children live in differ from the surroundings they study in.

Learning to wait begins almost at birth, not in fourth or fifth or even first grade. From this proposition, strongly supported by evidence, it requires an Olympic leap to suggest, as one author has that "the problems posed by the lower class can be solved fundamentally only if the children of that class are removed from their parents' culture." Or consider permitting the sale of infants and children to qualified bidders (though we are urged to reject the latter as morally wrong and likely to stimulate even more lower-class babies).[34] You need not destroy society in order to save it. It is not parenthood and families that must be torn apart but the needlessly ramshackle environments that stunt and warp children's ability to properly value the future and, ultimately, handle their life choices effectively.

Mandating Patience

In the United States, most state laws require that formal education begin at age seven and continue through age sixteen. These laws provide for a minimum acceptable quantity of schooling. Recent Supreme Court decisions have, in addition, addressed the need for a minimum acceptable *quality* of education.[35]

By the inescapable law of input and output, what children take out of school depends on what they bring into it. Ability to defer gratification is an essential input; its current nature and distribution give rise to severe internal contradictions in our present schooling structure.

Anthony Davids and Jack Sidman studied a group of high school students with superior ability; the average IQ was 126, and average age was about sixteen.[36] Some of the students were known to be underachievers while others had high achievements and were tabbed as future scientists. Each of the youths was asked what he or she would do if given 10¢, $1, and $100. Answers were divided into immediate, short-term, and long-term categories. The high achievers were found to be substantially more future oriented, as the following figures, giving the percent who chose immediate gratification, show:

	10¢	$1	$100
Underachievers	65%	40%	35%
High Achievers	30%	10%	10%

They conclude that in the conventional educational system, orientation toward immediate gratification will cause difficulties. To succeed in school, they suggest, children must inhibit certain behaviors and exert much self-control.

The law requires school attendance until sixteen. Economics and propensities lead some pupils to want to quit long before that age. The law seems about to require minimal educational capability. Impatience puts attainment of this minimum beyond many pupils. Some have argued that mandatory school-attendance requirements should be weakened or even abolished. There is little chance of this happening, nor would it be desirable. But faced with the contradiction between mandated education and children poorly equipped to use it, much more attention must be given to the children and much less attention to litigation and legislation.

Patience Has No Color

In urban America more than one black in four falls below the poverty line; for whites, the proportion is one in twelve.[37] Even well-meaning people fall into the trap of attributing present-orientation to race, when it is so clearly both a cause, and an effect, of poverty itself. In 1968, the year *The Unheavenly City* was published, Julian and Rita Simon pointed out that blacks save more of their current income than do whites whose income level is the same.[38] This fact was documented as early as 1944 in Gunnar Myrdal's *An American Dilemma.* It has been subject to intense econometric testing and has survived. Why, then, do ordinary people and some scholars believe otherwise? If saving behavior of a randomly chosen white and randomly chosen black are compared, the black saves less *because he is likely to earn less.* As the Simons note, saving is class linked because *income* is by definition class linked (income is how we mainly define and measure class) and saving and consumption spending are closely related to income. Blacks may save more of their income than whites, for a given income class, for many reasons—less access to credit, smaller liquid assets, or less job security. But race itself is not a cause.

Oscar Handlin said very clearly thirty years ago: "There is no evidence of any inborn differences of temperament, personality, character, or intelligence among races."[39] This is as true as it ever was, and it should be repeated again and again.

Patience and Inflation

The overriding importance of inflation, and the declining importance of other considerations, in present-future choice is a relatively recent development. During the Eisenhower Administration, consumer prices rose 1.4 percent a year on average, and during the Kennedy and Johnson years, about 2 percent. Yet to most people, inflation has a hoary head and an assured, permanent future. For the past five years less than one out of seven Gallup Poll respondents believed the rate of inflation would decline during the coming year. Erosion of the dollar's value has brought about a drastic devaluation of the future for both rich and poor.

At the turn of this century, Irving Fisher was convalescing from tuberculosis in Santa Barbara, California. His masseur there was a socialist. (Then as now, Marxists believed interest reflects the exploitation of labor by capital; Marxist countries evaluate investments by the number of years they take to pay for themselves, a back-door disguise of rate of return.)

Learning to Wait Begins in Childhood

"Interest is the basis of capitalism and is robbery," the masseur said.

"How much do I owe you?" Fisher asked.

"Thirty dollars," replied the masseur.

"Very well. I will give you a note payable a hundred years hence. I suppose you have no objections to taking this note without any interest. At the end of that time you, or perhaps your grandchildren, can redeem it."

"But I cannot afford to wait that long."

"I thought you said that interest was robbery. If interest is robbery, you ought to be willing to wait indefinitely for the money. If you were willing to wait ten years, how much would you require?"

"Well, I would have to get more than thirty dollars."

Irving Fisher smiled in triumph. "That is interest."[40]

Today a conversation of this kind would be very different. The masseur's inability to wait a century would not be primal. The worthlessness of thirty dollars in a century would be. It is astonishing but true that at the time Irving Fisher negotiated with the socialist, the general price level in the United States had *fallen* by more than 40 percent compared with post–Civil War levels. For some time after the turn of the century, money held its value well. The New York subway system was inaugurated in 1904. The fare was a nickel. The fare remained a nickel for forty-four years, until 1948. For someone born in New York at the turn of the century, a nickel would have the same symbolic buying power—a subway ride—from his infancy through middle age. During the course of their lives, people need a certain number of fixed stars to help plot a course. Not that long ago, the value of money was one of those stars. For those alive today, it is no longer, and it may never be again in our lifetimes. The implications for society extend well beyond the relatively narrow concerns of economics and time preference. In this book, I shall return repeatedly to inflation as a symptom of social conflict in which psychology and economics are intimately connected.

There is in fact no *logical* necessity for inflation to influence now-or-later choice. Irving Fisher theorized that the "real" rate of interest—the market rate of interest minus the annual decline in money's purchasing power—would in the long run be independent of inflation. He reasoned that in borrowing or lending, people would add the expected inflation rate onto their rate of time preference, so that expected inflation would more or less come out to actual inflation. According to this logic 20 percent interest rates with 18 percent inflation (about what we had for a time in early 1979) are effectively the same as 2 percent interest rates with stable prices. This is true, for instance, in countries where nearly everything is contractually linked to the cost-of-living index—wages, interest, and bond prices. This is called *indexation.* There are countries where inflation is so rapid that indexation is needed to keep labor markets and capital markets working; ironically, it seems to take rapid inflation to make inflation unimportant.

Today, in the United States, a small or large saver who wants to *contractually* guarantee the purchasing power of his savings ten, twenty, or thirty years hence has no way to do this. So-called purchasing-power bonds, whose principal is linked to a price index, are not available. Why this is so is, to me, a mystery. There seems to be ample demand. Businesses offering such bonds could pay much less in interest. If businesses are leery of undertaking such *contingent liabilities* (a debt whose sum is variable, contingent on future inflation), let governments take the initiative. Both liberal economists (James Tobin) and conservative ones (Milton Friedman) have called for creation of a purchasing-power bond, one of the few subjects on which they agree.[41]

There are powerful psychological reasons for such a bond. The public no longer believes governments can control inflation; the greater the skepticism, the greater the expected inflation. The faster money loses its future value in people's eyes, the faster it is spent, thereby converting cause into effect and verifying the premise that got the whole process going. There are antiinflation hedges, but none of them are certain. Once, the stock market was thought a good hedge; this has not been true since 1969. Real estate did well

—until late 1979. Gold and silver have soared, except during sharp drops. People who find financial markets mystifying, and are averse to risk, can find no escape from taking huge gambles with their savings. Because of uncertain future inflation, equivalent to a roulette wheel, people such as these have little choice but spend their savings on current consumption. If promises to curtail inflation are disbelieved, the proper approach is to try to insulate present-future choice from inflation's effects. A purchasing-power bond would be a good start.

Losing Patience

Are individuals singly and collectively becoming more impatient? Is this the age of instant gratification?

In his time Marshall thought "the character of man himself had changed"—but toward more patience. "[Man] has obtained a greater 'telescopic' faculty; that is, he has acquired an increased power of realizing the future and bringing it clearly before his mind's eye," he wrote in 1890.[42] A long look at interest rates bore him out. In medieval times interest rates were around 10 percent. They declined to 6 or 8 percent during the Renaissance and from the end of the Napoleonic Wars to the close of the nineteenth century, they fell even further. Marshall felt that discounting the future at a moderate rate was "sensible." But his successor, Arthur Pigou, adopted Marshall's telescope metaphor and reversed it. Pigou claimed people see the future myopically as if through the wrong end of a telescope, figuratively and literally. There remains in economics a strong tradition which holds that pure time preference (interest rates corrected for inflation, risk, and rising real incomes), if greater than zero, is irrational and requires state intervention.[43] (See the box on page 78.) Curiously, the two main institutions that funnel funds to poorer countries are poles apart on this issue. The United Nations assumes zero pure time preference, while the World Bank opts for market interest rates.[44]

ECONOMISTS ON TIME PREFERENCE

To secure a maximum of benefit in life, all future events, all future pleasures or pains, should act upon us with the same force as if they were present, allowance being made for their certainty. . . . But no human mind is constituted in this perfect way.

—WILLIAM STANLEY JEVONS

Our telescopic faculty is defective. . . . we, therefore, see future pleasures, as it were, on a diminished scale. . . . people distribute their resources between the present, the near future and the remote future on the basis of a wholly irrational preference.

—ARTHUR C. PIGOU

(Discounting) later enjoyments in comparison with earlier ones (is) a practice which is ethically indefensible and arises merely from the weakness of the imagination.

—FRANK RAMSAY

Pure time preference is . . . a polite expression for rapacity and the conquest of reason by passion.

—ROY HARROD

Individuals' choices over time are notoriously irrational. . . . if one is likely to be the same person five years hence, and to have roughly the same real income, the gift of a certain enjoyment, whether it be a crate of champagne or a visit to the Sistine Chapel, will add the same amount to the pleasures of a lifetime whether it is promised in five years or today. . . . The irrationality consists in discounting the future solely because of the passage of time. . . . there is no good reason why the State, qua custodian of future generations as well as the present, should adopt this irrationality as its own.

—MAURICE DOBB

Learning to Wait Begins in Childhood

If the goods we produce were placed on a continuum based on the immediacy of the enjoyment they bring, public goods—roads, bridges, and schools—would rank higher in deferred gratification than private goods. For that reason social critics measure social patience by the abundance of collective consumption. Tawney's *Acquisitive Society* complained that industrialized communities neglect the very objects for which it is worthwhile to acquire riches in their feverish preoccupation with the means by which riches can be acquired. Nearly forty years later John Kenneth Galbraith in *The Affluent Society* lamented the family in a mauve-and-cerise finned automobile, driving through billboard-blighted countryside, picnicking by a polluted stream, camping in a park that menaces public health and morals amid decaying refuse. He reflected vaguely on the "curious unevenness of their blessings." During those forty years the public sector's claim on resources grew more rapidly than at any other time in history, and since 1958 it has continued to grow. Today, public opinion appears to favor less public consumption. This is generally attributed to widespread disaffection with waste in government. But it can also be explained as impatience—the desire to consume privately, now, rather than publicly, for those alive both now and later.

If the "me" and "now" generation has succeeded the "lost" and "beat" generations, it is partly because inflation and uncertainty have made the future more distant and less attractive. And then, of course, there is television, always a convenient rationale for social ailments. Small children watch television for an average of thirty-one hours a week. There must be some relationship between the instant satisfaction of television and, for example, the fact that the little plastic put-together toys found in Cracker Jack boxes twenty years ago are being replaced by instant gratification toys. "Children are used to TV," the prize buyer explained, "where everything happens for them."[45]

What we find in popcorn boxes reflects what we find within ourselves. "We may well travel to the moon," Charles de Gaulle once reflected, "but that isn't very far. The greatest distance we have to travel lies within ourselves."

Conclusion

The economic and psychological approaches to present-future choice have been described and contrasted. Unlike economics—which usually posits that differences in people's impatience, or subjective interest rates, are smoothed out by borrowing and lending in capital markets—psychology makes patience, or willingness to wait, an aspect of personality that may vary over time and among persons.

Interpersonal differences in patience can partly explain why one person is wealthier than another, and why the ability to *generate* wealth, as well as wealth itself, is heritable. Buried deep in the bitter trap of poverty, impatience, and more poverty, there is a message of hope. What is learned can be unlearned. A more attractive, secure present can make the future more attractive too, and it can lead to action that makes it so.

For individuals the future "me" may speak only in muffled tones to the present "me," to his or her own detriment. As a result, for society, current generations make choices that leave too few resources for future unborn generations. This kind of present-future choice is like a two-person game, where the opposing player is permanently absent from the table because he does not yet exist. Pigou said government should correct the imbalance. But these days, governments seem to be as myopic as the people who elect them.

Not all now-or-later choices are monetary. Some of the most puzzling and socially disastrous of all economic phenomena involve incurring future harm from things that seem to yield insufficient present returns—smoking, obesity, addiction. Like St. Augustine, ordinary mortals prefer chastity and continence, but

Learning to Wait Begins in Childhood

not just now. Like Oscar Wilde, we resist everything but temptation.

At the start of his great career, Irving Fisher insisted in his doctoral dissertation, in 1894, that psychology lay beyond the concerns of economics. But in his seventy-fifth birthday talk at Harvard, he said, "Today, I would like to see a study, partly economic and partly psychological, showing how the human animal following his desires often misses satisfactions instead of attaining them."[46] He specifically mentioned narcotics.

In this, as in so many other ideas, Marshall got there first. "[Economics] has to analyze the influences which sway men in their choice between present and deferred gratification," he wrote. "But here, the post of honour lies with mental science."[47] We should have heeded him, in 1890.

Perhaps the most important now-or-later choice individuals face is education—forgoing current income and consumption for higher future income. The next chapter treats the private and social value of education and deals with psychological aspects of human capital.

PART II

People as Producers

4

YOU ARE YOUR OWN
MOST VALUABLE ASSET:
THE PSYCHOLOGY OF
HUMAN CAPITAL

LIKE a huge electronic wristwatch, the census clock blinks out the estimated population of the United States in big bright numerals. In 1968, when the clock indicated 200 million, there was a lot of fanfare. (Since as many as one person in twenty slips through the enumerators' nets, the actual 200 million mark was likely crossed years earlier.)

Another major landmark drew much less attention when it was announced. The 1970 Census showed that for the first time in history, a majority of adult Americans were high school graduates.[1] Today one adult American in every six has a college degree. Some day, perhaps sooner than we think, there will be more Americans who have college degrees than those who lack them.

Schooling is a major part of our lives. It is, as chapter 3 showed, one way that people postpone present gratification for future reward, and it is perhaps the most important of all present-future choices people face. By two-question logic, decisions about schooling require knowledge of what education is worth and what must be given up to get it. The main thing schooling requires us to give up is *time*—time that could otherwise be used to work and earn money. The value of education is measured by what it adds to the earning power of those who acquire it.

In economics, the dominant school of thought about education is called the *human-capital* approach. This chapter describes the theory and measurement of human capital and shows how psychology modifies and strengthens this concept. In particular, I shall discuss the relationship between personality and earnings, and the economics and psychology of testing ability and intelligence. One of the most absorbing of all debates—the nature of man in relation to his labor—both takes place in, and centers around, the classroom.

The Man, the Hoe, and How They Differ

> *Bowed by the weight of centuries he leans*
> *Upon his hoe and gazes on the ground,*
> *The emptiness of ages in his face,*
> *And on his back the burden of the world.* [2]

Jean Millet lived in abysmal poverty, little better than that of the French peasantry whom he painted. *The Man With the Hoe* (1863), eventually sold to the San Francisco Museum, probably brought a larger chunk of capital than Millet ever saw or dreamed of in a lifetime. A Californian, Edwin Markham, saw the painting and wrote a poem about it, which was published in 1899 in the *San Francisco Examiner.* His bitter protest against the landless, exploited hoeman was widely reprinted throughout Europe. Gold-rush wealth brought Millet's striking image to California, and

California sent it back to Europe in words a generation later, the message greatly amplified by the changing times.

Whether in ink or oils, *The Man With the Hoe* perfectly illustrates the theme this chapter addresses: the nature of man, the labor he supplies, and the capital he wields. Can there be any sharper distinction than the man—labor—and the hoe he plies—capital? Surely further discussion of the difference between labor and capital would be superfluous.

But the issue turns out to be far from simple. Consider the hoe. Where did it come from? Perhaps the man fashioned it out of wood and iron the day before. Nature supplied the wood, and man, the labor to hew and shape it. What about the iron? A blacksmith forged it—more labor. By patient teleology all capital can be traced back to labor.

Two hundred years ago economics began its odyssey by searching for a theory of value—a theory that would explain what things were worth. Adam Smith, and later David Ricardo, were certain they had the answer: the labor theory of value, which said that the value of a product was proportionate to the amount of labor needed to produce it.

The logical step from "capital is worth the labor (direct and indirect) used to make it" to "capital *is* labor" may be miles long, or millimeters short, depending on your point of view. Karl Marx took that step (perhaps that is why Paul Samuelson once called Marx a "minor post–Ricardian") and turned it into a powerful ethical proposition. Marx's basic axiom is: If all factors of production are labor, then labor should have as its due all output. Put another way, if wages compensate labor (in the present), and profits compensate capital (past labor), then workers deserve both wages and profits, as owners and suppliers of labor. (Milton Friedman once responded caustically to this argument by asking precisely how we should reward past labor, by building fancier tombstones?)

Not surprisingly, there is an utterly contrary point of view, one which sees the man as capital, rather than the hoe as labor. The hoeman, like the tool he holds, is an instrument for generating

87

output. He embodies skills acquired through long experience, skills that involved an investment of time and effort. The value of The Man With the Hoe can be capitalized as the present value of all the future services he will perform for rows of cabbages or beets, much like the value of a coupon-laden twenty-year corporate bond. His poverty stems not just from his landlessness, as Markham railed, but from the sparseness of the *human* capital he embodies and signifies.

What seems like a semantic quibble within economics turns out to be an inquiry into the nature and significance of knowledge and education, and the people they serve, a topic on which economics and psychology substantially overlap.

As for Edwin Markham, he himself was a teacher. Eventually he rose to become a school superintendent, overseeing the formation of human capital that America was to view as a just and efficient response to the hoeman's bent back.

Time Is Money

Ask a foreigner to characterize Americans in a few words, and you often hear, "time is money," expressing the American taste for haste in work and play. After all, wasn't it Benjamin Franklin who urged us to "remember that time is money"?

In fact, those three words came to typify *England,* not America. They appear in the English writer Edward Bulwer-Lytton's popular play *Money,* staged in 1840. By 1862 Victor Hugo could ask rhetorically in *Les Misérables,* "Take away *time is money,* and what is left of England?" (For Hugo, *cotton is king* defined America.) It was England, not America, that led us into the Industrial Revolution. With it came one of the ironies of prosperity: The more a labor hour can produce, the more a leisure hour costs in terms of lost output. In poor societies, time is small change and the pace of life is leisurely; in wealthy ones, time is big money.

"Time is money" captures the essence of human-capital theory. To study, to earn a college degree, to acquire a trade, takes an investment of time. Investing time in acquiring knowledge requires forgoing some earnings. According to Theodore Schultz earnings forgone "account for fully half to three-fifths of the total costs of high school and higher education."[3] Even if tuition, books, and room and board were free, there would still be no free educational lunch. To acquire formal education, what must be given up is mainly time and the earnings that time could otherwise bring in.

Even if "time is money" is not especially American in origin, the human-capital approach to education is. In his book *The Rate of Interest,* Irving Fisher, whom we encountered in the preceding chapter, saw *all* factors of production as forms of capital:

> All . . . income springs from capital-wealth, if land and man are included in that term, or if not, from capital and man, or capital, land and man. It may all be capitalized and hence . . . it may all be regarded as interest upon the capital-value thus found. . . . The income of the workman may be capitalized quite as truly as the income of land and machinery.[4]

This was written in 1907. At that time, Marshall held sway. In his *Principles,* Marshall flirted with the idea that human beings may be treated as a type of capital; and in places, he even seemed to embrace it. In the end Marshall's behavioral approach to economics clashed head-on with another fundamental Marshallian precept: Economics deals with entities that can be brought into common measurement using market prices. In an appendix entitled "Definitions of Capital," he decided to adopt Ricardo's definition of capital: "food, clothing, tools, raw materials, machinery, etc. necessary to give effect to labour."[5]

Marshall praised Fisher's "masterly argument," calling it "incontestable" from the "abstract and mathematical" point of view, but finally chose to define capital in a way that keeps "realistic economics in touch with the market-place."[6] Since human capital, unlike physical capital, is not bought and sold—only its *services* are offered for sale—its value can never be subjected to economics' ultimate polygraph, voluntary transactions in free markets.

Marshall's view held for generations. Not until Theodore Schultz's speech, "Investment in Human Capital" (to the American Economic Association in December 1960) and Gary Becker's volume *Human Capital* (1964) did the concept of human capital take firm root.[7] It was not quite in time to save economists from two major errors.

People (Not Just Plants and Ports) Are Producers

At the close of World War II economists mustered up their collective wisdom, furrowed their brows, surveyed the Western economies, and made two fundamentally wrong predictions, one on each side of the Atlantic. On this side, they predicted that when war spending dried up, and with it the jobs that war created, there would be a recession or a depression. Among the few who forecast inflation, rather than deflation, was psychologist George Katona. His postwar survey revealed large, pent-up demands for consumer goods and an equally large supply of stored-up purchasing power to pay for them.

On the other side of the Atlantic, economists surveyed the disastrous destruction wrought by war in Europe of plants and equipment and foresaw a long, slow road to recovery. With much of Europe's physical capital destroyed, they reasoned, it would take years and years to restore prewar production levels. With hindsight we now know that helped by generous and wisely dispensed Marshall Plan aid, the brains and muscles of European workers created a major economic miracle in West Germany, and only slightly lesser ones in France, Holland, Italy, and Britain. The reason we fell into this error, Theodore Schultz concluded in his A.E.A. address, is "because we did not have a concept of *all* capital and, therefore, failed to take account of human capital and the important part that it plays in production in a modern economy." We had forgotten to heed Marshall's precept: "Capital consists in a great part of knowledge and organization," and "knowledge is our most powerful engine of production."[8] War destroyed ports, roads, plants, and machinery. But it did not, could not, erase know-how. Morally, human beings are the ultimate value. Economically, they are also the ultimate instrument of production. This is the message of the human-capital approach.

Quantitatively, Schultz has estimated that between 1900 and 1956, the U.S. stock of human capital doubled three times, while nonhuman capital doubled only twice. This brought the "stock of education" to almost half the value of reproducible, physical capital in 1956, compared with 22 percent at the turn of the century. Today this ratio is doubtless much higher.

The inescapable conclusion is: America's productive capacity depends more on the quality, skills, and drive of the American work force than on the modernity and technical sophistication of American microprocessors and industrial robots. The remainder of this chapter shows how economics tries to value those skills, and how psychology treats personality as a kind of human capital.

What Are You Worth?

"How should I invest my money? Are stocks going up or down? How'd the market do today?" At cocktail parties, baseball games, or PTA meetings, admitting one is an economist very often elicits those questions. It is not easy to find the right answer. If you explain that economics is about markets but not necessarily about *the* market, narrowed eyes hint you know something and are hiding it. The efficient market spiel—if there *were* bargain stocks around, alacritous investors would have snapped them up, forced up their prices, and so removed them from the bargain racks (see chapter 9)—elicits outright hostility. Everyone knows people who made zillions in stocks, from Bernard Baruch to Aunt Maude. (In affairs of money and love, human nature is deliciously asymmetric; conquests are broadcast, defeats are played close to the vest.)

"Invest in yourself," I usually respond, with self-persuasion born of repetition, and I recite the chapter title. Though it sounds like the name of a warmed-over self-help book, it is literally true; you *are* your most valuable asset if you are an ordinary American. A strong, empirical case can be made for investing in improving your earning power, or even your capacity to enjoy life, and thus receiving a yield at least as high as the rate of return on conventional investments. It is a fact: In cold dollars and cents the average American's wealth in human capital exceeds his wealth in conventional forms (house, car, insurance, and securities).[9]

How much is a college education worth over a lifetime? Other things being equal, people with more education tend to earn more than people with less education. To measure this, it is accepted practice to adopt Irving Fisher's suggestion to *capitalize* workers' incomes—that is, to bring future dollars into relation with present ones with the help of interest rates. The higher the interest rate, the less a future dollar is worth compared to a present one. Since education provides benefits that accrue far off in the future, the higher the interest rate we choose for purposes of capitalization, the smaller the value of education becomes.

Some of the earliest calculations of the lifetime value of education were made by Hendrik Houthakker.[10] Using 1950 Census data, he found that at age fourteen, four or more years of college were worth (in present value) $280,989, using a zero interest rate to capitalize future income dollars, and measuring value in constant 1950 dollars. At a 3 percent interest rate, a college degree is worth an extra $106,269; at 6 percent, $47,546; and at 8 percent, $30,085. (To bring those sums to 1980 dollars, multiply by three.)

Notice how quickly the present value of a college education drops when future dollars are discounted at 8 percent rather than 3 percent or zero. It is easy to see how, by two-question logic, a college education would seem much more valuable, and worth investing in, to someone whose subjective interest rate is 3 percent, than to someone whose subjective interest rate is 8 percent. The latter impatient person would be willing to invest less than a third of what a patient person would invest in getting a college degree, according to Houthakker's figures.

Later, more sophisticated computations by W. Lee Hansen put rates of return to investment in schooling at levels above all but the riskiest of conventional investments.[11] (See table 4.1.) The basic assumption of all these calculations, though, is that the added income accruing to extra education can be attributed to the higher productivity that education causes. This assumption has been challenged; later, I shall discuss how. But first let us turn to an aspect of people as producers that economists usually choose to overlook: personality.

Table 4.1

Private Rates of Return to Investment in Schooling, Viewed at Age 14 for U.S. Men in 1949

	Percent, Before Taxes	Percent, After Taxes
Two Years of High School	12.7	12.3
Four Years of High School	15.3	10.4
Two Years of College	10.4	9.4
Four Years of College	12.9	11.5

SOURCE: W. Lee Hansen, "Total and Private Rates of Return to Investment in Schooling," *Journal of Political Economy* 81 (1963).

Can You Step on Roaches?

You are what you know, and what you think and feel. What you *know*—your cognitive characteristics—is the focus of human-capital theory. What you *feel*—affect, emotion, or personality—has been systematically banished from the list of variables economists research, debate, and measure. Yet if human beings are indeed producers, their personalities may have as much to do with their productiveness as their knowledge.

Which personality traits find monetary reward in the market-place? Randall Filer, an economics professor at Brandeis University, addressed this question with the help of a remarkable set of data.[12] Filer acquired information about 4,300 persons evaluated between 1967 and 1977 by Psychological Consultants, Inc., a private firm in Richmond, Virginia. PCI evaluates job candidates and current employees for purposes of hiring or promotion. In addition to conventional data on salary, education, and cognitive skills, each subject had undergone a Guilford-Zimmerman Temperament Survey.* Ten personality traits are measured quantitatively on a scale from zero to twenty. These traits are: general activity (or drive), restraint, ascendance, sociability, emotional stability, objectivity, friendliness, thoughtfulness, personal relations, and masculinity (fitting a traditional male role model).

For some twenty-five different groupings (by sex, education, profession, occupation, and industry), Filer found that overall, personality traits do indeed affect wages. Some personality factors emerged as more important than others. "By far the most important personality trait," Filer found, "appears to be general activity, or drive."[13] Moving from one standard deviation below the mean for this trait to one standard deviation above it would (other things being equal) add 6.5 percent to the monthly salary. Only for biology majors, wholesale- and retail-trade workers, and blue-collar workers was this trait not important.

The second most import important trait was ascendance ("desire to be on top"). Next are sociability and friendliness. Sociability (an

---

*Subjects are asked to answer yes, no, or ? to a set of three hundred items. Some examples (altered to avoid compromising the test and infringing on the copyright) are: Roaches, spiders, and bugs make your skin crawl; You feel sorry for caged animals; You would rather plan a trip than go on one; You deserve more pay than your boss; You often start things and then leave them in the middle; You would rather be a construction worker than an interior decorator; You like people; Waiting a long time at a red light makes you tense and irritated; What seems like friendliness is really a disguise for ambition; You do not dwell on past errors.

person's liking for social activities, conversation, and having many friends) is *negatively* related to earnings. Highly sociable people, Filer speculates, may be less likely to settle down and produce. Sociability seems especially deleterious to wages of managers and service personnel. Friendliness, tolerance for opposition, and respect for others boosts wages, especially for salespersons, blue-collar workers, and those in finance, insurance, and real estate.

Statistically significant, but less powerful, were masculinity, objectivity, and restraint. Finally, emotional stability, thoughtfulness, and personal relations appeared to have little effect on the individual's wages.

For two of the traits, Filer found that extremes do not pay. For those with very low sociability (in the bottom 16 percent), being more sociable brought *higher*, not lower, wages; a certain minimal amount seems necessary. By the same token, excessive friendliness (in the top 5 percent) *lowers* earnings. Apparently, being *too* tolerant can lower productivity.

One of Filer's most interesting findings is that the inclusion of personality variables in wage equations does not materially alter the magnitude or direction of other coefficients. Moreover, he adds, certain personality traits "seem to produce higher wages no matter where they are acquired,"[14] whether by going to college or by attending schools of hard knocks.

I conclude that if we are to regard people as human capital, the concept must be broadly interpreted to include personality as well as knowledge and verbal and quantitative skills. Perhaps if we economists had met more payrolls, or actually hired the people on them, we would have recognized this earlier and enlisted psychology to aid us.

With or without personality taken into account, how valid is the concept of human capital itself? Recent evidence has arisen to challenge it strongly.

More Pay for Less Performance:
Human Capital Reconsidered

Over the course of our working life, our earnings rise as our experience increases. Surely this is because the knowledge piled up in the school of experience—human capital—makes us more productive. Or is it?

Several recent studies cast serious doubt on the link between experience and productiveness. Gene Dalton and Paul Thompson studied the performance and earnings of twenty-five hundred engineers and managers in six technology-based companies.[15] For employees, supervisors graded the "contribution made to the company during the past year." Dalton and Thompson found that beyond the age of thirty-five, engineers' performance *declines,* but pay continues to rise. (See figure 4.1.) This may be related to the rapid obsolescence of an engineering education, whose "half-life" has been estimated at as little as five years. For top- and mid-level managers past their late thirties performance was also found to dip.

James Medoff and associates studied personnel files of two major American corporations.[16] These files included performance ratings for both professional and managerial jobs, and they were used to track age, pay, and productivity. Jobs were classified by grade levels. As expected, they found that college graduates earned more than less-educated workers. The reason for this, they found, was almost entirely because added degrees win jobs with higher grade levels. *Within* grade levels extra education brought relatively little extra pay, other things being equal. Their main finding was that within similar jobs, human capital (knowledge and experience) and performance were not correlated. Put another way: For both corporations, "those with less than a college education appear to have a much lower probability of being in one of the top two salary categories . . . than do those whose highest degree is a bachelors,

FIGURE 4.1

Annual Salary, Performance, and Job-Complexity Rating for Engineers

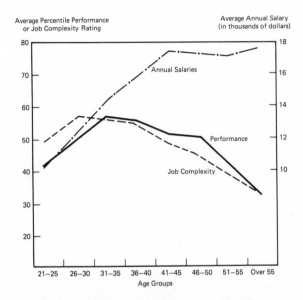

but not a lower probability of being in one of the two top performance categories."[17]

Medoff's moral goes well beyond the issue of human capital; it relates to the way economists go about testing their theories. He argues,

> Unlike physical scientists, economists typically are not involved in the collection of the data they use, and unlike other social scientists, economists generally avoid having contact with their units of observation. As a result, the proper data for testing numerous important beliefs that many economists hold have not been gathered and the knowledge of those who are likely to really know what is going on has been ignored.[18]

97

The largely unexploited "micro-micro" data (pertaining to individual workers in specific firms) of personnel files is just one example. There are many others.

Further evidence that is at odds with the human-capital approach is Jencks's finding that besides family background, the single most important factor contributing to a person's economic success is *finishing* college.[19] If what counts is diploma, cap, and gown rather than what is learned on the road to winning them, then a full four years of college should be worth a great deal more than two or three-and-a-half. This is in fact true. Some view education as a huge sorting machine that does not fundamentally alter the things it categorizes rather than as a factory, that transforms unproductive people into productive ones.

Human Capital or Olympic Hurdling?

The observation that additional knowledge generates additional income led to the theory that there was a kind of capital formation generated by investing in that knowledge. But no one has ever *seen* human capital, just as no one has ever seen an electron. Both are inferred from their "footprints," and this leaves considerable room for controversy, both in physics and in economics.

Just before the turn of the century, the English physicist Joseph Thomson announced to skeptical colleagues that "atoms are not indivisible, for negatively electrified particles [electrons] can be torn from them. . . ."[20] Skepticism in this theoretical inference turned to belief only when Charles Wilson, a Scottish physicist, invented the cloud chamber. His idea was to fire electrons through a fine mist of water droplets. Some of the droplets, he reasoned, would condense along the electrically charged path of the electron and mark a clear, visible trail, like the incriminating evidence of a child's muddy footprints across the carpet.

Physicists still argue sometimes over what exactly they have observed, and photographed, in a Wilson cloud chamber. Not surprisingly, in the context of human capital, economists also argue when they observe that educated people make more money than less-educated ones.

Consider the following view of knowledge diametrically opposed to that of human capital—one that students find especially persuasive at exam time. Schooling is a long series of Olympic hurdles. Running the course makes you no smarter, abler, or more productive. But the certificate you get at the finish line proves you are able to jump hurdles. *That* is useful information to an employer. In other words, the amount of schooling you acquire is an observable variable that "signals" the presence of an unobservable one—not human capital, but ability. You had the ability well before the starter's pistol fired. But since it is next to impossible to measure hurdlers' abilities at the starting line, especially if none of them has ever raced before, hurdle you must.

According to this model, schooling is really a screening device that sorts and categorizes people without in any way altering them. The *value* of knowledge lies not in how it improves people, as producers, but in how it helps differentiate innately good producers from poor ones. People with diplomas have observably higher incomes than those who lack them, it is argued, *not* because they acquired more productive skills, but because they succeeded in proving, in the schooling process, that they *had* those skills in the first place.

$E = R\ C$

There is a simpler, more direct way to sort and categorize people than to cram them into classrooms: psychological testing. There are two types of tests: those that measure ability—*maximum* performance—and those that measure *typical* performance, such as personality, aptitude, and so on. Schooling and testing, as filters, or sorters, are complementary. Prior to and during schooling, tests find use in channeling students into appropriate grades, schools, or vocations.

Psychological testing has become a legal and ethical issue that, as much as any other one, exposes the very core of the question, what kind of society do we want to fashion? To understand the issues involved, large doses of both economics and psychology are needed. Here are what I see as the main questions, along with some tentative answers.

DO PEOPLE DIFFER? HOW? HOW DO WE FIND OUT?

Ever since Stanford psychologist Lewis Terman supervised the Army Alpha Examination, a short test used to find suitable officer material in 1917, psychologists have been engaged in building tests to measure people's intelligence, ability, personality, and almost anything else that characterizes human psychology. Hundreds of different tests measuring cognitive ability and emotional adjustment point to the conclusion that people differ in all these aspects. An initial naive reaction is, *vive la différence.* Who would want to live in a world of 4 billion people all cloned from the same cell?

WHY DO PEOPLE DIFFER?

People differ because of inherent nature (heredity) or nurture (environment), or both. Fortunately this is an issue I can skirt in this chapter. The preceding chapter took a nurture position with respect to patience.

Without further evidence, suppose people are what they have learned and acquired from their environment—the nurture school. Then success at taking various tests will depend on how compatible the environment you grew up in is with the test you are taking. This has led to a search for an environment-free, or culture-free, intelligence test. One of the approaches has been to define test results according to an appropriate culture-related reference group: the culture from which the test taker is coming. Taken to its extreme, with each reference group optimally narrowed down to one person —yourself—all interpersonal differences could be made to disappear. Yet the reference-group approach to finding a culture-free test has become powerful and persuasive, accompanied by an enormous amount of controversy, which it richly deserves.[21]

IF PEOPLE DO DIFFER, SHOULD WE MEASURE HOW, AND HOW MUCH?

In one sense schooling and testing are messengers who bring bad tidings of social inequality. One reaction, an understandable one, has been to kill the messenger. After two earlier attempts, vetoed by then Governor Reagan, the California legislature finally banned intelligence testing. The famous *Larry P.* case brought a ruling in October 1978: The use of standard IQ tests to place black children in classes for the retarded violated both the California constitution and the Fourteenth Amendment.[22] Federally, The Education for All Handicapped Children Act of 1975 (PL 94–142) calls for the use of "nondiscriminatory" testing—like military intelligence, a near contradiction in terms—without clearly defining nondiscriminatory.[23]

The economics of testing suggests that if performance and ability tests did not exist, the market would soon invent them. George Akerlof's *market for lemons* model is relevant.[24] Suppose that in the used-car market, buyers can't tell the difference between good and bad used cars. Therefore, for a given model year and mileage, good cars and "lemons" will fetch the same price. Bad cars will quickly drive out good ones, since sellers (who *know* whether their car is a lemon or a "honey") will put only lemons on the market. Unless some way of helping buyers distinguish lemons from honeys is found, for example, certification or "testing," the used-car market may simply disappear, a consequence that can be of value to no one. There is no fundamental difference, then, between "Would you buy a used car from this man?" and "Would you buy this man?" Both the markets for cars and manpower need ways for buyers to determine quality in order for those markets to work well, or to work at all. An untrained worker may have valuable natural talents, Akerlof notes, but his talents must be certified by the educational establishment before a company can afford to use them. He quotes George Stigler, who once wrote that "in a regime of ignorance, Enrico Fermi would have been a gardener, Von Neumann a checkout clerk at a drugstore."

The economic benefits of ability testing can, in a rough way, be quantified. Hunter and Schmidt have shown that the use of tests to assign people to appropriate jobs can improve productivity by between 3 and 14 percent.[25] They show that estimated productivity gain, E, is proportional to the product of two parameters: R, the correlation between measured ability and "true" ability, or productivity; and C, the extent to which productivity varies within jobs. The equation is:

$$E = 5.0 \, R \, C$$

Fifty years of study of R, the validity coefficient, have yielded a stable and conservative value of 0.4. The few studies of C suggest values ranging from 0.16 to 0.7 (the coefficient of variation of output for a given job, assumed constant across jobs). Substituting in the equation gives values of E ranging from 3.2 percent to 14 percent. Even if these estimates are exaggerated, as Michael Rothschild has argued, sufficient economic profit remains from testing to give both tester and test taker an incentive to favor it.[26]

ARE TESTS THAT DISCRIMINATE DISCRIMINATORY?

This question is purposely phrased provocatively. The issue is, if people do differ, does sorting them make society less egalitarian?

You Are Your Own Most Valuable Asset

Michael Rothschild provides a persuasive example where ability testing yields a *more* egalitarian result than the absence of testing.[27] Here is my version of it. Imagine a world of only two types of jobs —for example, making steel and making computers—and only two types of ability—brains and brawn. Suppose making steel takes only brawn, and making computers, only brains. The annual wages for each type of worker in each type of job might be as follows:

	Making Steel	Making Computers
Brains	$ 10,000	$30,000
Brawn	$30,000	$20,000

If employers had no way of distinguishing brains from brawn, and workers had no way of certifying their particular abilities, people would be assigned at random. Assuming an equal number of jobs in computers and in steel, and an equal number of smart and brawny people, 25 percent of the labor force would be assigned to each of the four cells in the above table. The average income would then be $22,500 ($10,000 × .25 + $20,000 × .25 + $30,000 × .50). The standard deviation* of the distribution of income would be $8,292.

Now assume testing assigns people to the jobs they best suit— the brawny to steel making and the brainy to computer making. Everyone earns $30,000. Average income rises substantially. Inequality drops to zero. This is a highly abstract, theoretical example. Its sole purpose is to persuade, as Rothschild notes, that ability testing will not *necessarily* make income distribution less equal. Whether it does, or does not, in reality requires careful research on the relationship between various abilities and productivity—a topic in which economics and psychology are inseparable. To date there has been regrettably little such research.

*A measure of the degree of variation, or degree of inequality.

Conclusion

In his paper "Five Decades of Public Controversy over Mental Testing" Stanford psychologist Lee J. Cronbach—himself a pioneer contributor to testing—argues that "society needs to think once again about the kind of equality it would prefer and about the desired relation between productivity, social status and standard of living."

"Most of all," Cronbach reasons, "it needs to distinguish between education as preparation for service to society [that is, investment in human capital, for purposes of production], education as preparation to get more out of living [consumption, or investment for purposes of consumption] and education as a means of certifying social status."[28]

This chapter has spoken of all three aspects of schooling. All three are probably going on simultaneously, in proportions whose magnitude is more than a little unclear. Here is another instance where the science of behavior and the science of production, by failing to join forces, have left largely uncharted a treacherous piece of terrain over which we now march more or less blindly.

James Thurber, in a serious moment, once said that it is more important to know some of the questions than all of the answers. "The social scientist is trained," Cronbach observed, "to think he does not know all the answers. [But he is] *not* trained to realize that he does not know all the *questions.*" When he fails to understand this, "the social scientist's social influence is not unfailingly constructive."[29] In trying to understand people as producers, economics must call on psychology. Psychology can provide some new answers. More important, it can help us ask new questions.

5

THE SOCIAL LOAF:
PAY, PRODUCTIVITY, AND
THE SINS OF WAGES

IN their roles as producers, people help bake the social loaf—the total amount of goods and services available. Many of our social and economic ills can be described and illuminated by this metaphor. As consumers, people seek slices of this social loaf. When the slices people want add up to more than the whole loaf, the result is inflation. Higher prices are the market's way of reconciling what is wanted and what is available. (Chapters 6 and 7 deal with people as consumers, and treat the problem of inflation at length.) When people work less well and less hard toward baking the social loaf, there is less for all to consume. Productivity and the supply of effort are the subjects of this chapter. A common model of social conflict unites both the demand and the supply sides of the social loaf—the tragedy of the commons, encountered in chapter 2. In this chapter the model shows why it may pay a rational worker to shirk rather than to work. When everyone shirks, productivity growth plunges.

People are not machines. A drill press can be worked to capacity,

day and night. If it is properly maintained, it will not utter a word
—or squeak—of complaint. A drill press *operator,* on the other
hand, can choose to work at X percent of his potential capacity,
where X can be any number between zero and one hundred. In
Working, Studs Terkel quoted an auto worker in 1973:

> [Management] got all the technological improvements . . . but one
> thing went wrong. . . . We've been telling them since we've been here:
> We have a say in how hard we're going to work. They didn't believe
> us.[1]

If we are to understand people as producers, it is essential to
know what makes some workers put out maximum effort and
others put out the bare minimum. This is as important as knowing
how much people *could* produce if they worked flat out. Psychologists have long been interested in this question, as have some
economists. If there is any subject where economics and psychology should join forces, it is the problem of productivity. In this
chapter they do.

Taking Sides on Supply-Side Economics

The supply of goods depends on the supply of labor that produces
them. Lately some new economic policies have been built around
the word *supply.*

A group of *supply-siders* growing in size and influence now
challenges the conventional, orthodox *demand-siders.* Like physicists, athletes, politicians, and small children, economists like to
divide up into teams from time to time and square off against one
another. If, as the Talmud counsels, the rivalry of scholars increases wisdom, then the discipline of economics is bashing itself
about, trying to get smart.

The alleged distinction between Keynesian policies (identified

Pay, Productivity, and the Sins of Wages

with demand management) and non-Keynesian policies (associated with supply-side theory) does more to cloud current debate than to clarify it. Keynes wrote in a setting of depression stemming from insufficient demand. Between 1933, the low point of the American economy, and 1936, when Keynes's *General Theory* was published, gross national product grew by 50 percent.[2] This happened not because the *capacity* of the economy to produce goods and services grew by half; it happened because new demand elicited greater use of existing productive capacity, enabling previously idle men and machines to go back to work. Keynes's message to the world was not to insist that demand management is the cure to all our ills. His message was that left to their own devices, free markets tend to land us in some form of economic trouble, whether it is deflation or inflation, and appropriate intervention is needed. For inflation that intervention can comprise soaking up demand—a short-run plan—or boosting output by shifting resources from consumption to capital formation—a supply-side, long-run plan. To the extent that both demand-siders and supply-siders agree on the need for some form of intervention and policy measures, they are Keynesians. To choose up teams between these two camps is to dichotomize where no real split exists, since neither position excludes or contradicts the other. In fact, both camps should (but regrettably do not) share an important common conviction—the reasons we demand too much and produce too little have psychology at their core. Our problems in building a clear, realistic picture of the macroeconomy lie less in the somewhat artificial conflict between demand-side and supply-side than in our imperfect grasp of the psychology underlying both demand and supply. It is nevertheless true that in the postwar period, economics gave lavish attention to demand and treated supply like an orphan. Now that productivity clamors for immediate first aid, this imbalance is quickly changing to favor supply.

What Happened to Productivity Growth?

FOURTH CONSECUTIVE QUARTER

United States Economy Skips
Quarterly National Dividend

WASHINGTON, Dec. 28—The U.S. Economy, Inc., producer of
the Gross National Product, announced today that the national
productivity dividend of 0.75%, payable Jan. 1 to citizens of record
on Dec. 15, would not be paid. This is the fourth consecutive
quarter that the dividend has been skipped in 1979. Officials cited
general economic difficulties as the cause.

A spokesman refused to predict when the dividend would be
restored, but said top management was generally optimistic.

The above news story is, of course, made up. No newspaper ever
carried it. But the key fact it illustrates is true. For most of human
history the standard of living remained low and constant. E. H.
Phelps Brown showed, for instance, that for approximately six
centuries, between 1215 and 1798, the real income of English
construction workers did not rise.[3] In the United States, Abramovitz estimates that productivity grew barely at all—0.3 percent
annually—from 1800 to 1890.[4] From 1889 to 1919 Kendrick calculates that productivity growth accelerated sharply, to 1.7 percent,
and again accelerated during 1919 through 1942, to 2.2 percent,
despite the depression.[5]

In the two decades following World War II, productivity grew
3 percent annually, a historically unprecedented rate for such an
extended period. Small wonder that policy focused on demand
management during this period, with supply ticking along so
smoothly. Then something went wrong. From 1965 to 1973 the
productivity dividend lost a percentage point. In the following five
years it lost most of another point. In 1979 output per worker in
the private-business sector actually *declined* for four quarters in a
row. Since then it has recovered only a little. It can be no coinci-

dence that in 1979 consumer prices rose 13.3 percent, the highest rise since 1946.

"There is a mystery here," labor economist Albert Rees notes.[6] Why is output per hour in American manufacturing growing more slowly than in any other Western country, with the exception of Britain? Why has the U.S. economy stopped paying a productivity dividend to its citizens? What are the implications of the productivity growth slowdown, particularly with regard to inflation? Above all, how can the dividend be restored?

Productivity growth is crucial for several reasons. It is the main source for improving our standard of living. If our material comforts are more plentiful in the 1980s than in the 1970s or the 1960s, it will be because we are more productive. Conversely, little improvement in our living standards can be expected—despite the optimism of "top management"—unless we find ways to become more productive. Productivity growth is the closest thing to a panacea that economics has to offer. By two-question logic most policy measures require us to give up something to gain something else. For instance, soaking up demand may cut inflation but may also boost unemployment. The strengthened dollar, in comparison to other currencies, cheapens imports and hence the cost of living, but it harms exports and the balance of payments. Productivity growth, however, is nearly costless. Perhaps that is why it is such a favorite catchword. Squeezing more output from each unit of labor, capital, energy, or natural resources is almost blemish-free, if you believe more goods and services are better than less. By distributing a social dividend, Rees has argued, "productivity growth mediates social conflict" and "lubricates the clashes between competing groups." It also cuts the inflation that results from such clashes.

Drops of Sweat Replace Drops of Oil

A long list of possible explanations for the mystery of the disappearing productivity dividend exists. Maybe we are replacing drops of oil with drops of sweat, as Ezra Solomon has suggested, and by substituting human energy for that of fossil fuels, biting into productivity.[7] Another theory says we are working *less* hard, not harder. Are large numbers of people now convinced that hard work is unnecessary or, worse, uncouth, as sociologist Amitai Etzioni suggests?[8] Partial evidence is provided by the University of Michigan's Survey Research Center. A national sample of workers was asked to respond to the statement "I am not asked to do excessive amounts of work." They could choose one of four possible responses: Very true, somewhat true, not too true, not at all true. In his analysis of the data for 1969, 1972, and 1977, Randall Filer reports "an unmistakable increase in the proportion of workers who feel that they are asked to do excessive amounts of work."[9] Either jobs have been getting harder, Filer reasons, or workers *perceive* that they have—that is, standards of effort have fallen. Workers whose standards of effort have fallen are likely to invest less effort in a given job, with a resulting fall in productivity. It stretches credulity to suggest that jobs have become objectively harder. We are therefore led again toward perceptions and psychology, to ask *why* have effort standards declined?

The point I am trying to make should not be overstated. Some of our productivity problems lie in the realm of human nature, but a good deal lies beyond it. Punitive tax rates have lowered after-tax profit rates, slowed capital formation, and hampered embodiment of new methods and technology in new equipment. This, too, is in part a psychological phenomenon, related to the desire to consume in the present instead of save and invest in the future (which was discussed in chapter 3).

Technical solutions—tax concessions and depreciation provisions, for example—do exist. But neither perspiration, nor perspicacity, can be legislated. Human effort is an economic variable with psychological causes that demand study and attention if the productivity dividend is to be restored.

Effort Is a Variable

One of the economic variables economists watch most closely is *capacity utilization:* the ratio of actual output to the maximum practical output attainable with existing plant and equipment. During economic expansions the utilization rate is high—90 percent in 1965, for instance—and during contractions it is low—74 percent in the 1975 recession. Highly detailed data exist for various manufacturing sectors. In 1978 the auto industry worked at 95 percent of capacity and the aircraft industry worked at 70 percent, bracketing highest and lowest values for manufacturing in that year.[10]

There is a curious asymmetry here between physical and human capital. Utilization of physical capital is carefully tracked. But what is the capacity-utilization rate of workers? How much *do* laborers actually produce, compared with what they *could* produce in an hour, a week, or a month of labor? Conventional economics is greatly preoccupied with whether or not labor, capital, and other resources are employed as efficiently as they can be. An implicit assumption is the Gertude Stein–like principle that an hour of labor is an hour of labor is an hour of labor, in the sense that the effort level is constant. But anyone who has visited a shop floor, warehouse, or typing pool knows that effort is not a constant but is a variable, changing with time, place, and circumstance. How well and hard a given worker labors at job A is quantitatively more important to the size of the social loaf than if the worker should be doing job B instead.

Economists have a term for our success in allocating resources to their best use—*allocative efficiency.* Harvey Leibenstein, a pioneer of behavioral economics, has coined the term *X-efficiency* for the ratio of actual output to potential output of resources in a *given* use, particularly human effort.[11] This is a topic on which psychology has much to say.

Solving for X

The assumption that firms minimize costs—another way of saying firms squeeze the maximum output out of a given set of inputs—is an inseparable part of microeconomics. This implies everyone who works for the firm is maximally motivated. To assault this assumption, Leibenstein distinguishes between what he calls *principals* (owners) and *agents* (those who work for others). Most Americans work for others in relatively large establishments. Of the largest five hundred corporations in manufacturing, the top one hundred employ more than half of all the field's employees. Of the biggest fifty companies in retailing, the largest ten employ one worker of every two in the field. How much do managers know or care about employee performance? How much incentive do employees have to go all out? "The individual is the main economic actor," Leibenstein argues, "rather than the firm."[12] Where individuals have discretionary power over their effort, as most do, the psychology of motivation, drive, and achievement becomes relevant and important.

Readers with experience in the business world may be bemused that economists even question the existence of X-*in*efficiency. An entire branch of psychology, organizational behavior, is built on the assumption that X-inefficiency (the gap between actual and minimal costs) is alive and well. Yet mainstream economics for the most part continues to grasp the straw of cost minimization and defend it vigorously, as in George Stigler's challenging 1976 article, "The Xistence of X-efficiency."[13] Stigler argues that X-inefficiency

Pay, Productivity, and the Sins of Wages

is really illusory (the result of ignorance or mistakes) or the result of differences in production techniques.

How important is X-inefficiency quantitatively? In an interview in *Fortune* magazine, Leibenstein said "I would be amazed if X-inefficiency wasn't around the 20 percent level for the economy as a whole."[14] Twenty percent of a 2 trillion-dollar economy is an enormous sum. Moreover, all of it is pure waste. A relatively small increase in X-inefficiency could explain much of the lagging productivity growth in recent years. What, then, is the evidence on behalf of this particular type of behavioral economics?

Leibenstein reports he first stumbled on his theory because a research assistant was underutilized—X-inefficient. He and his assistant began examining reports of management-consultant teams, or technical-aid teams, in various parts of the world. They found many cases where costless improvements capable of yielding great savings were suggested to managers, but they were never adopted. The type of inefficiency involved, Leibenstein reasoned, was internal to the firm and was independent of resource misallocations due to taxes, monopoly, and so on that economists typically study. Since then the evidence has piled up. Much of it points to inefficiency in labor utilization, though other factors such as information flow and capital utilization may also be at fault.

- A study by John Shelton compared manager-operated and franchised fast-food restaurants.[15] Menus, accounting systems, volume, and so on were similar or identical. Owner-operated units averaged a 9.5 percent profit margin. Manager-operated units averaged a 1.8 percent profit. The principal-agent distinction stands out.
- Walter Primeux, Jr., compared forty-nine cities with two or more electric companies to cities with only one.[16] Competition, he found, reduces *costs* by an average of nearly 11 percent. Note that this is *not* an inefficiency due to monopolistic distortions. In economic theory, monopolies have as great an interest in minimizing costs as competitive firms do. In reality they are under less pressure to do so and, apparently, do not in fact minimize costs. Incidentally, Primeux carefully adjusted for economies of scale in his comparison.

113

- A study of the cement industry by Kim Clarke found productivity was 6 to 8 percent higher in unionized plants compared to nonunion ones.[17] If nonunion plants were fully efficient in the first place, where did the productivity gains come from after their workers were organized? Richard Freeman and James Medoff found that in general, unionized plants had 20 to 25 percent higher productivity than nonunion plants.[18]
- In Israel, following the general mobilization of reserves in the Yom Kippur War, the labor force fell by 15 percent, yet GNP declined by only 5 percent.[19] Other countries have had similar wartime experiences. War taps wellsprings of extra effort. Perhaps by utilizing X-efficiency less tragic events can do so as well.
- A British coal strike in 1974 led to a three-day work week in manufacturing. Labor and capital were therefore utilized at only 60 percent of their capacity; But output was more than 80 percent of its normal level.[20]

Lord Kelvin said that science begins with measurement. Measurements of X-inefficiency point to a major, necessary alteration of economic science—one in which effort becomes a variable, rather than a constant, for purposes of theory and experimentation.

Productivity and Pride

One reason lagging productivity growth has aroused concern in the United States is that it has *not* been a worldwide phenomenon. If rising X-inefficiency, lack of effort, or slumping productivity growth had characterized, for example, Japan as well as America, I am not sure that the topic would have taken on the same urgency.

Recently Dr. Mieko Nishimizu presented a difficult, scholarly paper to an academic conference in Japan, showing that the level of technology in Japan surpassed that of the United States sometime in the early 1970s.[21] Despite the dense, econometric nature of her work, she was mobbed by journalists. American newspapers have been carrying stories showing that since 1950, Japan's annual productivity growth rate has been quadruple that of the United States and projecting that by 1990, Japanese workers would actually be more productive than their American counterparts.[22] Even Canada has been catching up; there is evidence that productivity growth in Canada picked up after the 1974–75 recession, while in the United States it did not, even though, traditionally, economic patterns in Canada closely follow those of her southern neighbor.[23] National pride and honor now seem to hang in the balance and have taken on an importance almost as great as the concern over material well-being. The productivity problem, I believe, now aims its stake at the very heart of American industry—mass production and the assembly line.

Two hundred years ago, when Adam Smith addressed the question of why some countries are rich and others poor, he found the answer to wealth and poverty in an exceedingly simple syllogism: The division of labor determines productivity. The extent of the market determines the division of labor. Therefore, the extent of the market determines productivity.

"The greatest improvement in the productive powers of labor," he wrote, "and the greater part of the skill, dexterity, and judgment with which it is any where directed, or applied, seem to have been the effects of the division of labor."[24]

Smith's famous example is the pin factory. "The important business of making a pin," Smith explains, "is . . . divided into about eighteen distinct operations, which, in some manufactories, are all performed by distinct hands."[25] One man draws the wire, another straightens it, a third cuts it, a fourth points it, a fifth grinds it at the top to receive the head. Making the head takes several operations, as does putting the head on, followed by whitening the head, and putting the pins in paper. Ten people can make upward of 48,000 pins a day, he observes. They do this "in consequence of a proper division and combination of their different operations."[26] Had each worker tried to do all eighteen operations himself, he could not have made even twenty, or perhaps even one, pin a day, Smith contends.

Therblig and Drof on Pins and Needles

Clearly, the larger the market for pins and other mass-produced goods, the greater the possibilities for applying Smith's division-of-labor principle. Henry Ford comes to mind at once. Until his Model T, automobiles were an expensive luxury. Ford took off unneeded accessories, offered every color provided it was black, and began assembly-line production in 1907. By 1908 he had captured the market. His automobile rattled and clattered not because it was poorly made or assembled, but because manufacturing tolerances had to be large to permit interchangeable parts.

Henry Ford did not invent mass production, the assembly line, or even interchangeable parts. A competitor, Henry Leland, had earlier, in 1903, performed a dramatic experiment with spare parts. He took three Cadillacs to an English racetrack, took them apart, dumped all the parts into a huge common pile, replaced one set of parts with an entirely new set, mixed them all up, separated them again, reassembled the three cars, and had them driven around the track for five hundred miles. Ransom Olds mass-produced fifteen hundred Oldsmobiles in 1901.[27] But Henry Ford rediscovered Adam Smith's principle that productivity requires large production runs and a large market. The closed-loop feedback system Ford pioneered—long production runs mean higher productivity means lower prices means bigger markets means long production runs—became a dominant feature of industry in America and elsewhere.

As the first Model T rolled off the assembly line, a new principle was born. We may only now be reaping the seeds it sowed. The principle is: Productivity and the division of labor are limited by the extent of boredom they involve.

At roughly the same time that Henry Ford's assembly line was applying Adam Smith's eighteen-step pin-factory principle, a man called F. B. Gilbreth was inventing time-motion study.[28] As a seventeen-year-old bricklayer apprentice, Gilbreth carefully observed and classified each motion of the bricklayer. Bricklaying took eighteen movements, he noted. It could be reduced to five. The result: One man could lay 350 bricks an hour instead of 120. Gilbreth gave up a successful contracting and construction business later, and with his wife Lillian he began making detailed time-motion studies. All manual work, Gilbreth claimed, can be reduced to seventeen basic elements he called *therbligs* (Gilbreth backward, with the "h" and "t" interchanged). Efficiency requires finding ways to eliminate or combine as many therbligs as possible, or shorten the time for each one.

Therblig and *Drof*—the term for splitting big tasks into many smaller ones, which Henry Ford mercifully failed to invent—may spell names backward, but with them, American industry surged forward. Somewhere in the inexorable process of reducing automobile assembly down to such precise tasks as putting eleven rivets into part of a fender, and streamlining the way those rivets are drilled in, for example, intensely uninteresting and excruciatingly boring labor was created. Marx may not have been a great economist. But he did seem to understand the sociology of labor. Boil labor down to its dullest common denominator, he argued, and you detach the worker from the product he labors to produce. By definition, the smaller each laborer's task, the more infinitesimal a part of the finished good the laborer's sweat becomes. The god of efficiency may eventually be sacrificed on its own altar of division of labor and time-motion. The most striking example is the labor unrest at a new General Motors plant, the ultimate in mechanized efficiency, where working apparently was impossibly monotonous.

Everything but the Squeal

While Gilbreth was writing about bricklaying, and Henry Ford was conceiving his assembly line, another seemingly unrelated event was taking place. Upton Sinclair, an American writer, was writing his novel *The Jungle* for the socialist paper *The Appeal to Reason.* His subject was the packing industry. Based on his observations of the Chicago stockyards in 1904, Sinclair's novel aroused a storm of protest and quickly resulted in the Pure Food and Drug Act of 1906. Here is Sinclair's description of hog processing made efficient, well before Henry Ford's assembly line:

> The carcass hog was scooped out of the vat by machinery, and then it fell to the second floor, passing on the way through a wonderful machine with numerous scrapers which adjusted themselves to the size and shape of the animal, and sent it out at the other end with nearly all of its bristles removed. It was then again strung up by machinery, and sent upon another trolley ride; this time passing between two lines of men, who sat upon a raised platform, each doing a certain single thing to the carcass as it came to him. One scraped the outside of a leg; another scraped the inside of the same leg. One with a swift stroke cut the throat; another with two swift strokes severed the head, which fell to the floor and vanished through a hole. Another made a slit down the body; a second opened the body wider; a third with a saw cut the breast-bone; a fourth loosened the entrails; a fifth pulled them out—and they also slid through a hole in the floor. . . .[29]

This passage brings to mind the psychologists' ambiguous picture of a beautiful young woman or an old hag, depending on what you perceive. As just mentioned, legislators wrote tough new standards for the purity and cleanliness of the food Americans eat under the influence of *The Jungle*'s graphic portrayals of abattoirs. But what about the human beings? What about the hygiene of labor, rather than the hygiene of pork? The phrase "each doing a certain single thing to the carcass as it came to him" stands out. It is a telling comment on society that the gore being axed carried more weight than the miserable laborers wielding the axes.

A half century later scholars were still studying slaughterhouses and reporting how one man removes pigs testicles only and another does nothing but link sausages (once every three seconds).[30] Perhaps as the division of labor reaches its pinnacle, the deleterious effects of monotony and diminishing returns are becoming substitutes for legislation. Is this the message productivity figures carry?

It is undoubtedly true that mass production, division of labor, and resulting efficiency brought high productivity, and with it, high pay. There are many studies where job satisfaction is found to be inversely correlated with productivity. Workers dislike the work itself but like the pay, and they work hard for it. Moreover, technology itself may be solving its own problem. Microprocessors now handle dull mechanical tasks that human labor once performed. But where high pay or technology cannot or do not save the day, new attention must be focused on what it is that interests and motivates workers. Adam Smith's syllogism, and Henry Ford's artful application of it, must now be ground through the mills of psychology if American productivity is to climb at the rates it once did so effortlessly.

Were he alive, even Karl Marx would be amazed at the sheer size of modern corporations. A.T. & T. has about 1 million employees; General Motors has about as many employees as the city of Dallas has people. The Volkswagenwerk plant in Wolfsburg, Germany, employs over forty thousand and covers three hundred fifty acres; at capacity, it can turn out four thousand cars daily. For economists the crucial ratio may be four thousand cars divided by forty thousand workers, or a car per worker each ten days. This is very high productivity. For the assembly-line worker, the relevant ratio may be 1/40,000—he or she is one insignificant pinscrew in a forty thousand-part machine, and a very great perceptual distance away from the shiny vehicle at the end of the line. This *can*—though it need not—become low motivation and, eventually, low productivity. Why it does become so in some plants or countries and not in others is a topic that industrial psychologists study intensely. The time has come for their tools, approaches, and findings to be integrated into economics.

The Psychology of To and From

What is the appropriate relationship between what people contribute to the social loaf and the size of the slice each person gets? By the principles of theoretical socialism, none. "From each according to his abilities," Marx wrote in his *Critique of the Gotha Program,* possibly paraphrasing the French Socialist Louis Blanc; "To each according to his needs."

Stalin found the seas of this high-minded theory much too stormy and altered a single word: "To each according to his *work.*" To the extent that Communist-bloc countries believe capital is essential for growth and progress, they are as capitalist as the West; to the extent that they tie pay to productivity, and indeed they do, they are as market-oriented as America.

The growth of the public sector has, meanwhile, significantly and obviously altered Stalin's second principle in Western countries. There it now reads, "To each according to his work, less his fair share of the cost of collective consumption (taxes)." I will discuss the import of this significant shift, and the bearing psychology has on it, in chapter 10.

But the first principle, too, has undergone a subtle but major overhaul. As the division of labor becomes finer and finer, as production processes become more complex, as single plants approach the size of small cities, interdependence grows. Perhaps it now reads, for many of us, "From each according to what he or she perceives *others* are contributing (within the bounds of ability)." We may, as a result, face what the apostle Matthew described: "The harvest truly is plenteous, but the laborers are few."[31] In a setting of pay and productivity, the problem turns out to be generically similar to Hardin's tragedy of the commons.

"I pass with relief from the tossing sea of Cause and Theory," Winston Churchill wrote, "to the firm ground of Result and

Pay, Productivity, and the Sins of Wages

Fact."[32] Let us leave firm ground for a brief but necessary venture into the theory of effort.

Here are two somewhat technical scenarios that I call *Better Half a Loaf* and *The Sins of Wages*. In the first, acting according to self-interest leads to a result Dr. Pangloss would have loved: Everyone is best off. In the second, acting according to self-interest leads to an impasse Voltaire would have relished: Society is worst off. Only a thin hair separates the two scenarios. While working through these two examples, I invite the reader to ponder whether today we are all actors in the first little drama or in the second.

Better Half a Loaf . . .

"Better half a loaf than none," sayeth the Proverbist. In the following example, two workers find how true this is.

Al and Burt are bakers. They share equally the revenues from the sale of the loaves they bake. Like all bakers, they rise early. At the start of each work day, each must decide how hard to work. For simplicity, suppose Al and Burt each have an "effort" switch: A (Al's) and B (Burt's). Each switch can be in one of two positions: Off (loaf) or On (work hard). When Al works hard, A is equal to 1. When Al loafs, A is equal to 0. The same thing applies to Burt's switch, B. Each baker makes his decision regarding how hard to work independent of his partner. Neither knows what the other will do.

Suppose that the total number of loaves baked depends on how hard Al and Burt work, according to the formula:

$$100(A + B)$$

If both work hard, they bake $100 \times 2 = 200$ loaves. If only one works hard (A or B equals 1), they bake $100 \times 1 = 100$ loaves. If neither works hard, no bread emerges from the ovens.

If a loaf of bread sells for one dollar, Al and Burt will each have a daily income of $100 (A+B)/2$. (Remember: they share revenues equally.) If both bakers loaf, they earn nothing. If only one loafs, they share $100 and each gets $50. If both work hard, they each earn $100.

Like the rest of us, Al and Burt do not especially enjoy hard labor. In fact, each would be willing to pay as much as $25 to be able to loaf.

Each of the bakers, Al and Burt, can pick one of two strategies. This is therefore a game with four possible outcomes. For each outcome, here is what Al and Burt get, *with the implicit cost of effort, $25, deducted where appropriate.*

1. Both Al and Burt work hard ($A = B = 1$): Al earns the equivalent of $100 - $25 = 75; Burt earns $75.

2. Al works hard; Burt loafs ($A = 1, B = 0$): Al earns $50 - $25 = 25; Burt earns $50.

3. Al loafs, Burt works hard ($A = 0, B = 1$): Al earns $50; Burt earns $50 - $25 = 25.

4. Al and Burt both loaf ($A = B = 0$): No revenue or cost of effort; Al and Burt share zero.

In the language of game theory, both Al and Burt have a dominant strategy—that is, a strategy that is best no matter *what* the other player decides to do. The dominant strategy is to work hard. Here is why.

Suppose Burt loafs. Al reasons as follows: If I work hard, I get $25. If I loaf like Burt, I get zero. Better to work hard, even if I know Burt is exploiting me. I would rather be exploited than suffer the cost of mutual distrust.

Suppose Burt works hard. Al reasons: if I work hard, I get $75. If I loaf, I get $50. I do best if I work hard.

Therefore, no matter what Burt does, Al comes out ahead if he works hard. The same reasoning applies to Burt. If both Al and

Burt are rational, they will both choose to work hard. The result is a productive bakery and many social loafs with no private loafing. Precisely as Adam Smith argued.

A Yiddish proverb warns, "For instance is not a proof." Here is another 'for instance' with a very different ending. The only parameter changed is the implicit cost of labor. Al and Burt find themselves burdened by . . .

The Sins of Wages

Assume now that the implicit cost of hard labor is *$60*, not $25. (Everything else is as it was in "Better Half a Loaf.") Perhaps Al and Burt have become prosperous and now value leisure more highly. Perhaps fundamental changes in the work ethic make hard work less socially approved. As before, there are four possible outcomes to the game (note that the cost of effort, now $60, is deducted where appropriate, as before):

1. Both Al and Burt work hard (A = B = 1): Al gets the equivalent of $100 − $60 = $40; Burt also gets $40.

2. Al works hard, Burt loafs (A = 1, B = 0): Al gets the equivalent of $50 − $60 = −$10; Burt gets $40.

3. Al loafs, Burt works hard (A = 0, B = 1): Al gets $50, Burt gets $50 − $60 = −$10.

4. Both Al and Burt loaf (A = B = 0): There is no revenue or cost of effort; they share zero.

This is a different kettle of fish. The best strategy for Al now is to loaf. If Burt works hard, Al gets $40 if he works hard, and $50 if he loafs. If Burt loafs, Al gets −$10 if he works hard, and 0 if he loafs. It pays for Al to loaf; same for Burt. This is an instance where individual rationality collides head-on with social sensibility. A capsule description of the logic of this game is: *I would rather have nothing than risk being exploited.* Both players think and act on this. In the end, both are worse off than if they had cooperated. Action based on self-interest, narrowly defined, gives society the worst of four possible outcomes. When the invisible hand refuses to become calloused, no income at all crosses its palms.

Even a signed agreement between Burt and Al to work hard may not help much. Suppose it is hard to find out whether each is loafing or really breaking his back. Each partner has a strong incentive to violate the agreement and let the other person work hard while slacking off himself. When both yield to this temptation, they end up with zero again. Each may not trust the other enough to sign an agreement.

This type of game has been dubbed *Prisoner's Dilemma* by the Princeton mathematician A. W. Tucker.[33] It takes its name from the parable of two criminals who are arrested and interrogated separately. Each criminal is offered reduced punishment if he "sings." Neither knows what the other will do. The rational strategy is to sing. But if both sing, both get the full weight of the law. *Prisoner's Dilemma* has been used to represent a wide variety of social conflicts. It is essentially Hardin's tragedy of the commons, described in chapter 2. There, it was rational for each person to graze another bull. But when all did so, everyone lost. Here, in *Sins of Wages,* it is rational for each worker to slack off. When each does, there is no output.

The fact that game theory proves that the individually rational strategy in *Prisoner's Dilemma* is zero (zero effort, zero cooperation, or whatever) does not mean everyone will always *behave* that way. Characteristically, though social conflict is by definition a social and economic problem, most of the evidence seems to come from psychology. It suggests that the larger the group, the less each person tugs on the rope, figuratively.

Bonacich, Shure, Kahan, and Meeker (1976) theorize that a group decision to cooperate may be thwarted, or vetoed, by a small number of egoistic noncooperators (perhaps just one), and larger groups are more likely to contain such persons than smaller ones.[34] (See the discussion of *risky shift* in chapter 9.) Alternately, as *Prisoner's Dilemma* is played over and over again—for example, a work team attaches gasoline tanks day after day—the sequence of individual decisions acts as a kind of signal to other players. The larger the group, the more these signals become attenuated and weakened, particularly those that indicate willingness to cooperate and improve collective output or well-being.

Supporting evidence comes from an experiment by Lindskold, McElwain, and Wagner.[35] In a *Prisoner's Dilemma* context, they examined how individuals and groups respond to a threat of non-cooperation by an opponent. Individuals, they found, were much more likely to prefer a cooperative response than were groups who tended to prefer eye-for-an-eye threats as a response.

During the years when productivity forged ahead and yielded steady, large national dividends yearly, was society playing *Better Half A Loaf?* Have we lately been playing *Sins of Wages?* If so, why the change? How can we restore the better half of *Better Half?*

Social Loaf, Social Loafing

Loaf•er / lō-fer/, *n.* [18th-c. Western New England dial., "one who owns but does not actively work his farm"; prob. Hudson Valley D.; akin to LG. *lofen,* G. *laufen,* to run, as in G. *landlaufer* (cf. LAND-LOPER)], a person who loafs; lounger; idler.[36]

A psychologist named Bibb Latané has written interestingly on the phenomenon underlying *Sins of Wages,* which he calls *social loafing.* He supplies some interesting empirical evidence in his article entitled "Many Hands Make Light the Work," written jointly with Kipling Williams and Stephen Harkins.[37]

Latané begins by citing a fifty-year-old study by the German psychologist Ringelmann, which, curiously, was never published. Ringelmann asked German workers to pull as hard as they could on a rope, with one, two, or as many as eight other people. A gauge measured how hard they pulled. In theory the total force exerted by seven workers should be seven times that exerted by one worker alone. But Ringelmann found quite different results. Taken one at a time, individuals averaged 63 kilograms of pressure. In twos, they averaged 59 kilograms; in threes, 54; and in groups of eight, only 32, or a bit more than half. Put another way, four men pulling on individual ropes, and unaware that others were also tugging, could exert as much force as eight men (the *same* men, perhaps) pulling together. Many hands apparently do make light the work, Latané suggests, but not precisely in the way the proverb had in mind. The larger the group, the more tempting it is to "let the other guy do it," and the easier it is to disguise slacking.

Latané replicated Ringelmann's study by having groups of undergraduate males shout and clap as loud as they could. Effort was measured by a sound-level meter, expressed in decibels, and converted to dynes per square centimeter, the physical unit of work involved in generating sound pressure. The results are shown in figure 5.1.

We may understand only vaguely the meaning of "one hand clapping," as the Zen Buddhist saying goes. But the meaning of a dozen hands clapping is loud and clear: Six pairs of hands do not clap even three times as loudly as a single pair.

Once again, *perception* turns out to be crucial. Latané cites an experiment by Ingham, where only the individual's *perception* of group size was varied, but where in fact each person actually tugged on a rope *alone*. Merely *thinking* that others were pulling also caused "a substantial drop in output with increases in perceived group size."

What, then, is the solution? We clearly cannot discard the collective "bathwater" along with the capitalist "baby"—mass production—that splashed in it. As Robert Sutermeister has asserted, "from now on, our increases in productivity in this country will

Pay, Productivity, and the Sins of Wages

FIGURE 5.1

Latané's Experiment Showing Intensity of Clapping and Cheering Declines with the Size of the Group

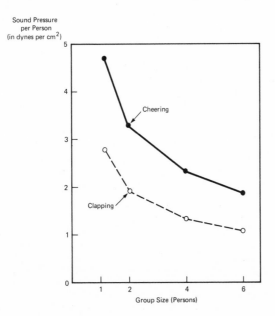

NOTE: Reprinted by permission of the publisher from Bibb Latané, Kipling Williams, and Stephen Harkins, "Many Hands Make Light the Work: The Causes and Consequences of Social Loafing," *Journal of Personality and Social Psychology* 37 (1979): 822–832. Copyright 1979 by the American Psychological Association.

depend above all on our ability to increase productivity of the nonmanual worker"—managerial, clerical, professional, technical, and service workers, salespersons and supervisors—who, as early as 1956, already made up two-thirds of the labor force.[38] Nonmanual work is in large part done in groups. Latané's conclusion, therefore, takes on extra importance. "Collective action," Latané reasons, "is a vital aspect of our lives. . . . Despite their inefficiency, groups make possible the achievement of many goals that individuals alone could not possibly accomplish."[39]

"The cure will come," he suggests, "from finding ways of channeling social forces so that the group can serve as a means of intensifying individual responsibility rather than diffusing it."[40] I believe it is significant that psychologists are already searching for cures to social loafing well before economists show substantial willingness to recognize the existence of the illness.

In another article Latané relates social loafing to the reasons for America's lagging productivity compared to other countries.

> While American society continues to emphasize individual accomplishment and self-fulfillment, it increasingly provides collective work situations in its larger organizations. Much attention has been given, in recent decades, to human-relations approaches to organization development. . . . we caution that any such approaches should weigh the potential losses in productivity from social loafing against any possible gains in worker satisfaction.[41]

Pay, Productivity, and Inflation

Despite widespread concern over productivity, inflation remains the predominant thorn in the side of the American public. In April 1981 a majority of Gallup Poll respondents felt prices would rise in 1981 by more than the 1980 rate of 12 percent. More than one person in three foresaw inflation of 15 percent or greater.[42] Debate over economic policy focuses largely on this single issue, and the consumer price index (CPI) has become the monthly parameter of political success.

How are the CPI and what we might term the *PEI—producer effort index,* or productivity—related? The answer to that question is another question: What causes inflation?

For prices to rise, people must be willing to pay more than is currently being asked for some good or service. Put differently, there must be either a contraction in supply, or an expansion in demand, or both. The end result is the same—at existing prices, a gap opens between the quantity people want to buy and the quantity sellers are willing to provide.

What is actually consumed cannot exceed what is produced (ignoring inventories). But what is demanded can far exceed what is available. The result is inflation. Inflation is one mechanism—a cruel, unnecessary, and undesirable one—for bringing people's wants into proportion with the means to satisfy them.

As Marshall constantly reminded us, market prices are set by supply and demand together. In this broad sense, every economist is both a supply-sider and a demand-sider. They part company over the *cure* for inflation and inflationary gaps—whether to hammer at demand curves and whittle them down or tug and pull at supply curves and pull them up.

The size of the slice from the social loaf that each person demands will be influenced by his or her perception of what *other* people are asking for. Moreover, the size of the *loaf itself* will depend on each person's skill and effort, in turn influenced by his or her perception of how much effort *other* people are exerting. Seen in this light, inflation is always and everywhere a social and psychological phenomenon, arising from interactions among people, both in supply and demand.

Chapters 6 and 7 deal with people as consumers. The behavioral model developed in them, used to explain and understand inflation, turns out to be another version of *Prisoner's Dilemma,* or Hardin's tragedy of the commons, where individual rationality collides with the social good. This and the preceding chapter dealt with people as producers. Here, again, how much and how well we produce turned out to depend in part on psychological links between the individual and the group of which he or she is a part.

Whether you believe inflation is essentially a problem of demand or a difficulty in supply, or, as I do, both demand and supply, the psychological foundations underlying the problem must be brought to light. Once they are, the appropriate solutions are much clearer.

Conclusion

The humorist Ambrose Bierce once defined labor as the process by which *A* acquires property for *B*. [43] At times, we are most serious when we are joking. A work ethic shot through with Bierce's definition—my effort helps you—can, when combined with the near-compulsion of individual self-fulfillment, produce a society, and social loaf, much different from that which Adam Smith described. It is a society that economics cannot hope to understand, let alone set right, without the assistance of psychology.

PART III

People as Consumers

6

BE HAPPY AND LIVE
WITHIN YOUR MEANS*

THE Apostle Paul said that love of money is the root of all evil.[1] George Bernard Shaw, a socialist, amended: *Lack* of money is the root of all evil.[2] I venture one more version: Lack of *understanding* of money and the ways people perceive it is one of the roots of our economic evils. The economic psychology of money, debt, and credit is the subject of this chapter.

Psychology cannot do much to remedy the intrinsic evil of loving money, or lacking it. But in concert with economics, psychological principles can reveal a great deal about how Americans feel about borrowing money and how they act on those feelings; explain why monetary *perceptions* are more important than monetary aggregates; and interpret the U.S. economy's abrupt nosedive, and equally abrupt recovery in the spring of 1980. This will set the stage for discussion of the psychology of inflation in chapter 7. This chapter and the following one show that psychology is as essential for understanding people as consumers as it is for understanding people as producers.

*even if you have to borrow to do it.

Incidentally, the chapter title is by Artemus Ward, whose humor could capture the American soul and spirit in just a handful of words.

Neither Borrower Nor Lender

A few words are worth a thousand pictures. In words and numbers here is one curious and absorbing aspect of the American economic scene. On a cloudless Sunday in April, an ordinary American drives his family to church in a brand-new yellow station wagon, bought the previous week. It was paid for with the help of a large car loan, with an interest rate well over 12 percent.

During the long sermon, the ordinary American (the O.A.) dozes a little and counts his blessings: nice family; good job; new car; money in the bank, securely socked away in a savings account and bearing interest—a little over 6 percent. His wife's elbow wakes him just before the collection. What's wrong with this picture? Quite likely, nothing.

Borrowing money at 12 percent and lending it at 6 may seem a little puzzling. But statistics show millions of Americans do just that. A Gallup Poll survey revealed that three Americans in four (they or their spouses) have a savings account.[3] Although the real rate of interest these accounts bear—the actual interest rate minus inflation—is negative, savings deposits still represent what the average American sees as the main bulwark against rainy days and hard times. The amount held in savings accounts totals over 1,000 billion dollars, roughly divided equally between banks and thrift institutions.[4]

The same poll showed that one American in four (again, they or their spouses) has a car loan. Automobile credit totals over 100 billion dollars and comprises nearly two-fifths of all installment credit outstanding. Financing the purchase of new cars by borrowing has long been commonplace, despite the relatively high interest rates on such credit.

According to this survey, 82 percent of Americans who have car loans *also* have savings deposits. Moreover, I would guess that for a substantial proportion of this group, the amounts held in savings accounts approach or exceed the amount of the car loan.

Why lend at 6 percent and borrow at 12 percent? If you have the money, why not just use it to buy your car—in a sense, lend to yourself at 12 percent (the interest you save) instead of lending at 6 percent to a thrift institution. That way, you pocket a profit of 6 percent on the amount you do not borrow, and cut the price of the car by a hefty sum.

On close interrogation the O.A. would probably claim he never even considered drawing down his savings account to pay for his new station wagon. That account, he would say, was built up dollar by dollar. It is his cushion for emergencies. True, Americans save mostly for old age and retirement; but half of all savers cite emergencies or "rainy days" as major motives.[5] "Suppose I spent the money in my savings account," O.A. might reason. "In four years, I would have an old heap of rust and no money in the bank either. I would have no car and no savings. This way, in four years, I still have the savings, and I can buy another new car in exactly the same way I bought this one."

The ordinary American's brand of rationality is not very appealing to conventional economists. An expert in two-question logic might argue that O.A. is throwing away several hundred dollars a year, and so are those who behave like him. If car-loan payments are a convenient means of forced saving, then why not sign a slip deducting fixed amounts from your salary for a company savings plan, for example, and make the installment payments to yourself instead of to a finance company?

Neither a borrower nor a lender be, if you get 6 percent and pay 12. But the ordinary American probably likes Shakespeare as much as he relished college economics. Three or four years hence, he will buy his next new car in precisely the same fashion.

Millions of words have been written on the *economics* of borrowing and lending, money supply, and capital markets. The literature on the *psychology* of debt and credit is much smaller. Without psychology's insights, it is hard to fathom the behavior of the ordinary American and millions like him or understand the link between money and economic activity or predict the next move of the erratic long-pursued North American heavy-billed consumer. In the end it is people who borrow, lend, and spend. It is *them* we must understand, not the chits, slips, ducats, and coins they pass around. How people use credit to smooth out gaps between their means and their wants is one of the keys we need to unlock the secrets of economic activity and its periodic dips and climbs.

Saving, Business Cycles, and Life Cycles

A visitor from deep space would not be overly impressed with how our lives are organized. "Lacks synchronization," he might report to his home planet. Biologists claim nature designed the human body to last for four or five decades. Now, we squeeze thirty more years out of it than its designer intended. On the average women live eight years longer than men. Moreover, three out of four men are older than the women they marry. The result of this differential mortality and age gap at marriage is more than 10 million widows in the United States, nearly 5 percent of the population.

If our biological life cycle is poorly set up, so is the economic life cycle. Wealth and income are not well synchronized with needs. The need for income peaks at age twenty-five or thirty, when houses are bought and furnished and children are being born and raised.[6] (See figure 6.1.) From that point on, needs decline steadily. But actual income follows a precisely opposite pattern. At age twenty-five or thirty, experience, training, and seniority are all low,

Be Happy and Live Within Your Means

FIGURE 6.1

Optimal and Actual Distributions of Income for American Urban Families

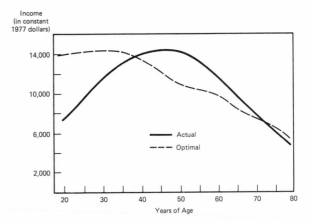

SOURCE: Adapted from Lester Thurow, "The Optimum Lifetime Distribution of Consumption Expenditures," *American Economic Review* 59 (1969): 328.

and so is income. Income peaks at about age forty-five. By that time our spending needs are only 70 percent of their highest level. As a result, wealth piles up. At ages twenty-five to thirty-four, average net worth—just when we have the youth and health to enjoy it— is only one quarter or less of its level at ages fifty-five to sixty-four. After retirement a little of this wealth is used up. But for those over sixty-five, net worth is still higher than at any other age except fifty-five to sixty-four. Part of this wealth consists of single-family houses, but a surprisingly large part is in liquid and investment assets.

Presumably, it would be eminently logical to borrow heavily early in life and repay the loan later on, to even out our spending patterns. But banks lend money to people, not to averages or curves. People partly act as their own life-cycle bankers. For the most part, though, over the course of the economic life cycle, what we spend lies much closer to what we actually earn than to the ideal income configuration defined by needs. In this sense, living within our means in a long-run perspective *does* justify borrowing, as Artemus Ward suggested. Yet despite the economic rationale for moderate and carefully considered borrowing, most Americans are exceedingly cautious and conservative in how they regard spending money they do not have. That caution has not prevented credit-fueled spending binges from propelling the economy into an upswing or slamming it into a downturn when the fuel is spent. Both the economic life cycle of the individual, and the business cycle of the whole economy, are intimately bound up with attitudes toward saving and borrowing.

Happiness $\pm$ Sixpence = Misery

Paradox is often a signal for caution in the face of complexity. Here is a fundamental paradox that characterizes the average American consumer. As previously stated, the American people are, have been, and will probably remain exceedingly conservative in their attitudes toward incurring debt. Like Dickens's Mr. Micawber, they profess that "Annual income twenty pounds, annual expenditure nineteen nineteen six, result happiness. Annual income twenty pounds, annual exenditure twenty pounds ought and six, result misery." For want of sixpence, "The blossom is blighted, the leaf is withered, the God of the day goes down upon the dreary scene, and—in short you are forever floored."[7] Whatever their ages, Americans shrink from debt. Extensive evidence will be cited shortly.

At the same time, there has been an explosion in consumer credit in the post–World War II era. A good part of it came in mortgages. But nonmortgage debt mushroomed too. A generation ago cash registers—big old mechanical ones that rang bells when they opened—had little signs stuck on them saying, "In God We Trust, All Others Pay Cash." The cash registers have disappeared, and so have the signs. In their place are red, white, and blue VISA signs,

Be Happy and Live Within Your Means

Diner's Club, American Express, Carte Blanche, MasterCard or Chargex signs—all inviting buyers to charge it.

In 1950 outstanding consumer credit amounted to one-eighth of disposable (after-tax) income. Twenty-five years later it had risen to one-quarter of disposable income. Including mortgages, people now owe over 1,200 billion dollars, six times what they owed in 1960.[8] During the past five years revolving installment credit shot up to top 50 billion dollars. In the same period the fraction of Americans who believe it is "not OK or never OK, to buy on credit" never dipped below 60 percent and lately has been on the rise (See figure 6.2.)[9]

Behind this apparent contradiction between Micawberian attitudes and macabre debts lies a story. The main character is the American consumer. The plot involves financial institutions that

FIGURE 6.2
Attitudes Toward Debt Remain Conservative While Installment Credit Soars

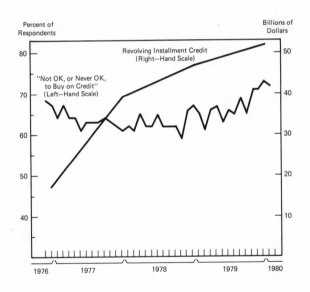

SOURCE: Attitude Toward Debt: Gallup Poll Survey, August 1979; Installment Credit, *Statistical Abstract*.

found ways to squeeze between chinks in antidebt armor. The sequel involves the onset of the steepest three-month drop in the GNP since 1945. The discipline needed to understand character, plot, and sequel is psychology.

Attitudes Toward Borrowing

Some people say that credit is a valuable asset which should be used to let them live the kind of life they want to live. Other people say that credit is something that is best to use as little as possible. Which comes closest to your own opinion?

This and other questions relating to borrowing and credit were part of a Gallup Poll national survey covering 1,538 Americans in August 1979. The answers reveal a fundamental reluctance to borrow. In answering the above question some 27 percent of the respondents said that credit was a "valuable asset." But fully 70 percent answered, "Credit should be used as little as possible." Only 3 percent could not decide; credit, apparently, is one subject where fence straddlers are few.

Objectively, a person's financial situation is defined by income, assets, and liabilities. Subjectively, when asked to choose "the one most important thing that the words 'financial fitness' mean to you," 39 percent said, "Being free of debt." The closest runner-up, a distant 15 percent, was the short-run version of the sixpence principle, "not having to worry about being able to meet day-to-day expenses." Being debt-free was picked by half the respondents as either first, second, or third in importance for financial fitness.

Overall, people expect their indebtedness to decline rather than to rise:

Not counting any mortgage you may owe, three years from now do you expect to have more debt than you have now, about the same

Be Happy and Live Within Your Means

amount, less than now, a lot less, or do you think you will have it all paid off?

Only one person in nine answered, "more . . . than now." One in four said, "about the same," and almost half said they anticipated "less, . . . a lot less, or . . . all paid off."

Asked, "Do you feel you are living within your means, or do you feel that you are buying too much and saving too little?" 85 percent of the respondents felt they were living within their means. The same percentage said they "hardly ever" or "never" had to borrow money to help pay "bills and everyday expenses."

Given these data alone, no expert would predict the recent explosive growth of credit buying. In the same survey, respondents were asked to react to hypothetical situations.

> If you suddenly found that next week you had to make an unexpected expenditure about equal to two weeks' income, where would you get the money from?

A bit less than half mentioned "savings account" first; only 23 percent mentioned borrowing. Taking out a loan ran slightly ahead of savings, but only as a second alternative. For a major unexpected expenditure equal to a month's income, a majority preferred using savings rather than buying on credit and paying in installments.

Is the unease borrowing arouses mainly an attitude of older people, raised in an era when money was coin and paper rather than plastic? This is not the case. The percentage of respondents who feel it is not OK, or never OK, to buy on credit, according to age, zigs upward significantly only beyond age seventy:

Age:	under 20	20–29	30–39	40–49	50–59	60–69	70–79	80–88
Percentage of Respondents:	63	64	66	63	69	67	84	93

How, then, do consumers profess to spurn debt, and by all accounts embrace it at the same time? Doing one thing while believing another is not a phenomenon economics likes to confront. Let us call the social psychologists in for consultation.

Cognitive Dissonance

Consistency may have been the "hobgoblin of little minds," to Ralph Waldo Emerson, but it is reasonable to assume that ordinary people prefer consistency to inconsistency. This is the basis of a theory of motivation known as *cognitive dissonance,* first elucidated by Leon Festinger. The basic premise is that people seek consistency in their values, ideas, and opinions. Dissonance—a clash between two or more beliefs—impels people to try to reduce it. *How* they do so is the subject of voluminous research, and it is a valuable tool in understanding behavior and attitudes.

Festinger's theory arose from a study of strange rumors following a 1934 earthquake in India.[10] In a region where there were sharp tremors but no damage or casualties, widespread rumors of impending doom and disaster circulated. If people normally avoid unpleasant things, such as anxiety, why did this happen? Festinger explained the phenomenon as stemming from dissonance between strong fear and apprehension caused by tremors and lack of a firm *reason* for such fears. The rumors provided a reason and reduced the dissonance.

In a classic experiment Festinger and Carlsmith had three groups of college students perform a dull experimental task.[11] One-third of them were then asked how they felt about it, and they said it was unpleasant. The two other groups were given another job before being asked their opinions. They were paid to introduce the next subject (waiting outside) to the task, by depicting it as pleasant and enjoyable. One group got one dollar apiece, the other, 20 dollars apiece. Dissonance arose between attitudes to the task and what the subjects were paid to say about it. Those paid 20 dollars rated the task much like the control group; payment bought hypocrisy and could justify it. Those paid one dollar rated the task more agreeable and pleasant than the other two groups. In the absence of a substantial reward, dissonance was reduced by changing the original attitude toward the task.

How can lenders overcome the cognitive dissonance arising from conservative attitudes about debt? Financial institutions' profits flow, of course, from lending people money. For some of these institutions, demand is more than adequate to soak up the supply available. But increasingly, there is competition for borrowers.

One way to attract those sought-after borrowers is to lend people money in a manner that does not arouse dissonance at all. If people can borrow without really seeming to do so, inconsistency between behavior and attitudes is minimized. The conflict between "I am going deeper into debt" and "Debt is wrong" need not arise if loans are sufficiently "unloanlike." Credit cards and bank-check credit have filled just such a role.

Plastic Money

Once, long ago, money was money—gold or silver coin, stamped with the king's head, issued only by him. Paper came next, still issued by the sovereign but backed by metal buried in deep vaults. Then came fractional-reserve banking. Private banks got the right to create money—by creating deposit balances for their borrowers —under the control of central banks. Textbooks showed various ways central banks could sop up money or make more, but it was hard to deny that *some* control over the money supply had devolved to commercial banks.

The latest development is private individuals creating money. The First National Plastic Bank of the Average American Family is here. I estimate that at least two American households in three hold either a VISA or MasterCard credit card. The credit ceiling on each card is usually $1,000. The average amount owed per credit card is now around $501.[12] This means that about 60 million households could, if they chose, each create $500 in money by utilizing their unused credit for a total of $30 billion.

Credit cards are not a new phenomenon. In fact, they came into being well before fractional-reserve banking. The term *credit card* was first used almost a century ago by a visionary lawyer, Edward Bellamy. He foresaw a cashless society where each citizen would get a yearly credit card from the government. The card would have tiers of squares representing dollar amounts, and every purchase would cancel out the appropriate number of squares.[13] As early as 1900 hotels were issuing credit cards to selected clients; and in 1914, department stores and gasoline station chains followed suit.

Diner's Club transformed credit cards from paying for particular goods to a general means of payment (for restaurant charges) in 1950. The first true *bank card* was issued in 1951 by the Franklin National Bank in New York—a bank whose name we now recognize not for its innovation but for its collapse—and Bank of America and Chase Manhattan soon followed suit.[14]

Bank cards went national in 1965. By 1972 BankAmericard and Master Charge each claimed 30 million card holders. At that time it was estimated that more than half of all families held at least one credit card. But only one in six of these cards were bank cards. The rest were issued by oil companies or specific stores. Today, VISA (the successor to BankAmericard) and MasterCard (the successor to Master Charge) each claims 58 million cards holders.

It is highly unlikely that 60 million American households will some day rise as one, as if on signal, and lend themselves another 30 billion dollars in spending power, anymore than they will all dash to the bank and draw out all their savings deposits in cash. But it is an exceedingly important and interesting new economic fact of life that people *can* write their own loans, almost without seeming to do so. In the end it is the change in how people *perceive* credit cards, not the cards themselves, that overshadows recent events. And the plastic revolution is not confined to credit cards alone.

The Disappearing Zero

Credit cards are not the only major new institution changing the economic landscape. Bank-check credit—interest-bearing checking accounts with preapproved credit—operates in similar ways. Once people felt strictly limited by the lower bound of their bank account, zero. Generations of comedians wrote jokes about overdrafts and bouncing checks. Today the zero point has been largely erased. Once everyone had a fair idea what his balance was or, at least, how far from zero it was. Today there is no need. For those with bank-check credit, the *sign* attached to the bank balance (plus or minus), let alone the amount, may not be known. Black ink and red have blurred together. By writing a check, the ordinary American may or may not be writing himself a loan. The key point is, he is unlikely to be much concerned about it.

In this way, competing commercial banks have, wittingly or unwittingly, found a way to slip through the cognitive-dissonance cracks. Paying for a purchase with a credit card is not really borrowing, the buyer tells himself, because it will be paid for at the end of the month. When the bills pile up at the end of the month, it is easy and natural to pay only part of the credit-card balance, perhaps a very small part. The dissonance between borrowing in this way and believing that debt is wrong and risky is therefore minimized.

Similarly, writing a check may pull one's balance below zero. This is equivalent to asking for a loan. But since writing a check with a positive balance is the identical act to writing one with a negative balance, and since it may not be at all *certain* that the account balance is negative, the debt-creation aspect can easily be overlooked. Again, one can borrow without really seeming to borrow.

Ironically, in the wake of disappearing zeros and plastic rectangles, *real* plastic money is in the offing. In inflationary times, paper dollar bills wear out quickly and need to be retired after eighteen months or so of use. Cost of printing replacements is about 50 million dollars a year. Experiments are being conducted with a tough plastic dollar bill, immune to inflation and rapid turnover.[15] Since plastic is made from petrochemicals, there is considerable logic in making dollars out of the very stuff they are needed to buy.

Think and Do

Putting new credit-creating power into people's hands does not necessarily mean that they will choose to use it. Much depends on their expectations.

Economists spend long hours pondering the state of the economy, how it got that way, and where it is headed. But ordinary people do not normally share that preoccupation. Most people spend very little time thinking about economic trends. When they do think about them, their thoughts rarely become clear-cut expectations. When they do exist, such expectations do not always suggest a course of action, nor are people always willing and able to carry out such action. Conversely, consumer behavior cannot always be traced back to precise patterns of reasoning. Links among economic news, expectations, and spending are complex and mysterious. Without a close alliance of psychology and economics, they will likely remain so.

"It is not to be supposed that we assume every action to be deliberate, and the outcome of calculation," Marshall wrote (rather wistfully, I think). "For in this as in every other respect economics takes man just as he is in ordinary life: and in ordinary life people do not weigh beforehand the results of every action . . . ."[16]

I invite the reader to respond to a question put to Gallup Poll interviewees.

> At any time in the past two years, have you added up all your basic monthly expenses to see what the total is—I mean, things like mortgage or rent payments, food, transportation, clothing, debt payments, and the like? (If yes: When was the last time?)

About 42 percent answered that they had added up only some of these things, and 7 percent said it had added up none of them. For those who had added everything up, half had done so two or more months ago.

Few of us, then, have up-to-date knowledge of spending on basics. We therefore have no precise knowledge of current total spending either. The model of the exacting consumer matching subjective value and objective price right at the precipice of his budget line, along which he or she skates with Olympic precision, is farfetched. Even when a clear consensus develops about where the economy is headed, and about people's own incomes and spending and how they are likely to change, actions based on those thoughts may still be ambiguous. Inflation expectations are a conspicuous example.

The anticipation of more rapid inflation should logically lead to stepped-up buying by consumers, who want to buy in advance of price rises. (This is sometimes called buy-in-advance spending.) If this is widespread, the very expectation can bring about the feared result, a kind of self-fulfilling prophecy. (Chapter 7 will deal at length with this mechanism, at the very heart of which lies some social psychology.)

There have been episodes of this sort, notably in 1978–79, when buy-in-advance spending fueled house- and car-buying binges. But at other times—for instance, inflationary periods during the Korean War and Vietnam War—the opposite has happened. To many people inflation means uncertainty and instability. In the face of uncertainty people become cautious. They become less ready to undertake major purchases, and they try to put away a bit more in savings, just in case. Empirically, then, the expectation of faster inflation has led both to higher savings rates and to lower ones, depending on the circumstances.[17]

In the absence of wars and other big disturbances, two opposing forces have traditionally operated to keep savings rates relatively stable. In good times strong incomes keep savings high, while the desire to spend keeps them low. In bad times concern for the future and worry over personal finances keep savings high, while the erosion of incomes keeps them low.

Credit-card consumer psychology appears to vitiate one of these forces. People may be strapped for funds and have little left over to save. But they appear to be unconcerned. Part of this lack of concern must be due to the pervasiveness of credit cards. The contingency nest-egg function of savings is now being supplanted, to some degree, by small colored rectangles made of plastic. They offer a discretionary means of evening out spending levels and tiding the family over temporary rough times.

To an accountant, charging a purchase with a credit card creates a debt or liability for the user. But credit-card holders seem to view them as a kind of "just in case" fall-back asset. They make it possible for us to continue to live within our means by borrowing, without really seeming to borrow.

Suppose, however, people's faith in two-inch-by-three-inch plastic safety nets is shaken? What then? The economy falls through a trap door.

Recession on the Analyst's Couch

When it finally arrived, the 1980 recession that economists had been predicting for a whole year hit the economy like Muhammad Ali's left hook, short and very sharp. During the spring quarter, output of goods and services fell by a record 10 percent, the biggest drop ever. (See figure 6.3.) Financial writers called it the *hit-and-run* recession. Close analysis suggests the term *psychological* recession might be more apt.

No one denies, least of all economists, that psychology (of consumers and businesses) exerts powerful influence on economic activity. How much people spend on cars, houses, and appliances and how much businesses spend on plant and equipment provide demand that influences production, employment, and prices. Spending plans, in turn, depend on both objective information and subjective opinions. Every squiggle in the GNP can therefore be attributed in some fashion to general, ill-defined consumption or investment psychology. The 1980 recession, however, was different. I believe its cause can be traced quite precisely to a distinct psychological mechanism of immense power, set in motion quite by accident.

On the face of it, the story of the spring 1980 recession is told by credit. In 1978 outstanding consumer debt (including mortgages) grew by 135 billion dollars. For the first three quarters of 1979, debt grew by 129 billion dollars. (This and the following figures are all annual rates and are therefore comparable.) In the last three months of 1979 the addition to the debt was $102 billion, and 94 billion dollars were added in January through March 1980.

Then, lightning struck. On March 14 President Carter dramatically announced that he was invoking martial-law powers of the 1969 Credit Control Act in an effort to clamp down on inflation. The gist of his message, covering forty pages of credit-control

FIGURE 6.3
The Psychological Recession of 1980

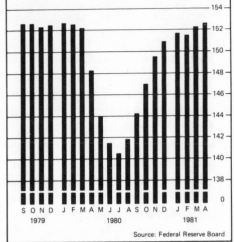

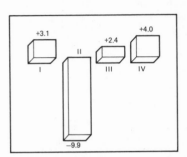

(a) Percent Change in Real GNP
(Annual Rate), for 1980,
Seasonally Adjusted

(b) Industrial Production
Index (1967=100), in 1980
January–December

Source: Federal Reserve Board

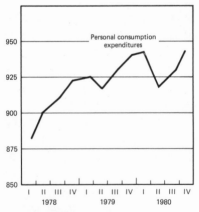

△ Billions of 1972 dollars, seasonally
adjusted annual rate

Source: Data Resources Inc., Commerce Dept.

(c) Private consumption
Expenditures (Annual Rate),
in 1978-80

NOTES: (a) *New York Times,* Jan. 18, 1981, p. 5 (International Edition), © 1981 by the New York Times Company. Reprinted by permission. (b) *New York Times,* May 16, 1981, © 1981 by the New York Times Company. Reprinted by permission. (c) *Business Week,* March 9, 1981, p. 71. Reprinted from March 9, 1981 issue of *Business Week* by special permission, © 1981 by McGraw-Hill, Inc., New York, N.Y. 10020. All rights reserved.

regulations, was that there would be a considerable reduction in the availability of credit.[18]

"Any time lenders increase the total amount of credit outstanding on charge cards, revolving bank-credit plans or other unsecured personal loans," it was announced, "they will have to make a 'special deposit' with the Federal Reserve System, amounting to 15 percent of the extra lending." The deposits would earn no interest.

The general message to lenders was: Interest rates would go up and the growth of credit would slow down. Prime lending rates quickly shot up to 19 percent.

The message to borrowers, as *they* perceived it, was quite different:

> You know those credit cards that stuff your wallet? And the $3,000 that Mr. Upshaw, the assistant bank manager, said you could draw on if you needed to? Carter and the bankers have done something to them, something complicated, it's hard to understand what. Whatever it is, you can't depend on them anymore. Using them is borrowing. They don't want you to borrow. If you do, they penalize you somehow.

The March 14 policy left scorched earth in shopping centers, department stores, and car showrooms. In April consumer debt rose by 24 billion dollars (annual rate). But in May it *declined* by $24 billion, and in June, by $34 billion. Compared with 1978, June 1980 saw a shortfall of consumer borrowing amounting to 169 billion dollars. This alone is enough to explain why the economy fell through a trapdoor.

Did the *supply* of credit contract, or was it the *demand?* The ultimate cause probably lay in the following process of thought among many Americans. Inflation is bad and unlikely to get better. But I'm OK, I have unused credit I can draw on in a pinch. But wait. Maybe I can't draw on it. Those new controls may mean it won't be available when I need it. Better cut back, cut spending, borrow less, pay cash.

Focusing attention on credit cards and bank credit brought

home to Americans that their use was *indeed* explicit borrowing, that such borrowing was quantitatively large, and that those in charge wanted to discourage it and had the means to do so. In terms of cognitive dissonance, antiborrowing attitudes were strengthened, and at the same time, the nature of actions clashing with those attitudes (borrowing money) was made explicit. No wonder many consumers resolved the dissonance by paying off their debts rather than adding to them.

Until March 14 people had run up a lot of debt, mostly inadvertently. At the end of the month, the most pressing bills would be paid, and when the money ran out, credit-card debt could be put off until next month. It might not have even been considered a debt. After several months of this, debts would pile up. The March 14 announcement called attention to this debt. Until then, I believe people were concerned about owing money not because they were afraid they couldn't repay it, but because they weren't sure if it was right to borrow in the first place. A policy that spotlights the issue and transforms latent worry into overt anxiety has enormous impact, not by slicing the supply of credit but by slashing the demand for it.

This is why I call the recession a psychological one. It turns out to have been a large-scale uncontrolled experiment in social psychology. The bill came to 60 billion dollars—the cost of a 10 percent drop in the GNP for three months.

The experiment ended. Controls were dismantled in the summer of 1980. Consumers have short memories and quickly returned to old habits. By August credit-buying had returned to its January peak, despite high interest rates. The economy recovered, interest rates dipped and then soared again, and the 1980 recession became the property of those who study history rather than those who live it. If we are to avoid reliving this mistake, we must learn from it. One of the major lessons relates to the economics of supply and demand.

Ever since the Great Depression showed how insufficient purchasing power could throw one man in four on the dole and let grass grow under assembly lines, macroeconomics—inspired by John Maynard Keynes—has posited that the level of economic activity is largely *demand*-determined. To help inflation, cut back demand. To fight recession, crank up spending.

During the 1970s Keynes fell from favor. Stagflation was born. As inflation and unemployment climbed together, they led to dissonance by suggesting that demand was both slack (hence unemployment) and excessive (inflation). Ingenious explanations were devised to patch up the conventional Keynesian model so that it could account for stagflation. But economists turned increasingly from the demand side of the economy to the supply side. Studies focused on, for instance, cost-push inflation and the relation between productivity growth and inflation. The idea that our economic fate, and ills, may be principally determined by supply became popular. Supply quickly rose to take its (rightful) place, at the GNP crossroads next to demand or perhaps slightly ahead of it.

Then, along came March 14, 1980. Massive amounts of purchasing power disappeared. The economy itself delivered a painful and much-needed reminder that aggregate demand, or the lack of it, remains a potent force, capable, if mistreated, of causing great ruin. That the lesson was not sharper and longer we owe not to clever policy but to habit, inertia, and abiding faith in the permanence of inflation—forces that proved stronger than inhibitions about debt.

Interest Rates or Money

On Saturday night even economists do not normally talk about discount rates and money supply. But late on October 6, 1979, they probably did. Federal Reserve Board Chairman Paul A. Volcker had just announced a major new plan to bolster the dollar and battle inflation. Bankers, gathered in New Orleans for their annual convention, puzzled over the hurried announcement of a set of fairly conventional measures—higher discount rates (interest rates paid by banks to the Federal Reserve) and higher reserve requirements. Some of them took note of an underplayed and understated part of the program—the announced intention of the Federal Reserve Board to switch their attention from interest rates to the money supply.[19]

Traditionally, U.S. monetary policy, for which the Federal Reserve Board and its chairman are responsible, has focused on interest rates. Hiking interest rates makes borrowing more costly for companies and consumers. This should slow down inflation and help cool off the economy. Cutting interest rates produces the opposite effect. The Federal Reserve claims it has the means to steer interest rates very close to declared target levels.

For years a group of economists had offered cogent arguments that it is the money supply, and not interest rates, that really matters. With appropriate lags, monetary growth tracks inflation closely. The Federal Reserve, they claimed, should zero in directly on the growth rate of money, not on the cost of borrowing. Paul Volcker's Saturday Night surprise announcement marked official acceptance of this view.

Historically, Federal Reserve control over the money supply has been much weaker than its control over interest rates. Former Chairman Arthur F. Burns repeatedly attested that he could not control the amount of money with precision. Since 1975, when Congress demanded that the Federal Reserve make public its money-supply targets, there have been some very wide misses.

Paradoxically, controlling the money supply became the official cynosure of monetary policy right around the time that the Federal Reserve's *ability* to control it was seriously weakened. One of the major factors contributing to that weakening was the growth of credit cards and bank-check credit. Just as the Fed said it intended to guide the *actual* money supply, the *psychological* money supply was galloping off into the distance.

$M_1, M_2, \ldots M_7$, or $\ldots M_\psi$?

Money is what people think it is. The official definition of money is what economist *think* people think money is.

There is a whole string of moneylike assets vying for inclusion in this definition. Cash and demand deposits are money beyond question; they are classified M_1. Add savings and time deposits; that is, M_2. (Midway between M_1 and M_2 is a recent hybrid, M_{1+}, which includes savings deposits and checkable deposits at thrifts.) Subscripts march on as assets with less and less "moneyness" are included, all the way down to M_7.

The relevant M is M_ψ. The Greek letter ψ (psi) stands for psychological. Money is what people *perceive* to be spendable liquid assets. This is an elusive concept, hard to measure or pin down. It appears in no statistical abstract or Federal Reserve Board bulletin. But if any kind of money matters, this is the kind that does.

Money supply figures for the second quarter of 1980, or the period preceding it, show no drastic changes; certainly none large enough to explain why the GNP fell out of bed. It is apparent however, that the psychological money supply (which includes available but unused credit, from credit cards and other sources) plummeted. Imposition of credit controls, even weak ones, planted doubts that unused credit could be counted on as a source of emergency funds. Government, lenders, and a helping hand from the media conspired to persuade consumers that they had a lot less spending power at their disposal than they thought. The result was a recession.

With a large margin for error, the Federal Reserve Board can control the growth of M_1 or M_2 by such means as open-market operations (buying or selling bonds to banks and people). Controlling M_ψ is infinitely harder and trickier. It may not, in fact, be possible.

One of the continuing battles in economics has been monetarism versus fiscalism. Lately the balance has tipped toward monetarism; the October 6, 1979, Saturday Night shift bears witness to this. Just when a close, stable link between measured monetary aggregates and economic activity seems established, the elusive consumer arises and proves this view wrong.

Conclusion

Jay Schmiedeskamp and I recently canvassed a group of economic forecasters. Only one-third of them said they relied mainly on econometric models. The remainder said they used judgment solely or a combination of models and judgment. They cited a wide array of variables they found useful, including the full panoply of subscripted M's. Our overall impression was one of substantial theoretical disarray and disagreement, with insubstantial attention to the thoughts, feelings, and sentiments of the consumer.

The last word on the subject belongs to Marshall. "The economist needs three great intellectual faculties," he wrote. "Perception, imagination and reason: and most of all he needs imagination, to put him on the track of those causes of visible events which are remote or lie below the surface and of those effects of visible causes which are remote or lie below the surface."[20]

The 1980 recession taught us that below the surface of the consumer's mind lies a complex psychology capable of causing abrupt and serious economic distress. At the core of that psychology lie attitudes toward borrowing. Understanding those attitudes, perhaps even harnessing them, is well within economics' means—with the help of some borrowed theory from psychology and a healthy dose of Marshallian imagination.

Inflation is like a crowd at a football game. No one is willing to be the first to sit down.

President JIMMY CARTER,
in a television address,
October 25, 1978

NOTHING CAN REPLACE THE DOLLAR, AND SOON WILL: COMMON INFLATION AS THE TRAGEDY OF THE COMMONS[1]

AT a football game, parade, or any event with large crowds, if everyone remains seated, everyone can see fairly well. A person can improve his view by standing, at the expense of the person behind him. When *that* person stands and then another and another, soon everyone is standing; the whole crowd sees no better, and probably much worse, than if all were seated. It is the nature of football games that exciting moments soon pass. As if at a signal, everyone sits down, until the next long pass or end run.

Inflation is indeed, as President Carter claimed, like a crowd at a football game. In the economy, if everyone remains moderate in his wage, price, and spending behavior, everyone can do fairly well. Prices stay stable. A person can improve his lot by hiking prices or by demanding high wages, at the expense of the person who buys from him or who employs him. When *that* person follows suit and

157

then another and another, soon, everyone is acting immoderately, rushing out to buy goods before they get more expensive. Everyone is no better off, and probably much worse off, than if all had acted moderately from the start.

It is the nature of inflation that such behavior does not go away by itself. Unlike behavior at a football game, no one willingly "sits down" during an inflationary period. To do so would entail a sacrifice, at least a perceived one, that few people would voluntarily accept. That is why inflation is always and everywhere a social phenomenon. Both the road to understanding the *causes* of inflation, and the path to developing a *cure* for it, lie partly in psychology's territory.

Hardin's tragedy of the commons model was first encountered in chapter 2. There it illustrated how the invisible hand of competitive efficiency gives way to the clenched fist of egoism. We met this model again as *Prisoner's Dilemma* in chapter 5, which dealt with pay and productivity. Some readers will have spotted the essential features of the tragedy of the commons in the football-crowd inflation metaphor—each economic actor, unwilling to be exploited by other actors, behaves in such a way that everyone is worse off. In this chapter I will argue that common inflation is an instance of tragedy of the commons, or *Prisoner's Dilemma*.

This idea is neither new nor original. It is firmly based on the writings of John Maynard Keynes, whom I will quote extensively. What appears on the surface as a purely economic phenomenon—an inappropriate relationship between the amount of money and the amount of goods and services available for purchase with that money—turns out to be an inappropriate relationship among *people* and not just *things*. Ample evidence exists to support a social psychology theory of inflation, and some of it will be presented later.

Economists widely accept the general principle that psychology has direct bearing on the rate of inflation. At the heart of modern macroeconomics are theories of how people shape their expectations about future prices. In these theories, however, cognitive psychology and learning theory, which are clearly relevant, still are not allowed even to peep over the transom. I expect that one day they will walk right in the door.

Deflation the Rule, Inflation the Exception

Events of the past decade have fixed deep in human perceptions the idea that inflation is a permanent feature of our existence. History proves it is not. A long view shows deflation is equally common.

Around the third week of each month, the Bureau of Labor Statistics (BLS) announces consumer price index figures for the preceding month. There is considerable fanfare, especially when some sort of record is set. In January 1981 the BLS announced that consumer prices rose 12.4 percent in 1980, compared with 13.3 percent in 1979. A modern record was thus set (you can look it up): Not since 1918–19, war or postwar years, has inflation topped 10 percent for two years in a row.[2] This dubious achievement comes to remind us that two-digit inflation is an historical rarity, not a permanent house guest.

The producer price index (PPI) reflects the cost of over 2,800 different commodities used to make other goods and going back well over a century, is the oldest continuous statistical series the BLS publishes. From PPI data we learn that there were fairly brief bursts of inflation that erupted after the Civil War and the First and Second World Wars. These periods of inflation were generally followed by collapsing prices and long, drawn-out bouts of deflation and recession, as in 1873–96 and 1930–39. Producer prices were actually lower at the start of World War II than they were at the close of the Civil War!

If deflation is the rule, rather than the exception, it is the pain of brief bursts of inflation that indelibly marks psyches. In Europe short, sharp spurts of hyperinflation left permanent psychological scars. In approximately eighteen-month periods between 1921 and

1923, prices in Austria rose by 1,000 percent; in Hungary, 2,630 percent; in Poland, 24,402 percent; and in Germany, by 250,723 percent.[3] (Only Czechoslovakia escaped the ravages of a destroyed currency, a story itself worthy of a book.) Nearly everyone has seen pictures of baskets of krones or marks or of children building playhouses with piles of paper notes. *Inflationsangst* is still a dominant economic and political reality in Germany, even though no more than one person in every ten recalls 1923 firsthand.

Objectively 1 percent of deflation may be 100 times worse than 1 percent of inflation, as Abba Lerner once said.[4] But it is periods of inflation that seem to tread heaviest on the economic, political, and psychological landscape.

"Experience in the 1950s and 1960s, in America as well as in many other countries," George Katona observed, "indicated that slow and gradual increases in the price level could prevail over several years without disturbing confidence in the currency or affecting past habits and behavior patterns."[5] Hilde Behrend, author of numerous articles on the psychology of inflation, noted that in the mid-1960s researchers were startled to find that inflation meant little to people, "even to educated respondents."[6] As late as 1976, a minority of Americans said inflation had a "great deal of effect" on their lives (39 percent). By 1978 the minority became a majority, 58 percent. It has remained so.[7]

Once, when asked whether they had heard news about unfavorable changes in economic conditions, Gallup Poll respondents primarily mentioned falloffs in income, employment, or output. As late as December 1977 inflation still ran second. Since March 1978 inflation has consistently been tabbed as the main "economic bad news," generally ahead even of energy shortages.

A new economic reality has taken root. Inflation once lurked well below the threshold of public awareness. At intervals, it would emerge from the depths briefly, following wars (for example), explode into full view, and then sink from sight again. Lately inflation has persisted. Though our thresholds of inflation-awareness have risen, inflation itself has kept ahead of them. Like the early mammals, inflation seems to have emerged from the primeval waters for good.

In 1890 Alfred Marshall could still write, "We may throughout this volume neglect possible changes in the general purchasing power of money. Thus the price of anything will be taken as representative of its exchange value relatively to things in general, or in other words as representative of its general purchasing power."[8] Today he would have to build a thick, high hedge around that assumption or abandon it entirely.

What's Wrong with Inflation?

Inflation is now perceived to be as evil as it is permanent. But why? What if prices rise 1 percent a month? So do money incomes, in general. To help answer this question, let us look briefly at Israel. Like America, Israel set its own modern inflation record in 1979 and 1980—*triple*-digit inflation (110 percent and 133 percent, respectively) for two consecutive years.[9] In recent years monthly price rises in Israel have exceeded annual price rises in some industrial countries.

I once took part in a meeting of economics professors with the governor of the Bank of Israel, who was pressing—unsuccessfully, it turned out—to put together a wage-price package deal among labor, business, and government.[10] A leading economist raised the question that heads this section, with serious intent, not as devil's advocate. He pressed us for objective answers. It was not easy to supply them. Despite the horrendous inflation in Israel, floating exchange rates kept exports buoyant and imports slack. Wages tied to the cost of living index, and adjusted quarterly, prevented mayhem in labor markets. Bonds linked to the cost of living index preserved capital markets. Even tax brackets are linked to prices in Israel. This relative insulation of real incomes from price changes protects people from inflation; but by doing so it also protects inflation from people, and thus perpetuates it.

In the end our best response was that people dislike triple-digit inflation intensely, they *perceive* it as an absolute evil, and that in itself is a reality. But the factors underlying that perception are not easy to pin down.

Suppose you give someone a $100 raise. Then suppose prices rise and soak up $60 of that raise. The *real* increase is $40. Now, offer that same person a $40-a-week raise, with steady prices. Most people much prefer the latter alternative according to Lester Thurow.[11] Their reasoning reflects a kind of reverse money illusion. They see the $100-a-week raise as *theirs,* with inflation unjustly robbing them of most of it. The fact that excessive money incomes sometimes *cause,* and sometimes are *generated by,* inflation is not clearly understood.

The shrinking purchasing power of the dollar is well known to all. We have all seen charts showing how $1.00 in 1940 was worth 80¢ in 1945, 50¢ in 1955, about 25¢ in 1976 and 20¢ in 1980. In other words what $1.00 buys today you could buy with 20¢ in 1940.[12] Put another way, it took twenty-four years dating from 1945, for the buying power of $1.00 to fall by half. The next halving took only a decade. At current inflation rates of 12 percent, the value of $1.00 will be halved in only six years. (Take comfort; at Israeli inflation rates the purchasing power of the currency is halved every eleven *months.*)

Currency Debauched

What these numbers all scream is "Currency Debauched!" What they fail to reveal is that although $1.00 today buys what 20¢ bought in 1940, we earn, on the average, more than *ten* times as many paper dollars today than we did in 1940. Real living standards have risen enormously.

Everyone knows this. Everyone knows he lives better than his parents and grandparents. Still, the dollar certainly is not worth much these days. Right or wrong, inflation encourages the Ogden Nash syndrome: "Oh money, money money, I'm not necessarily one of those who think thee holy. But I often stop to wonder how thou canst go out so fast when thou comest in so slowly."[13]

Inflation exacts a real tax from our sense of well-being in at least two ways. Over the economic life cycle, many important *when* choices must be made—when to spend, or when to save to spend another day; when to go out to work, or when to go on studying; when to switch jobs in favor of lower-paying ones with faster advancement; when to change employers or occupations; when to sell short-term Treasury bills for long-term bonds. All these decisions involve great uncertainties. These are inescapable. With inflation, another common uncertainty is added: What a future dollar will buy. Inflation tends to shorten horizons and encourage present consumption and present gratification. It *need* not have this effect. If inflation puts in our pockets as many extra paper dollars as it debauches, it leaves us neither better nor worse off. But there is real anomie from the uncertainty inflation induces; the resulting myopia may make us excessively present-oriented (see chapter 3).

Another inflation tax arises in connection with *this-or-that* choices. Two-question logic demands that we know value and cost. We generally get that information in the form of absolute prices: how many dollars each thing costs. We then convert absolute prices into *relative* prices: how much one thing is worth compared to another. All economic choice is based on relative prices.

If prices are stable, or even changing at a constant rate, relative prices don't change. Like riding a bicycle, you learn them once and never forget them. But with inflation they don't work that way. It is an empirical fact that the more rapid the general rise in the price level, the more sweeping the changes in relative prices. As Milton

Friedman said in his brilliant Nobel Prize address, the more volatile the rate of general inflation, the harder it becomes to extract the signal about relative prices from the absolute prices: The broadcast about relative prices is, as it were, being jammed by the noise coming from the inflation broadcast.[14] When inflation is very rapid, such as 10 percent a month, I can attest that the static is so bad that you turn off the radio, buy what you need whatever the price (even economists find it hard to tell what is expensive and what is cheap), and then stop buying when you run out of money. The resulting inefficiency of such a random process must be enormous. So is the inefficiency involved in investing time and effort in learning new prices once a week, only to have them change again.

Under rapid inflation everything is simultaneously cheap and expensive. It is cheap because it will cost more tomorrow. It is expensive because it costs more today than it did yesterday. When that dissonance grows severe, it causes great anxiety for many people, and the price system creaks and groans and starts to break down. It is hard to say which is greater, the psychological costs incurred or the real loss of output due to inefficiency.

Fiorello La Guardia once barged into the airport terminal that bears his name, burst into the restaurant, and shouted, "What I want is a complete meal in this place for thirty-five cents—including coffee!" (The restaurant complied.)[15] Today, you can't buy the *coffee* for thirty-five cents. But so what? A meal at La Guardia Airport takes a smaller bite out of the average budget today than it did then.

I think it boils down to this: As we journey through life, an uncertain and risky trip at best, we look for familiar milestones and signposts along the way. The dollar is one of the most familiar of those signposts. The significance of the dollar is what it can *buy*. Once, what a dollar would buy was a constant, reliable unit of measurement, like the inch, gallon, or kilowatt, but much more pervasive and important. This is no longer true. People have been deprived of their signposts. They have been replaced with question marks. The damage is extensive.

Common Inflation as the Tragedy of the Commons

If we have a poor understanding of the psychological damage inflation causes, then our understanding of the underlying mechanism that generates inflation is even worse. I suggest we return to Keynes, the elusive, "real" Keynes. Keynesian economics has come to mean pump-prime spending by government to lessen unemployment or knee-jerk tax hikes to cut demand and spending. Higher spending and higher taxes are currently at the wrong end of a popular trend, so it is natural that the theory allegedly underlying them should be unfashionable. I contend, however, that Keynes himself had a behavioral theory of inflation utterly different from today's nearly unrecognizable versions of what he supposedly taught and wrote. At the core of Keynes's theory is, clearly and unmistakably, tragedy of the commons and *Prisoner's Dilemma*, though Keynes did not use those terms. The most persuasive evidence is Keynes's own words.

Keynes as a Behaviorist

Just prior to World War I, John Maynard Keynes wrote an article for the *Economic Journal* that predicted a brief war, since neither side could afford the costs for long.[16] The costs were indeed heavy, but the war dragged on. Sadder and wiser, Keynes again took pen in hand on the same subject in 1939. He wrote a series of three articles in the *London Times*—somehow, they were leaked to the *Frankfurter Zeitung* and were published there first—on how best to distribute the economic burden of the impending war among the British people.[17] He later pulled together the articles into a remarkable little book entitled *How to Pay for the War* (1940). Written for laymen, this work never got the academic respectability bestowed on his opaque, hence respectable, *General Theory* (1936). Despite its brevity it contains a full-blown theory of inflation built on real and fundamental psychological laws of human nature. I think Keynes's teacher, Alfred Marshall, would have approved.

At first Keynes saw inflation as the havoc resulting from conflict over slicing up the national-output pie (or cake) among competing groups: a *zero-sum game* in game-theory language. Keynes cautioned,

> The man in the street must learn to understand . . . that [in wartime] the size of the civilian's cake is fixed. . . . Each individual can increase his share of consumption if he has more money to spend . . . but . . . he can only do so at the expense of other people. . . . If all earnings are raised two shillings in the pound and are spent on buying the same quantity of goods as before, this means that prices will also rise two shillings in the pound; and no one will be a loaf of bread or pint of beer better off than he was before.[18]

But Keynes quickly realized that it is not simply a zero-sum game ("My gain is your loss") but a *negative-sum game* ("my *attempted* gain becomes both my loss and your loss."). The chief result of the inflation stemming from distributional battles over a fixed-size "pie" or "cake" is that "consumers' incomes pass into the hands of the capitalist class . . . so that they alone . . . would be the principal owners of the increased National Debt—of the right, that is to say, to spend money after the war." This fierce unfairness—working classes at one and the same time spill their blood on foreign soil, literally, and drain their blood, figuratively, into the veins of the wealthy after the war—occurred after World War I. Keynes never forgot it.

"If prices go up," Keynes reasoned, "the extra receipts swell someone's income so that there is just as much (excess demand) left over as before. . . . Wages and other costs will chase prices upwards, but nevertheless prices will always . . . keep 20 percent ahead [on Keynes's assumptions]. However much wages are increased,the act of spending these wages will always push prices this much in advance."[19] Readers may spot here a *multiplier* arithmetic. Keynes's well-known multiplier effect generally pertains to unemployment. An extra dollar of spending, Keynes showed, would generate many times that amount in added output and employment as it passed from hand to hand. The same effect works at full employment, except it is *prices,* not employment, that multiply upward.

So far, this is conventional economics. Now, enters human nature.

Why then, Keynes asked, do trade unions push hard for higher money wages?

> A demand . . . for an increase in money wages to compensate for every increase in the cost of living is futile, and greatly to the disadvantage of the working class. . . . the leaders of the Trade Unions know this as well as anyone else. They do not want what they ask. But they dare not abate their demands until they know what alternative policy is offered. This is legitimate.[20]

In Keynes's eyes the crux of the problem was that moderate, prosocial, antiinflationary behavior (such as limiting spending or wage demands) conferred large benefits on those who behaved *im* moderately.

> An individual cannot by saving more protect himself from the consequences of inflation if others do not follow his example; just as he cannot protect himself from accidents by obeying the rule of the road if others disregard it. . . . We have here the perfect opportunity for social action, where everyone can be protected by making a certain rule of behavior universal.[21]

In another vivid passage, Keynes wrote, "What is to the advantage of each of us regarded as a solitary individual is to the disadvantage of each of us regarded as members of a community. If all alike spend more, no one benefits. Here is the ideal opportunity for a common plan and for imposing a rule which everyone must observe."[22]

In the metaphor of Hardin's tragedy of the commons, if I graze another bull (that is, spend), there is less for others, and they lose; if everyone tries this, we all lose (through inflation). To prevent this, some rule or agreement or social convention is needed. As a simile, inflation is like *Prisoner's Dilemma;* if I "sing" (spend), my silent accomplice gets life; he knows this, "sings" too, and we both look at bars (inflation) for years, unless something protects us from ourselves.

This model shifts the focus from things—money, goods, and prices—to *people* and how they respond to opportunities for short-term gains at others' expense. The shortcoming of conventional antiinflation theory and policy is that it has failed to see the problem as one of *Prisoner's Dilemma.* Economics has remained a prisoner of worn and outmoded ideas, while the behavioral model that welds inflation to social psychology has been overlooked for forty years.

Games People Play

Keynes once said that "economics is a science of thinking in terms of models, joined to the art of choosing models which are relevant to the contemporary world . . . . Good economists are scarce," he continued, "because the gift for using 'vigilant observation' to choose good models, although it does not require a highly specialized intellectual technique, appears to be a very rare one."[23]

One good model-building technique is to listen to what people are saying. What people—and some good economists, including Alfred Marshall—say suggests that behavior toward uncertain inflation is a venture in game playing. Like all games, there are sharp conflicts of interest among the players. Each player has several moves or strategies. Above all, each player must remember, as in chess, poker, or blackjack, that his or her payoff depends not only on the player's own move but upon other players' moves over which he or she (the first player) has no control.

Consider the following labor-management game. Each side vies for shares of the national income—real wages and real profits,

Common Inflation as the Tragedy of the Commons

respectively. Each wants as big a slice as it can get. This is legitimate, Keynes reminded us. Labor has two strategies—demand small wage increases or large ones. Management also has two strategies—boost prices a little or a lot.

If labor asks for a small wage increase and management hikes prices a lot, labor loses. Fear of losing keeps wage demands high. If management raises prices moderately, and labor asks for (and gets) big wage hikes, management loses. Fear of losing makes price increases steep. Lack of confidence in the other side prevents compromise. Habit maintains immoderate strategies once they begin.

Consumers also take part in a rather nervewracking game. For simplicity consider you and me and two houses for sale. Each of us can buy a house now or wait and buy it later. If I choose to buy now while you wait, you will pay more when you buy, owing to the tighter supply and general inflation. If I choose to wait and you buy now, I end up paying more. My best strategy is to buy now, even if my present dwelling is perfectly adequate. If *both* you and I buy now, chances are we will both pay high prices and lose out.

These two games—involving labor versus management and consumer versus consumer—each describe a kind of *Prisoner's Dilemma.* For each the individually rational strategy, if adopted by everyone, leads to collective ruin. In Adam Smith's economy, what is good for me, you, business, labor, and General Motors as individuals is good for the country. In *Prisoner's Dilemma,* what seems good for me is bad for the country, and sooner or later bad for me too. Seen in this light, inflation is a moral illness with psychological causes and economic symptoms. Its prognosis is chronic, unless radical surgery on human nature is performed (unlikely) or Spartan controls are imposed on spending (unpleasant). In his tragedy of the commons version, Garrett Hardin concludes that in some cases, there are no "technical" solutions. *Prisoner's Dilemma* research from psychology, mentioned in chapter 5, shows just how hard it is to elicit prosocial (cooperative) behavior; the opportunity to shaft the other player is ever-present, and ordinary mortals find it easy to resist everything except the things they want.

Do people in fact *perceive* they are trapped in a *Prisoner's Dilemma?* In an early economic application of *Prisoner's Dilemma* to ghetto expansion, Smolensky, Becker, and Molotch note that "perceptions, whether based upon fact or not, govern behavior."[24] It is as important to learn what game people perceive as it is to determine the objective nature of the game they are playing. The following section provides some empirical evidence.

The Illusion-of-Money Illusion

To measure how well Americans understand the dilemma inflation poses, the following question was put to a random national sample in August 1979, as part of the Gallup Economic Service survey:[25]

> For people who work for a living, how well off they are depends not only on the wages they earn, but also on the prices of things they buy. [The respondent is shown figure 7.1 by the interviewer.]
> In your opinion, which of these four categories is the best, from the point of view of *working people?*
> In your opinion, which of these four categories is the best, from the point of view of *Americans as a whole?*

The results were illuminating. They reveal, I believe, considerable diversity, sophistication, and, if anything, an aversion to inflation quite the opposite of the *money illusion* (mistaking extra paper dollars for extra purchasing power) that economists purport to observe.

Of some fourteen hundred people who answered, three out of eight chose *different* outcomes for working people and Americans as a whole. Five out of eight felt that the interests of working people and all Americans coincided. The latter group was about equally divided between those who felt a large wage rise and a small price

Common Inflation as the Tragedy of the Commons

FIGURE 7.1

Respondents are asked by Gallup Poll interviewer to pick the outcome (1) best for working people and (2) best for the American people as a whole.

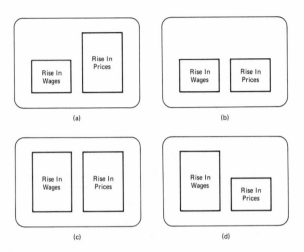

NOTE: Reprinted from S. Maital and Y. Benjamini, "Inflation as Prisoner's Dilemma," *Journal of Post Keynesian Economics* 2, no. 4 (Summer 1980): 459. By permission of M.E. Sharpe, Inc. Publishers, Armonk, N.Y. 10504.

rise were optimal and those who felt a small wage and price rise were best.

Less than half the sample—fewer than I had expected—felt that a large wage increase and a small price rise were best for working people. One person in three chose a *small* wage and price rise as best. A very small fraction—one in eight—picked large wage increases and large price increases.

A surprisingly large fraction—42 percent—believed small wage increases are best for working people. A narrow majority favored large wage increases. They divided up as follows:

- "My gain is your loss": Close to one-half felt *real* wage increases benefited workers at the expense of others (that is, small wage and price rises were picked best for all Americans). This is consistent with *Prisoner's Dilemma.*

- "Dictatorship of the proletariat": One-quarter felt real wage increases were best for workers and all Americans.
- The remaining one-quarter was split up among several diverse patterns.

When results are tabulated for various groups, those who are white, over sixty-five, and independent tend to see small wage and price rises as best for workers and society as a whole. (See table 7.1.) Black-white differences are particularly stark. No consensus or dominant opinion emerged. From the data I sense that most Americans do understand the social conflict inherent in the wage-

TABLE 7.1

Choice of wage and price combinations, by political party, age, and race

	Percent of Group Who Chose:		
	Small wage and price rise best for workers and all Americans	Large wage and small price rise best for workers and Americans	Large wage and small price rise best for workers; small price and wage rise best for all Americans
Whole Sample (N=1,390)	27	26	15
Republicans	28	22	20
Democrats	23	31	11
Independents	31	22	16
Under 35	23	25	18
35–64	29	26	14
65+	30	29	6
Black	10	37	3
White	28	24	16

price nexus. Similar results have been obtained in other countries. In a survey in Britain in 1973, 60 percent of the respondents said prices could not be stabilized without limiting wage claims.[26] But those who were aware of the link between wages and price felt that the only way to protect themselves from losing out was to agitate for pay increases—just as Keynes claimed.

To Have Money Is to Halve It

Novelists build characters by what their fictional people say and do and what others say about them. Poll results show what people think and say about inflation. But what do they *do* about it?

For one thing, "Americans assume inflation will continue, so they're spending more and more, buying now because it will cost more tomorrow," according to Henry Kaufman of Salomon Brothers. The previous chapter chronicled the long labor pains of the hesitant 1980 recession, predicted small and born hefty. What kept the economy buoyant so long was the *better-buy-now* mentality. What made this mentality possible was the availability of credit.

Milton Friedman insists that "inflation is always and everywhere a monetary phenomenon" and "a reduction in the rate of monetary growth is the one and only cure for inflation."[27] But better-buy-now fever, underlying inflation, is hard to starve in a world of credit cards, automatic loans, and NOW accounts. Even if money *is* freely available, to generate inflation someone has to decide to use that money. Inflation is always and everywhere a psychological phenomenon whose outward expression is monetary.

It is not solely consumers who stampede from money to goods. Companies do it too. "In this inflation economy," a corporate official is quoted as saying, "companies realize that goods are as important to have as is cash. They know a building will cost more tomorrow than it does today."[28]

America has seen four major episodes of buy-now-and-beat-inflation psychology in the post–World War II period: 1950 (the outbreak of the Korean War), 1968–69 (the Vietnam War), 1973–74, and 1978–80. These episodes have generally lasted from six to eight months, although the 1973–74 binge lasted a full year and the latest one more than a year and a half. In August 1979 more than one American in four responded yes when asked, "Have you or your family bought anything during the last few months because you thought it would cost more later?" Of those nearly half bought a house or house improvement or a car. In contrast, George Katona reports that in 1969 and 1970 only about one person in eight responded affirmatively to the same question, and those who did generally mentioned small items.[29]

Inflation creates an Alice in Wonderland unreality, where to have and hold money is to halve its value; where nonborrowers are sorrowers; where time is a waste of money; and where a penny spent is a penny saved. (See the accompanying box on pages 175–76.) Even when draconian credit measures restore reality abruptly, as in March 1980, and the GNP plummets 10 percent in one quarter, life quickly returns to abnormal again and when things settle down it is better to owe money than to own it.

If the causes of inflation are psychological, then to some extent so is the damage it wreaks. "Inflation is the problem of the stick with two short ends," Arthur Okun once said. "The individual who has bet wrong on future inflation is convinced he's got the short end and someone else must have the long end. But in a general inflation even the winner may wind up getting shorted. . . . A significant real cost of inflation is what it does to morale, to social coherence, and to people's attitudes toward each other." Inflation gives vent to, and may even temporarily mitigate, distributional conflicts. But once underway, that process opens a Pandora's box of greed, self-interest, and lack of trust.

Common Inflation as the Tragedy of the Commons

Put Your Money in Trust

At the heart of the game-theory inflation process just described lie inflation expectations—what people *think* about future price rises. Four decades ago, Sir John R. Hicks gave expectations center stage in his theory of economic dynamics. He identified several sorts of influences operating on price expectations. According to Hicks some of those influences—the weather, political news, state of health, psychology, market superstitions, crop reports—have to be treated as autonomous. They may affect economic events "in mysterious and indirect ways; but we cannot hope to do anything about it."[30] (Another type of influence, past and present prices, became a central part of Hicks's *Value and Capital*).

One thing we can do about those autonomous influences is to make the psychology of inflation expectations less mysterious. If inflation is indeed a *Prisoner's Dilemma,* lack of trust must be a fundamental, attitudinal source of the problem. In October 1975 my wife and I tackled this subject.[31] Through the Israel Institute for Applied Social Research's monthly survey, a random sample of 515 Israeli adults was asked the following questions, among others:

> Some people tend to believe in the promises of others; other people, less so. How do you regard yourself, compared with your friends? Do you believe in the promises of others as they do?
> (a) Much more than they do; (b) More than they do; (c) Less than they do; (d) Much less than they do; (e) Just like they do.
> During the coming year, a rise in the price of the goods you buy is anticipated. Assume that you spend at present I£ 300 per week. In your opinion, how much will it cost you to buy the same things in one year?
> (a) More than I£ 500; (b) Between I£ 450–I£500; (c) Between I£400–I£450; (d) Between I£ 350–I£400; (e) Between I£300–I£350; (f) Less than I£300.

INFLATION PROVERB: A PENNY SPENT IS MONEY SAVED

Alice called the class in modern proverbs to order and wrote on the blackboard. "A penny spent is a penny earned."

"That's not how Benjamin Franklin said it," protested the Mock Turtle.

"Of course not," interjected the Mad Hatter. "Times have changed, maxims have changed. A penny saved today is a penny lost tomorrow."

"Precisely," said Alice. "And a thing bought today is worth more tomorrow."

"I see, I see," said the Mock Turtle. "Completely logical. A penny spent is a penny saved.

The Red Queen entered and immediately demanded: "Have you finished, have you revised the ancient verities?"

"Not yet, not yet, if it please your majesty," responded Alice.

"It doesn't please me at all," answered the Red Queen. "If time is money, haste ceases to be waste."

"Yes, yes, your majesty," said Alice. "That explains our new proverb: 'The sooner money is spent, the less you have to lose, and the more you have to gain!' "

"That's why time has become a waste of money," declared the Mad Hatter.

Alice wrote "Time is a waste of money" on the blackboard, and asked: "Any other suggestions?"

The Mock Turtle raised his hand, and said: "He that isn't a borrower is sure to be a sorrower."

"Brilliant, brilliant," exclaimed the Red Queen. "Parting with money is now sweet sorrow. That justifies the annual increase in our national debt."

"Indeed, yes," said the Mock Turtle. "The greater the debt the richer the nation. The roads, the airports, the palaces, the royal art and property go up in value. Thus, the more one owes, the richer one becomes."

"Excellent, excellent," said the Red Queen. "Write this: 'Debt has lost its sting.' "

Suddenly, the Mad Hatter cried out, "Now I know why money is the root of all evil. The longer you have money, the sooner you halve it."

Common Inflation as the Tragedy of the Commons

"I've been thinking of Gertrude Stein's proverb, 'A rose is a rose is a rose,' " put in the March Hare. "It could be modernized into 'A dollar is a quarter is a dime is a nickel!' "

"Don't go any further," cautioned Alice. "We daren't be penny-wise and sound foolish."

"The Bible says, 'Money answereth all things,' " said the Mock Turtle, "but nowadays things answer for money."

"Very good, very good," said the Red Queen. "Write on the blackboard, 'Things answer for money.' "

"Let's not forget the oldest proverb of all," said the March Hare. "Money talks."

"But more and more weakly," amended Alice. "It's better to owe money than to own it."

"But oh! if you don't have money and need it, oh, oh, oh!" complained the March Hare.

"That's correct," said the Carpenter pensively. "If you don't have money to buy things, then money is more valuable than things."

"Incorrect," replied the Mock Turtle. "Since things now answer for money, one merely sells things to get money. One good turnover deserves another."

"And the moral of all this, if it please your majesty," said Alice, "is: 'When there's too much money, there never is enough of it,' " and she wrote that on the blackboard.

"That's why a lot of money goes a short way," said the Carpenter. "What used to be conspicuous consumption is now imperceptible. Somebody ought to write an 'Owed to Wealth.' "

The Red Queen thought for a moment and then said with finality, "It's a brand new world in which wisdom is noncents, debt is wealth, and a penny saved is a lesson unlearned," and picking up her train, she swept out of the classroom.

JOSEPH A. LIVINGSTON,
Philadelphia Inquirer,
Wednesday, February 14, 1979

The first question was a self-evaluated measure of interpersonal trust. We conjectured that people who were less trusting would tend to anticipate higher rates of inflation. They would, we reasoned, put less credence in government pronouncements and anticipate more self-serving inflationary behavior on the part of others. The second question served as a direct measure of expected inflation. To our surprise we found that (lack of) trust was the strongest statistical predictor of expected inflation, ahead of income, age, and other socioeconomic variables. The mean expected rate of inflation for October 1975–October 1976 was 55 percent—almost precisely the inflation rate for calendar year 1974, but well above the *actual* rate for the forecast period, which turned out to be 38 percent. Although war inevitably tows inflation in its wake, this *over*estimate was a result of Israel's post–October War inflation, which people seriously *under*estimated. It reflects a "once burned, twice wary" mistrust. Now deeply rooted, this attitude must inevitably make controlling inflation in Israel very difficult. In the United States too, William Fellner wrote, "inflationary expectations have become deeply imbedded because the public does not trust governmental anti-inflation intensions."[32]

Trust not in money, Oliver Wendell Holmes once advised, but put your money in trust.[33] He was half right. We trust not in money, but we put our money in goods, not in trust, and trust in goods, not in God, or in each other.

What Is the Solution?

If inflation is *Prisoner's Dilemma,* how can we be paroled? If it is a tragedy of the commons, how can the common tragedy be given a happy ending?

Not everyone agrees that it should be. Self-interest may be both bad morals and bad economics, but it is good genetics. Ethologists and sociobiologists see competition for scarce resources as part of an essential selection process. Applied to inflation this view disputes the possibility of altruism or sustained cooperation among members of society, or even their desirability as a potential solution.

Invisible-hand advocates argue that the solution lies in identifying the true source of the problem—not competition and greed but *lack* of it. The tragedy of the commons would be a comedy, they claim, if the commons were made uncommon by vesting property rights. The first man who fenced some land, called it his, and found people naive enough to believe him, was, Rousseau said, the true founder of civil society. Once common land is *owned* by someone, overgrazing may still occur, but if it does, it taxes only the offender himself. This may be true. But how can we build a fence around inflation and vest property rights in stable prices? The best things in life are free not because they are limitless and indestructible, but because specific rights to them cannot and should not be assigned to individuals. The competitive ideal of n persons powered by self-interest competing freely for goods where n is large is, for common-resource problems, ideal for collective chaos. Each person, as only $1/n$ of the whole, sees the damage his egocentric behavior imposes on others as minuscule. But in the cruel arithmetic of society, a small pain summed over large n becomes a very big one. The aspirin of laissez-faire slogans doesn't help.

The term *social contract* has become fashionable. Rousseau used it to mean a tacit agreement by all individuals to abide by the *general will*, by which the state is governed. It has come to mean a kind of voluntary agreement by various social groups not to seek gain at others' expense; specifically, in Britain, for example, this has meant wage moderation in return for price and tax moderation. But it is sometimes forgotten that Rousseau applied it solely to his ideal state of 20,000 homogeneous people of similar interests and character, and warned against extrapolating it beyond that framework. One could envision a social contract in Hialeah, Florida in 1950, but not in the United States in 1980 or even Hialeah, Florida, in 1960.

Dealing with inflation as a combined social, psychological, and economic blight must begin with Mancur Olson's principle of collective action: "Rational self-interested individuals will not act to achieve their common or group interests . . . even when there is unanimous agreement in the group about the common good and methods of achieving it."[34] Each person in the group knows he or she can become a free rider, practicing rapacity and applauding (and benefiting from) everyone else's temperance.

Biologists, psychologists, and some economists have all arrived at similar destinations by widely differing routes—the recognition that, in Hardin's words, "mutual coercion, mutually agreed upon by the majority affected" may be the only way out; if injustice results, "injustice is preferable to total ruin."[35] In the context of inflation, mutual democratic coercion implies some form of mandatory wage-price controls.

Controls: The I's Have It

A two-to-one majority of the American people favors imposition of compulsory controls on wages and prices. A three-to-one majority of American economists *opposes* them.

A CBS/*New York Times* national telephone survey in January 1980 found that 65 percent of adult Americans were willing "to have government enforce limits on both wage and price increases."[36] Gallup Poll results show a consistent majority in favor of controls dating back to April 1978. In contrast, a random sample of 221 members of the American Economic Association found that 72 percent *dis*agreed with the statement, "Wage-price controls should be used to control inflation."[37] Of some thirty such statements, only one (attributing oil-price rises to big oil companies) got a larger fraction of disapproval.

It is tempting to cite economists' opposition to controls as a powerful argument in controls' favor. But there are stronger rea-

Common Inflation as the Tragedy of the Commons

sons. When it comes to controls, with buying powered by the fears and egoism of inflation the I's have it.

Wage-and-price controls have been implemented three times: during World War II, the Korean crisis, and 1971–74. Opponents of controls often label the last two episodes as failures. This is far from obvious.

A few weeks after the first U.S. troops landed in Korea, Congress gave President Truman authority to impose wage-and-price controls without having to ask Congress for it.[38] Truman's use of selective controls, and his call for voluntary restraint, failed. The Federal Reserve Board boosted interest rates—to 1.75 percent! Declaring a national emergency, Truman installed machinery similar to the Office of Price Administration in World War II—a Price Stabilization Office, run by Michael DiSalle, and a Wage Stabilization Board, with members from labor, business, and the public. On January 25, 1951, a wage-and-price freeze was announced. Bitter controversy broke out. But the numbers speak loudest. After rising nearly 10 percent during 1950, and nearly 5 percent in the preceding quarter, consumer prices rose less than 1 percent from February through May 1951. Coupled with three stiff tax increases, controls gave stability to post–Korean War America—a stability not enjoyed during and after Vietnam a generation later, when the Great Society became the Great Inflation.

Were Nixon's Phase I–Phase IV controls a complete failure? The evidence is mixed.[39] One estimate shows they lopped 2 percentage points off inflation. Another study indicates wages rose 2.0 to 3.6 percent less than they would have in the absence of controls (though Phase I and Phase IV were inevitably followed by wage "explosions"). Nixon-era controls may simply have *repressed* or *postponed* some inflation; but, as all true procrastinators know, deferring something may annihilate it, especially if inflation expectations slip downward a notch or two. The Nixon controls were poorly supported by those charged with running them—"expect astounding price increases," said the Secretary of the Treasury in August 1973, eight months before controls ended—and their removal was poorly timed. It is difficult to think of a less suitable date for abolishing controls than the oil-shock period of April 1974.

"In a very real sense price control is a psychological measure," George Katona argued. "Making sacrifices equitable represents a paramount function of all controls and a precondition of public approval for them."[40] If current inflation results mainly from people trying to avoid sacrifices which they feel others are successfully evading, controls can work, provided they are *perceived* as fair, equitable, and nondiscriminatory and provided that people understand that voluntary restraint is unlikely to succeed.

"It may well be rational for individual trade union members and others to press their claims for remuneration in times of inflationary pressure," William Baumol wrote in 1952, "even though inflation affects them adversely. A voluntary abstention from wage-raise demands by one particular union will do little to relieve the overall inflationary pressure, and will indeed put its members completely at the mercy of rising prices."[41]

"In these circumstances," he concluded, "rationality may require recourse to a coercive arrangement."

Conclusion

At the start of the previous decade, President Nixon said in his Economic Report to the Congress, "We have learned that there is a human element in economic affairs—habit, confidence and fear—and that the economy cannot be managed mechanistically."[42] Events since then have tried to teach us this lesson again and again. But we have, I am afraid, proved poor pupils; we repeat the poorly-remembered past, as Santayana foretold.

Leonardo da Vinci once said that if theories are generals, experiments are the soldiers. In Scandinavia and Western Europe interesting experiments with various forms of social contracts, wage-and-price controls, and national incomes policies have been underway for some time. In some countries these measures have been notably successful in moderating inflation. (In war, soldiers always precede generals; in science, only rarely.) Nonetheless, perhaps in the case of inflation, experiement-soldiers will pave the way for new and more insightful theories. Some form of incomes policy framework (a national agreement on wages, prices, and taxes) for the United States, by the end of this decade, is far from improbable.

Failing this, and assuming that Kant's categorical imperative— act in such a way that if others also acted thus you would benefit —will not be universally embraced, we may need to learn to do without a stable currency. In time the current generation raised with inflation may find it less aversive than their parents did. But at the moment, the message heard in subways, coal mines, shop floors, and offices is loud and clear: Nothing can replace the dollar. Heal it.

PART IV

People as Risk Takers

8

TAKING CHANCES
AND/OR AVOIDING THEM:
SOME ODDITIES OF ODDS

"OUR CONSTITUTION is in actual operation," eighty-three-year-old Benjamin Franklin, returning to America after nine years in France, wrote to his friend M. Leroy. "Everything appears to promise that it will last; but in this world nothing is certain but death and taxes."[1]

In Ben Franklin's world, and in our own, nothing was or is certain except uncertainty itself. Increasingly we must choose from alternatives whose probabilities are vaguely known and dimly perceived. Death and taxes are no exception. In the long run we are all dead, Keynes said; but in the short run, he might have added, we are all odds in a mortality table. With the magnitude and extent of evasion on the rise, taxes can also be uncertain, as much so in 1982 as in 1764. That year, Franklin reached London, charged with persuading George III to stop soaking the Colonies. After trying for eleven years, he gave up and came home. It is interesting to speculate how American history would have looked had he succeeded. (Chapter 10 explores the topic of tax evasion further.)

Death, taxes, and a great many other aspects of life lie firmly in the realm of uncertainty. The burden of decision under risk can sometimes be averted, or lessened, through insurance. But uncertainty *itself* remains a permanent and sometimes dominant feature of the human condition. I can insure myself to the hilt against the chance of being struck by lightning, but no Lloyd's of London policy ever forestalled a lightning bolt.

Investing money, choosing an occupation or a college, changing neighborhoods or cities or countries, all these and many others reflect decision making in the absence of certain knowledge of the outcome. Economics, the science of choice, has worked out an intricate, rigorous theory of behavior toward risk. The foundations of this theory were laid by Oskar Morgenstern, an economist, and John von Neumann, a mathematician, in their book *Theory of Games and Economic Behavior* (1944). The axioms, or basic principles, they laid out then still underlie the economics of uncertainty. At the time von Neumann and Morgenstern felt these principles were "plausible and legitimate, unless a much more refined system of psychology is used than the one now available for the purposes of economics."[2] A generation ago no such new system of psychology was in sight. Today, thanks to some brilliant empirical and theoretical work, an entire new system of behavioral axioms has sprung up. These axioms try to depict how people take chances, and/or avoid them in reality, and they are all firmly rooted in countless experiments and surveys. Most of psychology's axioms of uncertainty directly contradict those of economics. When welded to the decision framework of economics, these psychological axioms provide a powerful new way of viewing economic behavior and markets.[3]

This chapter opens with an exposition of the economics of taking chances and its fundamental principles. Then, evidence from psychology assaulting those principles is compiled. Economics and psychology each have axioms to grind, it emerges, but those of psychology are sharper. A new behavioral theory of risk and uncertainty results, a joint product of the logic of choice and the science of behavior, with the promise of helping us make wiser choices in an ever more uncertain world.

Two-Question Logic with Coins and Dice

Economics, applied to decision making, boils down to the questions, What is it worth? and What do I have to give up to get it? Answering these two questions helps us choose between this or that, or between now and later.

When the alternatives we are comparing are *certain* ones—for instance, selling a house in the suburbs for a condominium in the city—a rational decision does not require exact, numerical answers to the two questions of two-question logic. All we need is a *greater than* or *less than* comparison. If something is worth more than what we sacrifice to get it, we choose it. If it is worth less, we reject it. If it is worth the same, we are indifferent. In other words, when people choose among certain alternatives, all they need to do is describe those choices to themselves in terms of *better than, worse than,* or *same as.* There is no need to determine that a Park Avenue apartment yields 275 happiness units while a Garden City bungalow brings only 235.

Suppose, though, that choice involves some risk: this or this, or that, with the first comma separating two distinct alternatives. You can have, for example, a certain *that* or a risky *this or this,* with a coin flip or a toss of the die deciding which. How does one answer the question, What is it worth? when *it* is not a single certain result but rather two or more different possibilities, each with its own likelihood?

Take, for example, the decision whether or not to buy a state lottery ticket. You can choose between keeping the price of the ticket—five dollars, for instance—in your pocket. Or you can part with the money, buy a ticket, and end up either with "this" (no prize at all) or "this" (a small, medium, or million-dollar windfall).

A simpler example is flipping a coin with a friend for a twenty-dollar bar tab. Heads she pays, tails you do. You can opt for Dutch treat and forgo the gamble or be a sport and flip for it. For lottery tickets, bar tabs, gambling, insurance, and many other decisions of this sort, two-question logic as I described it earlier in this book requires some extensive renovations. It is no longer enough to merely *compare* alternatives. Now we need to be able to attach numerical "happiness," or utility, values to each. Here is why. Suppose we posit a happiness scale whose low point is zero and whose high point is one. If you flip for the bar tab, and lose, paying twenty dollars, let the result on your happiness scale be zero. If you win, gaining a free ten dollars' worth of drinks, let your happiness number be one. Now, how should you decide whether to gamble or not?

If you opt for Dutch treat, the certain outcome is that you pay for your own drink and are ten dollars out of pocket. Clearly, paying zero beats paying ten dollars. Equally clearly, paying ten dollars beats paying twenty dollars. This is the *better than, worse than* ordering that sufficed for choice under certainty. But it is no longer enough. Knowing that alone is not sufficient to make a rational decision.

Assuming the coin you flip is fair, five times out of ten you end up paying twenty dollars and five times out of ten you pay zero. On the *average* your happiness scale will read 0.5. If you bet, think of it as one-half of zero plus one-half of one.

What does your happiness scale read if you pay your own tab, ten dollars, ten times out of ten? Suppose it reads 0.3; in that case, you would do well to flip for it. Suppose it reads 0.7; in that event, you would do better not to. That point is, unless we *know* how much better not playing is than gambling and losing, and how much better gambling and winning is than not playing, we cannot choose rationally.

Two-question logic, applied to uncertainty, turns out to be nothing more than taking a weighted average of the "happiness" outcomes for each risky eventuality, with the chances, or odds, of each outcome serving as the weights. This is known as the *mathematical expectation of utility;* it is simply the probability of an outcome times the utility of that outcome summed over all possible outcomes. (At various points in history, economists called *happiness* "happiness" [Bentham] or "utility" or "rareté" or "ophelimité." It is unfortunate that "utility" has won the day. Most people take the word to mean Webster [1] "the quality or property of being useful," rather than Webster [7], in *economics,* "the power to satisfy the needs or wants of humanity." I think we should have stuck with Bentham.)

Do-It-Yourself Happiness Scale

To fully understand the role of a numerical utility function, or happiness scale, in choice under uncertainty, I suggest the reader try to build his own by working through the following example:

Suppose you have a good job and earn $40,000 a year. You are offered the choice of: (a) staying at the same salary, or (b) working on commission. If you choose (b) you will earn *either* $36,000 or $48,000, depending on how well sales go (in this example, a matter of luck, not diligence).

Clearly, your choice of (a) or (b) will depend on how likely it is that you get the $48,000. For each of the five following sets of odds, say whether you prefer (a) or (b) or find them about equally good.

	Prefer (a)	Prefer (b)	About the Same
10 % chance to earn $48,000, 90 % chance to earn $36,000	☐	☐	☐
30 % chance to earn $48,000	☐	☐	☐
50% chance to earn $48,000	☐	☐	☐
70 % chance to earn $48,000	☐	☐	☐
90 % chance to earn $48,000	☐	☐	☐

I expect most readers would pick a certain $40,000 income over a one-in-ten or even three-in-ten chance to earn $48,000 rather than $36,000. I suppose most of us would welcome a nine-in-ten chance to earn $48,000 over a certain $40,000.

Suppose you felt that 50/50 odds (for $36,000 and $48,000) left choice (a), the certain $40,000, and choice (b), the gamble, equally good in your eyes. On your happiness scale set $36,000 equal to zero, and set $48,000 equal to one. (Since we are interested in *relative* happiness for income between those two levels, we are free to set the top and the bottom of the scale wherever we wish.)

If you chose (b), and worked on commission, then over a long period of years you would earn $36,000 half the time and $48,000 half the time. Half the time, your happiness scale would be at zero, and half the time at one. On the average, it would equal 0.5— one-half times zero plus one-half times one.

Now, recall that (a) and (b) were perceived as equally good. If the happiness number for (b) is 0.5, then it must be 0.5 for (a) as well. The income for (a) is $40,000. Thus, a certain $40,000 gets a happiness number of 0.5.

The above calculations lead to one more number that is highly revealing of attitudes toward risk. Notice that if you chose (b), over many years your income would average out (the odds of the higher salary are assumed to be an even, 50/50) to $42,000 (midway between $36,000 and $48,000). Being indifferent between a sure $40,000 and a coin-flip gamble on $36,000 and $48,000 means you are equally happy with $40,000 (certainty) or a gamble that pays $42,000 on the average. In other words, you place a value of $2,000 on the the certainty of a fixed salary. If forced to work on commission, you might consider buying "wage insurance" (*if* such insurance were available; markets for many kinds of insurance do not exist) and would be willing to pay up to $8,000 in premiums every year. For such insurance, if you earn the high salary, you net $40,000 ($48,000 minus the premium, $8,000). If you earn the low salary, the insurance company makes up the difference and pays you $12,000; minus the premium, you again net $40,000.

Some Oddities of Odds

One year in two the insurance company pays you $12,000. On the average, then, the policy costs the company $6,000 a year. But the premium you are willing to pay is as high as $8,000 a year. The difference between the premium you are willing to pay and the fair actuarial (or no-profit) premium is $2,000; this difference measures the degree of risk aversion, or the monetary value of eliminating risk.

To build your own happiness scale, go back and see what odds of getting $48,000, for you, make (a) and (b) seem equally preferable. If, as described above, those odds are 50/50, the calculations worked out below match your happiness scale:

Income	$36,000	$40,000	$48,000
Happiness Number	0	0.5	1.0

Notice that the additional happiness you get by going from $36,000 to $40,000 is worth one-half unit—0 to 0.5. To get the next half-unit of happiness takes *twice* that sum, or $8,000 ($40,000 to $48,000). This reflects the result that the more income we have, the less additional happiness each $1,000 brings. There is a direct connection between this principle, known in economics as *diminishing marginal utility*, and behavior toward risk. The link between risk aversion and the happiness scale will be discussed later in the chapter.

Von Neumann and Morgenstern set up a rigorous set of conditions or axioms that together guarantee the existence of a numerical happiness scale. Much of their work was done at the Institute for Advanced Study in Princeton. Another famous Institute scholar, Albert Einstein, once said, "I refuse to believe God plays dice with the world."[4] Einstein was stating his opposition to Niels Bohr's quantum mechanics, where electrons follow coin-flip, probabilistic patterns. Even Einstein, though, would have admitted that *people* play dice with the world. If such dice didn't exist, someone would have had to invent them. In fact, the Egyptians and Assyrians did and left versions of them in their tombs. Von Neumann and Morgenstern's theory in its time provided a powerful tool for understanding *how* people might play dice with the world. But time plays dice with theories. New evidence has come along to supplant their axioms. What follows is a simplified description of those axioms and the psychological set that deserves to replace them.

Nine Axioms Have Nine Lives

Nine basic axioms still form the foundation of the modern economics of uncertainty, and they have since they were formulated by Von Neumann and Morgenstern in 1944. Distilled and simplified, they read:

1. For any pair of objects or events, people have "a clear intuition of preferences . . . (their) system of preferences is all-embracing and complete."

2. People's preferences are consistent and do not embody internal contradictions.

3. Consider two events, *A* and *B*. Suppose a certain *A* is preferred to a certain *B*. Then, this implies that a one-in-a-thousand chance of *A* is better than a one-in-a-thousand chance of *B*. (For one-in-a-thousand you can substitute any probability between zero and one.)

4. Suppose *A* is preferred to *B,* and *B* to *C.* No matter how desirable *A* itself is, its influence can be made as weak as desired by attaching a sufficiently small chance to it.

5. The way a choice is "packaged," or expressed, makes no difference. If a bet is broken into two parts, or combined as one part, the choice should be the same. This is the anti-Proctor & Gamble axiom of gambles. It essentially means no pleasure derives from the act of gambling itself or the way the gamble is "marketed."

All these principles lend themselves to empirical tests by offering people choices and observing what they pick. With important exceptions economists have avoided such research. Psychologists have taken up the slack. What they have found shows, in general, that there are many and varied oddities in our behavior toward odds that clash with the above principles. Let us look first at their findings about consistency.

The A, B, C's of $A > B > C$

If you prefer the flavor almond over butter pecan, and butter pecan over chocolate, then you should logically pick almond over chocolate. This is known as the *transitivity axiom:*

> If you prefer A over B, and B over C, you should prefer A over C.

This assumption seems harmless. It implies nothing more than the internal consistency of preferences. Surely consistency is indispensable for any theory. Where can any theory take you if it does not assume that people make consistent choices? Under risk *or* certainty, two-question logic seems to demand transitivity.

Economists tend to argue, with considerable persuasion, that people are not perfect. They do make errors. But, they claim, theories about people must assume they do not err, because a theory of errors is a contradiction in terms. A standard response from psychology is, people are *consistently* inconsistent. Their preferences, for example, tend to be intransitive, but depart from consistency in systematic ways, which can be measured, explained, and studied. According to experimental work by psychologists, it turns out that even the following weak version of transitivity does not hold.

> If you choose A over B more than half the time, and B over C more than half the time, then you should choose A over C more than half the time.

In a famous experiment Amos Tversky presented a group of eight Harvard undergraduates with a series of gamble cards (see figure 8.1.)[5] Subjects were shown various pairs of cards and asked to choose the one they would prefer to play. They were told that at the end of the session they would be able to play one of the gambles they had picked, and their payoff would be the result of that gamble. Overall, choices of six of the eight subjects were not even weakly transitive.

One of the students said, There is a small difference between Gambles A and B, or B and C, and so on, so I would pick the one with the higher payoff. However, there is a big difference between Gambles A and E or B and E, and so on, so I would pick the one with the higher probability. When asked if he thought this type of behavior might lead to intransitivities (that is, inconsistencies), he

FIGURE 8.1
Tversky "gamble cards"

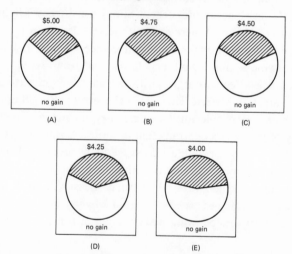

Legend: The shaded area of each circle represents the chances of winning the sum above the circle. Subjects choose from a pair of cards offered them. For pairwise choices, (A,B), (B,C), (C,D), (D,E), subjects tended to choose the higher dollar prize. Most however, picked E over A, when asked to choose between the two.

NOTE: Reprinted by permission of publisher from Amos Tversky, "Intransitivity of Preferences," *Psychological Review* 76 (1969): 31–48. Copyright 1969 by the American Psychological Association.

replied, I do not think so, but I am not sure. At the conclusion of this and another experiment, interviews revealed that subjects thought (a) people's preferences *are* transitive and (b) *should* be transitive. Many found it difficult to believe they had exhibited inconsistencies in their own choices.

Tversky offers the following plausible example of a common type of intransitivity.

> Consider . . . a person who is about to purchase a compact car of a given make. His initial tendency is to buy the simplest model for $2,089. Nevertheless, when the salesman presents the optional accessories, he first decides to add power steering, which brings the price to $2,167, feeling that the price difference is relatively negligible. Then, following the same reasoning, he is willing to add $47 for a good car radio, and then an additional $64 for power brakes. By repeating this process several times, our consumer ends up with a $2,593 car, equipped with all the available accessories. At this point, however, he may prefer the simplest car over the fancy one, realizing that he is not willing to spend $504 for all the added features, although each one of them alone seemed worth purchasing. [The article was written in 1968, hence the low prices.]

Economists David Grether and Charles Plott[6] point out that when offered the choice of playing one of the following two bets, a large proportion pick the first.

(a) Probability Bet

(b) Dollar Bet

(a) If a randomly thrown dart hits the line, you get nothing; otherwise, you get $4.

(b) If a randomly thrown dart falls in the shaded area, you get $16; if it falls elsewhere, you get nothing.

But when asked to place a monetary value on the bets, the majority place a a higher value on the *second*. Why don't people consistently prefer the bet they think is worth most? Pursuing this question, Grether and Plott had a group of economics and political science students choose, for various pairs of bets, which they would prefer to play. Later, for the same bets, subjects were asked for the *smallest* price they would ask for selling a ticket to (that is, the right to play) the bet. Both *P-Bets* (probability bets) and *$-Bets* (dollar bets) were offered.

For P-Bet choices, more than half were *in*consistent with subjects' selling prices. (That is, people said they preferred bets that they later said they would sell more cheaply.) This *preference reversal* phenomenon was even *stronger*—70 percent chose inconsistently—when decisions were made for real money. Much less inconsistency was observed for $-Bets. Out of ninety subjects, more than one-third were consistently inconsistent, that is, reversed their preferences every time they chose a P-Bet.

Their carefully designed experiment led Grether and Plott to reject many different explanations for inconsistency, including boredom and lack of incentive, falsifying prices for the purpose of strategy, *anchoring* (focusing on probabilities or on dollar values instead of weighing both together), confusion and misunderstanding, and unsophisticated subjects.

If indeed consistency is a paste jewel only cheap men cherish, then our preferences can cut glass. One conclusion that follows is that the *order* that choices are made among paired alternatives can make a difference in the winning choice. For transitive, or consistent, preferences, order makes no difference.

A Bird in the Hand

Another type of consistency requires that if one event is preferred to another when both are certain, the same event should be preferred in a world of uncertainty, provided both events become equally uncertain.

> If you prefer certain outcome A to certain outcome B, then you should prefer a coin-toss chance to win A over a coin-toss chance to win B.

This is the so-called *substitution axiom,* and it seems to make good sense. It clashes, however, with the four-hundred-year-old proverbial wisdom of Cervantes who wrote that a bird in the hand is worth two in the bush. It turns out that Cervantes wins. Answering the following two questions will show why.

- Which would you prefer, a 100-percent certain, one-week vacation in England, or a 50/50 chance to win a three-week tour of England, France, and Italy?
- Would you rather have a 10-percent (that is, one-in-ten) chance to win a one-week vacation in England, or a 5-percent (one-in-twenty) chance to win a three-week tour of England, France, and Italy?

If you chose England in both cases, you support the axiom. Experiments show, however, that eight persons in ten pick a certain week in England over an uncertain Continental tour, but seven persons in ten pick the *latter* option for a low-odds gamble.[7] Note that for each of the above two questions, the odds of getting England are double those of getting the Continental tour. The axiom says that you should make the same choice in each case. Cervantes says that *certainty* has its own virtue. Cervantes, it appears, was right. Many people appear to reason that a sure prize is worth more than an unsure, but more attractive, one. However, if both prizes are risky, it pays to pick the bigger one. Apparently raising odds from one-in-ten to certainty (a factor of ten) is more powerful than raising them from one-in-twenty to one-in-two (also a factor of ten).

Here is another example. Most people pick a one-in-a-thousand chance to win $6,000 over a chance to win $3,000 at half those odds. That result is reversed, however, when the bet is a 45-percent chance to win $6,000 versus a 90-percent chance to win $3,000. Here, the vast majority pick the second choice.[8]

With the help of a Princeton undergraduate, Cynthia Phillips, I tried these and other questions on a group that was highly experienced in dealing with odds—gambling supervisors at an Atlantic City casino. We thought that the *bird-in-the-hand* effect would *not* exist among those who work with probabilities every day. We were proved wrong. Our risk-experienced subjects exhibited much the same behavior that psychologists found among people less accustomed to dealing with odds.

"Go for the sure thing," one of them said. "Don't take the long odds." But when the odds are long for both choices in a pair, people apparently pick the one with the bigger prize.[9]

From these results does it logically follow that certainty per se is desirable? Not always, it turns out. Human beings are more complex than the axioms that try to portray them.

Take Calculated Risks: People Shun Fair Bets

This is not really regarded as one of von Neumann and Morgenstern's axioms. But it very often accompanies them when they are applied to economics problems. It says that people are averse to risks. Given a 50/50 (coin-toss) chance to win or lose one thousand dollars, most people would turn down the bet, this proposition states. Put another way, it says that people would be willing to pay considerable amounts to *avoid* such bets, that is, buy insurance.

There are at least two good reasons for believing in risk aversion. First, people *do* buy insurance, and they pay large amounts for the privilege, well beyond the actuarial value of losses. Second, it turns out that risk aversion follows necessarily from another cornerstone principle of economics: Successive increments to income add less and less to happiness, or utility. This is the principle of diminishing marginal utility, mentioned earlier.

The assumption of diminishing marginal happiness is plausible and has a long history. It is interesting that a mathematician and a psychologist, separated by different disciplines and two centuries, arrived at precisely the same equation to express this idea.

Daniel Bernoulli, an eighteenth-century Swiss mathematician and philosopher, argued that a 1 percent rise in income adds the same *amount* to happiness, whatever the income. This implies diminishing marginal happiness; if at $10,000 another $100 adds one unit of happiness, then according to Bernoulli, at $100,000 it takes ten times that, or $1,000, to add the same one unit of happiness: His equation is:[10]

Happiness = Constant × Logarithm (Income Divided by Constant)

Bernoulli said that the constant in the bracketed term was the cost of the "barest necessities."

An American psychologist, L. L. Thurstone, empirically established the following formula in 1931:[11]

Satisfaction = Constant × Logarithm (Amount of Commodity Possessed) + Constant

Thurstone's formula is for a specific commodity. But it can easily be translated into Bernoulli's equation, which applies to all goods taken together, that is, income. Thurstone's equation derives from what he calls "our most fundamental psychological postulate," namely, that "motivation is inversely proportional to the amount already possessed." This, in turn, is an economic expression of Fechner's law—the intensity of a sensation increases proportionately with the magnitude of the stimulus.

Even if one does not accept the Thurstone-Bernoulli equations, it is hard to escape agreeing with Marshall that "the utility to anyone of an additional £ declines with the number of pounds he already has."[12] It follows, Marshall continued, that gambling involves an economic loss, even when it is conducted on fair and even terms. Or, in other words, people are averse to risk. To understand this, consider an even-odds bet to win or lose $1,000. By diminishing marginal utility, winning $1,000 *adds* less to happiness than losing $1,000 *subtracts* from it. Thus, by the "happiness-scale" calculus explained earlier, since winning and losing are equally likely, on the average, happiness will be smaller if we take the bet than if we decline it. The *degree* of risk aversion depends on the rapidity with which incremental happiness declines with income.

If diminishing marginal utility seems to be a self-evident truth and implies risk aversion, why then do people gamble, often at highly unfavorable odds? (Saying that people gamble simply because they *enjoy* gambling is one of those tautologies that, because it explains everything, explains nothing at all. See below, p. 204.) Milton Friedman and Leonard Savage suggest that for certain income ranges, the utility of each additional dollar *increases*. [13] This does lead to risk affinity. But it is hard to square it with observed behavior. If there were rising marginal utility, people would try to *concentrate* their incomes, rather than spread them out evenly over their life cycle as in fact we observe them do.

The same line of argument has been used to "prove" the principle of diminishing marginal product, which states that each additional laborer working on a given amount of land yields less and less additional output. Suppose this principle were *not* true. Suppose each additional worker added more to output than the previous one. We could then, it was once said, grow all the world's wheat in a flowerpot. Similarly, suppose the added happiness from $1,000 grows as income increases. We should then expect to find people running around with dice, coins, and cards, betting on the weather, baseball, or the sex of an unborn infant.

Wheat is grown in Saskatchewan—an area rather larger than a flowerpot. But people *do* bet, on anything and everything. And people—often the same ones—go to great lengths to avoid bets. Doubtless, people are more interesting, and less predictable, than soil.

"Old Blood and Guts," General George Smith Patton wrote the following advice to his son, then a cadet, during World War II: "Take calculated risks. That is quite different from being rash." [14] He wrote those words on D-Day. He then gambled on driving his

Some Oddities of Odds

Third Army across France on dangerously thin gasoline supplies. The gamble worked. What for Patton was a "calculated risk" was, for nearly everyone else, a horrifying gamble. Patton's tanks, in front of the German lines beyond Metz, remind us how hard it is to squeeze flesh-and-blood—especially, blood and guts—into rigid axioms.

I suspect that a survey done around the gaming tables in Las Vegas would reveal that some of the high rollers carry six-figure insurance on their lives and possessions. The joint presence of risk aversion—reflected in insurance—and risk affinity—shown by gambling—is a behavioral contradiction economists have long grappled with, just as they have wrestled with the relationship of attitudes toward risk and entrepreneurship (see box).

BIRDS WHO SHUN THE BUSH

"There's your friend again Henry!" Mrs. Spearman remarked, delighted that her husband seemed to be in a holiday mood.

Henry Spearman looked up and watched the antics of a pearly eyed thrasher which had alighted on the next table. Unlike the more cautious birds on the island, the mischievous thrashers took advantage of the open-air dining room and each morning pilfered scraps from vacated tables that had not yet been cleared.

"Look at how close he is to us," Mrs. Spearman said as the bird pecked at an English muffin. "I wonder why other kinds of birds don't fly in. There are so many tablescraps available it seems unfair that the thrashers get them all."

"Nothing unfair about it at all, Pidge. It is simply a matter of choice. The thrasher appears to have a preference for taking risks which other birds do not share." Spearman had once written an article delineating the importance of risk taking in a free-enterprise system and decrying the absence of this entrepreneurial spirit among contemporary businessmen. "Just like people, some birds are no doubt risk lovers and others are risk averse."

MARSHALL JEVONS,
Murder at the Margin, pp. 149–50.

Taking Chances and Avoiding Them: Gambling and Insurance

"He is no wise man," Samuel Johnson wrote, "who will quit a certainty for an uncertainty."[15] Risk aversion is a highly plausible postulate. It explains the trillions of dollars of insurance coverage. But, Nobel Prize–winning economist Kenneth Arrow admits, there is one common observation that speaks against the prevalence of risk aversion, namely, that people gamble. Let us emulate the preacher, he suggests, who touched on a subtle theological point and then told his congregation, "Brethren, here there is a great difficulty; let us face it firmly and pass on."[16]

Let us, instead, dwell on the issue for a few paragraphs. Official estimates put amounts spent on gambling in the United States in 1974 at 22 billion dollars, about one-fourth of that illegal—surely a huge underestimate. (See table 8.1.)[17] Only about 18 billion dollars of that is paid back in winnings, the rest going to bookies, casino operators, and others. In illegal numbers games only about one dollar in two goes for winnings, making it the worst gamble around. Five adults in ten, or about 88 million people, admit to gambling. That is hard to square with pervasive risk aversion.

Early on, governments found lotteries as good as taxes for plucking the most feathers with the least squawking. Well before the Revolution, lotteries were used extensively in the United States, both by state governments and for specific projects. The Continental Congress ran a lottery to raise money. Lotteries are currently undergoing a big revival. In 1977 thirteen states ran lotteries, raising 500 million dollars net of prizes. In states that sponsor lotteries most adults have purchased at least one ticket, and 45 percent buy at least one a month. The most attractive prize structure, it has been found, is to give out two-thirds of the prize money (like numbers-game runners, governments give back only one dollar in two) in large numbers of little prizes of two dollars to five

TABLE 8.1
Gambling and Insurance

A. Gambling

	Total Spending (billions of dollars, 1974)	Adults Who Gamble (as a percent of all adults)*
LEGAL GAMBLING:	17.3	44
Horses at track	7.9	14
Off-track Betting (NY only)	1.0	14
Legal casinos	6.1	9
Bingo	1.7	19
Lotteries	0.6	24
ILLEGAL GAMBLING:	5.1	11
Sports books	2.3	2
Horse books	1.4	2
Numbers	1.1	3
Sports cards	0.2	3
Casino Games	0.1	n.a.
TOTAL:	22.4	48

*Some adults gamble both legally and illegally; hence the total is less than the sum of sub-totals.

B. Life Insurance

(1978)

Policies (in millions)	Value of Policies (in billions of dollars)	Benefit Payments (in billions of dollars)	Life Insurance Premiums (in billions of dollars)	Coverage per Insured Family	Coverage as Fraction of Disposable Income
401	2,870	28.6	36.6	$40,800	229

dollars—to inspire confidence—and the rest in a very few large prizes, to promote publicity and dreams of instant wealth.

The persistence of lotteries over history and their pervasiveness over the globe make them a "commodity" almost unexcelled in generality and breadth of market, Milton Friedman and Leonard Savage have noted. Long ago, Adam Smith noted people's "absurd presumptions" about their own good luck, especially among the young. Lottery data, plentiful and underused, can provide helpful clues.

For both lotteries and other forms of gambling, risk affinity does seem to be related to age. Three persons in four over the age of sixty-five claim to be *non*bettors, while about the same ratio for ages eighteen through twenty-four claim to be bettors.

A great many of the same people who appear in part A of table 8.1 also appear in part B, as insurance buyers. Benefit payments by life insurance companies are roughly equal in size to official estimates of spending on gambling.

Prior to 1860 life insurance in America was a you-have-to-die-to-win proposition, mainly for burial-fund purposes. Between 1895 and 1920 life insurance grew into almost a social norm; by the end of the period, average coverage equaled average annual family income. Depression and war forestalled further growth. But from 1946 to the present, coverage both broadened and deepened. Insured families are now covered for more than double their yearly income, on the average; more than 400 million policies are in force.

Economists aside, very few people lose sleep over the apparent contradiction between buying insurance and gambling. To most of us it is eminently logical. At least one economist has found a way to reconcile the two. Insurance eliminates *future* risk, Benjamin Eden argues; gambling provides *present* risk.[18] There is no clash between the wish to know now what our *future* income or wealth will be, he argues, by insuring, and the addition of a little *present* spice to life by gambling.

Some Oddities of Odds

Triumph and Defeat

In Rudyard Kipling's land of "If," defeat and triumph are treated alike. But in the real world, affinity for risk or aversion to it depends on whether or not we are taking the risk to achieve some gain or avoid some loss. A chance at triumph, it appears, looks quite different from a hope of avoiding defeat, as work by Amos Tversky and other psychologists has shown. Their findings suggest that people shun risk for gain but willingly take risks to avoid loss.[19]

Offered a choice between a 90-percent chance to win $3,000, or a 45-percent chance to win twice that, $6,000, six times as many people pick the smaller, more certain prize than pick the bigger, less certain one, according to Tversky. This is true, even though mathematically, the expected value of each bet is the same—$2,700 (the probability of winning times the prize).

Now, put minus signs in front of the prizes. Make the choice between a 90-percent chance to *lose* $3,000, or a 45-percent chance to *lose* $6,000. Which would you pick? The results are completely reversed. Nine persons in ten now prefer risking the larger, less probable loss.

In short, people are risk averse for *gains,* but fond of risk for *losses.* Cynthia Phillips and I found the same result among our twenty casino supervisors. Only eight out of twenty of them preferred the bigger, less likely *prize;* but sixteen picked the bigger, less likely *loss.*

Apparently, in the pursuit of liberty from losses, certainty—like moderation—is no virtue, while extremism (risk) in the pursuit of gain *is* a vice. Just to muddy the waters further, it is not always clear whether gains or losses are involved. Mathematically, the following two choice problems are identical.

- You have been given $1,000. Now choose between a 50/50 chance to *win* another $1,000 or a certain $500.

- You have been given $2,000. Now choose between a 50/50 chance to *lose* $1,000 or a certain loss of $500.

Most people (84 percent) in the first choice problem pick the $500 prize and avoid the coin-toss for $1,000.[20] This implies aversion to risk, for *gains*. At the same time a large majority (69 percent) in the second choice problem would rather gamble on losing $1,000 instead of paying a certain $500. This implies affinity for risk, for *losses*. That is, people appear to prefer taking a fair bet in place of a certain loss, when the average loss from the bet is the same as the certain loss. Where you stand on certainty, psychologists tell us, depends very much on where you sit—looking up at black ink, or down at red.

Form and Substance

We just saw that switching minus signs to plus, or vice versa, can radically alter decisions. This is a particular instance of a more general finding, which says that the way risky choices are presented to people can have a major impact on their ultimate decision. One of the von Neumann-Morgenstern principles holds that:

> The manner in which choices are offered, and their order, does not matter.

Committee chairmen, salesmen, and parents all know how choices can be influenced by judiciously setting up the order in which the alternatives are offered. It also turns out that, in contrast to the axiom, the *form* bets are presented in takes on its own substance. This is particularly true for so-called compound gambles, that is, bets on bets.

- Would you prefer a one-in-five chance to win $4,000 or a one-in-four chance to win $3,000?

Some Oddities of Odds

The majority chose the bet with the larger prize: $4,000, at 20-percent odds.

- Here is a two-stage bet. In stage 1 you have a 75-percent chance to win 0 (in which case the bet ends), and a 25-percent chance to proceed to the next bet. In the next bet, stage 2, you can choose between a certain $3,000 or an 80-percent chance to win $4,000. Before stage 1 begins, you must make your stage 2 choice (between the certain $3,000 or the risky $4,000). Which do you prefer?

Here nearly eight people in ten preferred the $3,000.[21] The two sets of choices above are formally the same. To see this, note that in the second one, just as in the first, there is a 25-percent chance of winning a certain $3,000, and a 25-percent chance of winning an 80-percent chance at $4,000, that is, a 20-percent chance at $4,000 $(25/100 \times 80/100 = 20/100)$. But most people reason that since the stage 1 risk is the same for each of the two stage 2 choices, stage 1 is therefore irrelevant, and hence they choose what they see as the "bird in the hand" ($3,000).

Experiments have shown that few people know how to combine the probabilities of independent events by multiplying them. One study of 143 college students found that not one of them knew this law.[22] It follows that choices where the risks are calculated in advance will elicit different behavior from choices where people themselves make the calculations.

A corollary of the axiom on p. 208 is that the act of gambling itself is not attractive, and it provides no pains or pleasures independent of the gains or losses it entails. One of the entrenched principles of the economic theory of the consumer and risk taker is that people do what they enjoy and enjoy what they do—the so-called revealed preference postulate. Nothing could be simpler, after observing the extent of gambling in this country, than to assume that it affords pleasure per se. Von Neumann and Morgenstern rejected this idea, and after them most economists, because it begs the question, What is it about gambling that people find pleasurable? The observation that people gamble because they like to may be true, but it doesn't take us very far. It is curious that the same revealed preference tautology that economists find so comforting in consumer theory is rejected in the theory of risk taking, in both instances for precisely the same reason.

The Dice Have Good Memories

How people perceive odds has been a most fertile hunting ground for psychologists searching for biases and flaws in reasoning. Their searches are usually successful. The reason is not hard to find. Probabilities are generally expressed as a ratio (one-in-ten) or a percent (10 percent). But many people are uncomfortable with ratio or percent calculations, and they use rules of thumb or rough guesses instead, especially when tangled in the brambles of probability laws. One of the most common, erroneous rules of thumb is that dice or cards or the roulette wheel or coins have memories. That is, after a long string of heads, tails is due, or after a long string of red, black is due.

In chapter 2, I examined how children develop. A general rule is that as they grow older, children learn to reason better. But the *maturity of chances* fallacy—the idea that an event which hasn't happened for a while is due—is a startling exception.

Ross and Levy ran experiments involving a series of random events with both children and adults. They found that when the series began with a run (the same outcome several times in a row), adults and tenth graders predicted the next event on the basis of the *dice have memory* fallacy, feeling it likely the run would end. But younger children (up to sixth grade) did *not* predict less frequently occurring results, nor were they influenced by runs. Ross and Levy concluded that "as people grow older, rather than acting on an increasing belief in event independence, they make predictions as if even random events were dependently related over short series."[23]

Another bias psychologists have known about for many years is that people tend to both overestimate, and overweight, small probabilities and underweight large ones.

Earlier I argued that people avoid risk for gains, and accept risk for losses. At the same time, large majorities *accept* a one-in-a-thousand chance to win five *thousand* dollars rather than take a sure five dollars, and they *reject* a one-in-a-thousand chance to lose five thousand dollars, preferring to lose a sure five dollars. This implies *overweighting*—giving small chances more weight than they deserve, even when the precise chances are correctly known. Played many times, the above bets would bring average wins, or losses, to five dollars. The pattern of preferences observed can be made consistent with gain-risk-aversion and loss-risk-affinity only by positing that small given probabilities are treated as if they were much larger. This is overweighting.

When people have to make their *own* calculations of the likelihood of rare events, they tend to *overestimate* them. I think death is a common instance. Our own subjective estimates of the risks of dying in a car crash or of a heart attack are, I believe, higher than those in mortality tables. Insurance companies put this particular bias to their own good use.

Taken together, overweighting and overestimating suggest that rare but costly disasters will be excessively feared, and rare but munificent gains will be overly anticipated. This is consistent with both gambling at bad odds and buying fire and life insurance. It is not consistent with the way economists tend to view the world. Misperceived probabilities are 'errors' and cost us money. Desire to maximize happiness or profit or income should, over time, wipe out such errors, the economic view holds. But there is strong evidence to the contrary.

Conclusion

In an address on Britain's BBC television, Baron Nathaniel Mayer Rothschild— a direct descendant of the Nathan Rothschild we met in chapter 1—argued that we are much more conscious of risks today than we were one hundred years ago.[24] We are better educated, he asserts, and have the communications media tracking down risk and informing us about it whenever it materializes. But, he implies, we may not have made much progress in evaluating, comparing, and dealing with risk. As a start toward a useful "risk accounting," he urges that risk be stated in simple language, such as one in one thousand, and that the unit of time be stated (per week, month, year, or decade).

Even with appropriate risk accounting, we need to deepen our understanding of how we behave toward risk. The axioms of von Neumann and Morgenstern served economics well for a generation. But they deviate seriously from what we now know about what people think and do. Marshall's call, a century ago, for "a careful analytic and inductive study of the attractive or repellent force which various kinds of risk exert on persons of various temperaments" has been answered—by psychologists.[25] Their axioms make strong bricks for reconstructing the economics of uncertainty. Let us put them to use.

9

Growth is sometimes kept within reasonable bounds. But at times, increases are almost incredible. Irregularly, in periods of five to ten years, there occurs one of the weirdest of all phenomena. No one knows for sure why it starts. In innumerable hosts, acting apparently on a common subconscious simultaneous impulse, they press forward. The mad rush is on. No obstacle stops them. They resist fiercely all efforts to halt them. A few survivors make it. But most pay a heavy price for excessive prosperity.

WHAT DO PEOPLE BRING TO FINANCIAL MARKETS BESIDES MONEY: SAVING, INVESTING, AND THE ECONOMIC PSYCHOLOGY OF GROUP RISK[1]

IN NORMAL TIMES financial markets are pretty dull. Few of us pay close attention to the Dow-Jones Average or Standard & Poor Industrials. Once in a while, panic sets in; prices spiral downward. Everyone—bystanders and participants alike—is drawn into the whirlpool. The ink is barely dry on newspaper accounts of the last such episode, the Great Silver Plunge of 1980.

The outward expression of financial crises is dry, technical, and economic in nature—percentage declines, volume, margin calls, and paper losses. The inner mechanism is psychological. All markets, financial or otherwise, are arrangements where goods, money, and real and financial assets change hands. It is vital to remember that the hands are *human* and are attached to thinking, feeling heads and bodies. To make markets reveal their secrets, you must ask Who? not just What? or When? For financial markets in particular, can there be any doubt, in Nathan Rothschild's time or in ours, of the crucial role psychology plays?

There can be, and there is. The economics of stocks, bonds, commodities, and foreign exchange bashes headlong into the psychology of investor behavior. Unraveling this conflict will lead us into some of the history of financial panics, the theory of efficient markets, locus-of-control, portfolio analysis, group risk taking and a mean-variance approach to human destiny. Where the previous chapter concentrated on *individuals* and the way they perceive and deal with risk, this chapter concentrates on *group* behavior and relies on the tools and concepts of social psychology.

Speaking of groups, the epigraph at the beginning of the chapter does not refer to panic-stricken stockholders. It is an account, drawn from several sources, of the decennial death march of the lemmings.[2]

Of Mice and Men

The fecund *Myodes lemmus,* Lapp cousin to the American meadow mouse, doubles its numbers, in good times, twice a year. In a decade, a single pair doubling itself twenty times becomes 1,048,576 lemmings—two raised to the twentieth power. Caught in the irresistible sweep of 200 percent a year compound interest (paid semiannually, in lemmings), only the most cynical of lemming mathematicians could fail to believe the following lemma: Hell, this is going to last forever.

Then Nature knocks. The incredible march begins. Plague and predators slash many zeros from their numbers on their way to the sea. The remaining zeros plunge into the frigid Barents Sea or the Atlantic Ocean. And the handful left behind, who didn't hear the call or ignored it, begin work again on the powers of 2.

Theorems about rodent behavior in general cannot be deduced from the single-minded suicide of the lemmings, any more than the psychology of ordinary people can be deduced from dementia praecox, or the economics of financial markets can explain headlong panics. But from time to time, men, like mice, leap off cliffs of groundless speculation; the pathology of speculative bubbles is instructive. As Galbraith notes, "one can relish the varied idiocy of human action during a panic to the full, for, while it is a time of great tragedy, nothing is being lost but money."[3] Investing money, like college politics, is deadly earnest because so little is at stake.

"I can calculate the motions of the heavenly bodies," Sir Isaac Newton wrote, "but not the madness of people."[4] Newton had an IQ of 190. His intelligence and mathematical skills did not keep him from losing £13,000 in the South Sea Bubble. The South Sea Company, formed in 1711, was given exclusive trading rights with South America in return for retiring all of England's national debt. In 1720 the expectation of immense profits drove prices per share up nearly 1,000 percent in just a few months. Collapse of fraudulent companies brought down prices per share and, with them, Her Majesty's Government. (See figure 9.1.) Property of the directors was seized, and investors eventually got back one-third of the company's original capital. But the bubble was not yet pricked.[5]

In 1825–26, a century later, 770 banks stopped payment owing to failure of other South Sea companies. As a result of this panic, families in Yorkshire were reduced to eating bran. In four years, two hundred thousand people emigrated to Europe and America

FIGURE 9.1

Forever Blowing Bubbles: Speculation Then and Now

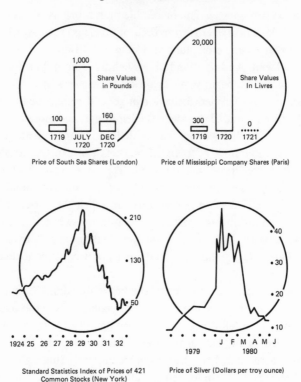

SOURCE: Lester V. Chandler, *America's Greatest Depression: 1929–1941* (New York: Harper & Row, 1970); Steven Plant, "After Silver and Gold: Some Sober Thoughts on Speculative Bubbles," *Economic Commentary*, Federal Reserve Bank of Cleveland, May 5, 1980.

as a direct consequence. They, at least, did not relish the South Sea idiocy. For them, much more than money was at stake.[6]

Roughly contemporary with Robert Harley and John Blunt's scheme in London, John Law was wooing the Duke of Orléans with a similar idea. Law set up the Compagnie d'Occident (later, Compagnie des Indes) to colonize and cultivate the banks of the Mississippi. Shares of the company had to be paid for one-fourth in coin and three-fourths in public notes *(billets d'état)*. Frenzied demand for the shares naturally drove up the demand for these *billets,* and the French government took full advantage by printing enormous quantities of them. Law's efforts to limit paper issue were unavailing. The Mississippi Bubble burst, and Law fled in December 1720. He died in Venice nine years later. Born too soon, his attempts to establish a Central Bank predated the Federal Reserve System by two centuries.

A great deal has been written about the Great Crash of 1929.[7] On October 29, 1929, Black Tuesday, 16 million shares changed hands, and the Dow-Jones industrial average fell thirty points (around 10 percent). The preceding day was even blacker—the Dow-Jones fell thirty-eight points!—and paper losses totalled 14 billion dollars, but for some reason that Tuesday, rather than Monday, has been singled out. As often happens, a brief rally ensued. That Wednesday, the Dow-Jones *rose* twenty-eight points, almost wiping out the previous day's losses; not until August 1971 was this single-day rise equaled. From then on, it was all downhill. When stocks hit bottom in 1932, they had fallen in value by 83 percent from September 1929 peaks. The fiftieth anniversary of the Great Crash in 1979 sparked a flurry of television, newspaper, and magazine debates on *can it happen again?* The authoritative answer was given several months later by gold and silver markets.

In early 1979 the price of gold was less than $200. A year later, its price had surged beyond $800 an ounce. From its peak of $850 on January 21, 1980, gold plunged to $650 two days later and hit bottom at $480 on March 17. The case of silver is even more extreme. Silver sold for $2 an ounce in the early 1970s. For brief periods in mid-January 1980, the price topped $50. It then collapsed to $14.80 in late March. Financial losses of the Hunt family ran to hundreds of millions of dollars. Ramifications of the burst bubble were sufficiently extensive to require active intervention on the part of the Federal Reserve System. The drop in silver prices brought the Dow-Jones average down twenty-five points in one hour.[8]

While not quite as frequent as the quinquennial-to-decennial lemming parade, financial bubbles, panics, crises, and collapses are not rare. Pick at random one year in the period 1763–1930. The odds are one in seven that you will pick a year when *some* sort of crisis was going on. Years of financial crisis were: 1763, 1773, 1793, 1799, 1814, 1825, 1826, 1831, 1837, 1847, 1857, 1866, 1873, 1884, 1885, 1890, 1892, 1893, 1907, 1914, 1921, and 1929.[9] If the history of financial panics proves anything, it is the following theorem, enunciated by J. M. Barker, which I believe should be engraved in large letters on a larger-than-life bronze statue of *Myodes lemmus* and placed in front of the six stately Greek columns of the New York Stock Exchange:

> Whenever you have a group of people thinking the same thing at the same time, you have one of the hardest emotional causes in the world to control.[10]

Unlike the lemmings, you can't always save yourself by sitting tight. "Nothing is more suicidal," Keynes admonished, "than a rational investment policy in an irrational world."[11] Keynes spoke knowledgeably. A brilliant speculator, he succeeded in increasing King's College's capital by a factor of ten. Kipling was wrong, it does not always help to keep your head when everyone else is losing his. In their sprint to the sea, lemmings flood over Hardin's commons and chew them to the roots. An investor caught in a panic who, like the high-minded prisoner in *Prisoner's Dilemma,* sticks with his assets simply subsidizes those who rush to sell and thereby salvage at least something, even though they contribute to the downhill slide and aggravate it.

When you next tot up your life savings and ponder what to do with it, recall Barker, Keynes, and the small Scandinavian rodent. They serve as a stark contrast to the economics of rational expectations, discussed later in this chapter.

What Do People Bring to Investing Besides Money?

Do Americans Save?

When buying stocks or bonds or mutual funds or cocoa futures, most people use the verb *invest.* To an economist, to *invest* is to add to the stock of producer goods (goods used to make other goods), by building a plant, buying a machine, or increasing inventory. Buying common stock—even new issues—is not investment, in this sense, but simply a change in the form of assets, from cash to securities. This semantic difference can lead to considerable confusion. So can the definition of *saving.* For economists, to *save* is to refrain from spending, thus freeing resources for other uses, such as investment, exports, or public consumption. But most people regard *discretionary* saving only—deposits in savings accounts, purchase of securities, and so on—as true saving. Pension deductions, mortgage payments (principal only), and repaying installment credit are all saving to the economist but not to the average person. This is more than a semantic distinction. People act on their perceptions, not on textbook definitions.

Paul Samuelson's influential textbook *Economics*—approaching 3 million in sales since 1948, its dozen editions having shaped how we think as much as Marshall's *Principles,* which ran to eight editions—makes the following assertion: The most important distinguishing feature of capitalism is that *saving* and *investing* are done by different economic agents with different motives (families and firms, respectively). Financial markets and intermediaries work to match the supply of savings with the demand for them, in exceedingly simple and in wondrously complex ways.

The questions Do Americans save? How? How much? logically precede discussion of how they invest. There is a great deal of exceptionally interesting psychology involved in saving behavior.

Most saving in America, according to George Katona, is done by those between the ages of forty and sixty who have above-average incomes.[12] In the sixth chapter I argued that over the economic life cycle, needs and the means to satisfy them are poorly synchronized. Figure 6.1 showed a large gap between actual and required (or "optimal") income up to the age of forty. At that age the two curves cross, and means exceed needs as income continues to rise and desired spending declines. From this we should expect to find *dis*saving (that is, spending exceeds income) among young people and saving among older ones. Overall, such a pattern is found, but—owing to difficulties in borrowing against the collateral of a hopeful future alone—the camellike hump of life-cycle spending is likely smoothed out much less than many people would prefer. I think if we could, most of us would like to shift more wealth from middle age to our twenties and thirties and perhaps in the other direction, too, toward old age. Indeed, saving does accelerate in middle age, more with a view to retirement than to pay off accumulated debt. More than half of all personal wealth is owned by people fifty or older. Surveys show the major reasons for saving are old age and retirement and to build a cushion for illness, unemployment, or emergencies. Saving is thus not just the faint shadow cast by spending. People actively decide how much to save. The habits, values, and emotions that motivate saving are no less powerful than those that motivate spending.

I discussed in chapter 7 the long-standing, deep-seated American abhorrence of debt. The puritan value of abstinence, saving, and accumulation is closely related and almost as strong. At times the desire to spend and consume conflicts with the desire to abstain and save. A study by Hamburger, Holmes, and Mukai showed that the larger the sum of discretionary income, the greater the cognitive dissonance between spending and saving.[13] The dissonance is dispelled either by a change in behavior (that is, altering spending) or by lowering the weight of either "spend!" or "save!" signals.

The fraction of disposable income that is saved usually *rises* during recessions. Normally one might expect people to *dis*save in hard times as they draw on past savings built up precisely for this purpose. But precisely the opposite occurs. Even the *expectation* of an economic downturn can cut into spending and sometimes cause the very result people feared. Until the early 1970s inflation expectations worked the same way. Katona notes that "the most common response to accelerated price increases between 1951 and 1971" was "postponement of purchases," an expression of "malaise and anxiety as well as resentment of the higher prices."[14] For reasons elaborated in chapter 6, buy-now mentality has taken over. It is not surprising to find the savings rate plunging to record lows in the past two years.

Wealth is the accumulated value of past savings. The composition of personal wealth in 1972 was such that real estate—mainly houses—and corporate stock each made up about 30 percent; cash and savings deposits, 13 percent; and bonds, 6 percent.[15] (The remaining 21 percent was comprised of insurance equity, notes, and other assets.) By now, real estate's share has grown and corporate stock's portion has dwindled as housing prices rose faster than common stock during the 1970s.

Behind this composition of personal wealth lurks a peculiar problem. At retirement the wealth of many people consists wholly, or in large part, of the houses they own. To convert that wealth into spendable form, as many would like to do, requires selling the whole house and moving. You can't sell just the porch, or the yard and the front bedroom, as you can sell two or three hundred shares. People in this situation find themselves *house rich* and *income poor.* So-called reverse mortgages have been tested to deal with this problem. Under this plan home owners deed their house to the bank in return for regular cash payments and the right to continue to living in it.

A large chunk of "wealth" (apart from human capital, discussed in chapter 4) does not appear in statistics. Martin Feldstein has estimated the present value of future social security benefits ("for most Americans, . . . the major form of saving") at 2 trillion dollars for 1971, two-thirds as large as conventional private wealth.[16] He and others have argued that the existence of social security has led people to cut their savings drastically, specifically by some 35 percent. Capital stock, gross national product, growth, and even real wages are all lower as a result, it is claimed.

George Katona and Phillip Cagan independently researched this issue; each used two groups of families, those covered by private pension plans and those not covered (the comprehensive nature of social security means there is no control group, which makes it hard to study social security's impact on saving directly). Both Katona and Cagan found those covered by pension plans saved *more* of their incomes (apart from pension savings) than those not covered. Cagan explains this by a *recognition effect* (pension plan coverage increases awareness of retirement needs). Katona applies the *goal gradient* theory from psychology (the closer you are to your goal, the more you intensify your efforts): "Being assured of some, for many people insufficient, funds after retirement, the attainment of adequate funds for one's old age no longer appears an insurmountably difficult task; being closer to the goal stimulates people to work harder to achieve the goal, and therefore collective retirement plans promote individual saving."[17]

Both the Cagan and Katona studies were done in the early 1960s. Have times changed? Joseph Friedman recently studied seven years' worth of data from the Social Security Administration's 11,000-person panel of people approaching retirement.[18] He found that in the few months just before retirement, the rate of savings accelerated greatly, as Katona conjectured. Retirees gradually liquidated their assets in amounts of roughly 10 percent of their annual income. His findings "do not support the hypothesis that Social Security or pension wealth reduce the accumulation of ordinary assets. On the contrary, the evidence indicates a positive association between the two kinds of assets."

Despite Social Security, Americans will continue to set aside part of their incomes as savings—albeit less than the Japanese or Germans—and their personal wealth will keep on growing. Part of their asset portfolio is stable, fairly illiquid, and easy to evaluate: their houses. Part arouses controversy, befuddlement, anxiety, bemusement, desperation, hope, and fallacy: corporate stocks. Of all the topics economics tackles, the stock market arouses the most interest of all among ordinary people. Despite this bottomless fascination, less than 1 percent of the contents of introductory economics textbooks (for instance, Samuelson's *Economics*), by weight or volume, address the subject. Specialized journals discuss financial markets in words—*martingale, random walk, stochastic dominance,* and so on—opaque to the nonspecialist.*

What happens when the psychological theory of collective risk taking confronts the economic theory of security markets? The remainder of this chapter searches for some answers.

The Meaning of Mean-Variance

In the previous chapter I modified two-question logic to take into account uncertainty. Further modification is required to adapt it to financial investments.

For some financial assets, the simplest answer to the question, What is it worth? involves some rate of return, or rate of interest, that the asset pays. A straightforward formula can convert rate of return into a price. In 1978, for example, after-tax rates of profit on stockholders' equity for American industry were, on the average, 15 percent. Rates of return for individual stocks, of course, varied widely around that mean.

The fact that rates of return vary from year to year, and from company to company, means that a single-number answer to What is it worth? is not sufficient. Consider two assets, A and B—a Treasury bill, for example, and a Canadian penny mining stock. Suppose we expect both to pay an 11 percent rate of return in the coming year. The Treasury bill estimate is virtually certain. The mining-stock parameter may be an average of a whole range of possible rates of return, from 0 to 22 percent. Security A has a 0 standard deviation, or *spread,* around its 11 percent mean return;

---

*These terms are used to discuss the alleged random, nonsystematic nature of changes in stock market prices.

Security B has a standard deviation of 6 or 7 percent or so around its 11 percent mean. B is clearly riskier. If people generally shun risk, they are likely to prefer A over B. To get them to buy B, a higher average rate of return will have to be offered.

Two-question logic in financial analysis, therefore, demands a two-parameter answer to What is it worth?—a measure of central tendency *(mean)* and a measure of spread, or dispersion *(variance)* for each asset. Similarly, every portfolio (collection of assets) can be described rather completely by two parameters—the expected (mean) rate of return and its variance.

With the help of algebra, the mean-variance profile of an investment portfolio can be computed from means and variances of the individual assets that comprise it, together with information about whether rates of return of component assets rise or fall together (known as *covariances*).[19]

A key finding of portfolio theory is that a combination of two assets may be less risky than either of the assets taken separately. This can happen if the rate of return on one asset tends to rise when the other is falling, at least some of the time. Long ago, Cervantes knew the wise man "did not venture all his eggs in one basket"; if he were writing today, he might say that the wise investor diminishes risk by diversifying (owning a range of assets).

Mitigating risk by diversifying is rational even for investors who like risks. Overall, financial markets are usually characterized by risk aversion; that is, to convince people to put their money into riskier (less certain) assets, a higher average rate of return is needed. Investors who don't mind risk can "sell" that propensity for a higher rate of return rather than waste it on unnecessary risk through failure to diversify.

Americans Put Stock in Stocks

Although portfolio theory is quite general and applies to a wide variety of assets, its widest application is in analyzing in which combination of shares to invest. Because of the nature of combinatorial mathematics, the number of different possible portfolios is enormous. There are 17 trillion ways to pick 10 stocks out of 100 possible ones. And the New York Stock Exchange alone lists 2,184 separate issues.

At last count about one American in nine owned corporate stock. Through life insurance, savings accounts, and so on, a great many more have an indirect stake in the stock market. Despite these figures, the influence of share prices on the average family is probably small. For six out of every seven stockholders, total holdings amount to less than $25,000 (in 1969 dollars). Katona reports that in the course of twelve months, the majority of stockholders reported neither buying nor selling shares. The real significance of the stock market probably lies in its role as a kind of thermometer to measure the "temperature," overall health, and optimism of the economy.

There are about 140 stock exchanges around the world. The New York Stock Exchange, far from the oldest, dates back to 1792. Alexander Hamilton consolidated Revolutionary War debts by selling Treasury bonds. The need for bond brokers arose, and twenty-four of them, together with Hamilton, founded what is now the NYSE.

Charles Dickens visited America in 1842. In his *American Notes,* he had this to say,

> This narrow thoroughfare, baking and blistering in the sun, is Wall Street: the Stock Exchange and Lombard Street of New York. Many a rapid fortune has been made in this street, and many a no less rapid ruin. Some of these very merchants whom you see hanging about here now, have locked up money in their strong-boxes, like the man in the

Arabian Nights, and opening them again, have found but withered leaves.[20]

There are said to be one-quarter of a million millionaires in America today. I suspect relatively few of them made it to six zero's directly and solely through the stock market. And as Dickens laments, there are more than a handful of *ex-*millionaires who got that way through common miscalculation of common stock. Even so, I have found that a surefire way to prick up the ears of a slumbering audience, or classroom, is to talk about whether stocks in general, and certain stocks in particular, are likely to rise or fall.

How in fact *do* you make money in the stock market? What follows is an imaginary conversation between an economist (E) and a psychologist (P) about the economic theory of efficient markets. Economics explains why you probably can't make much money in the market; psychology helps explain why you *think* you can—and perhaps in fact you can.

A Random Walk with a Martingale

P: What does your *efficient-market* theory say?

E: Nothing more than this: *Prices fully reflect all available, relevant information.*

P: Sounds fairly harmless, as theories go.

E: You won't think so when you see where the theory leads us. It leaves little room for psychology. Probably no more than what Marshall already told us: Risk-averse people will trade in low-risk markets; risk-affinitive people will drift into high-risk markets. But whatever the market, if it's efficient, your chances of making big profits are very small.

P: Why is that so?

E: By definition. Look, what did that millionaire advise? Buy low, sell high? If you buy low, knowing the price will rise, that means you have information about the price *that is not fully expressed yet in the price itself.* Unless it's "insider" information—there are strict rules on that, by the way—that no one else has, chances are that lots of other people know what you know too. Quick as a wink, the added demand shoots up the price as you and others try to pick up some profit. Unless you're first in line, you are buying *high,* not low.

P: I see the hint of a paradox here. What makes markets efficient is the existence of large numbers of quick-thinking, well-informed people out to make money. The whole theory is based on the presumption that nobody *believes* it. If enough people believed markets were instantaneously efficient, they wouldn't waste time and money looking for profit opportunities; soon, prices wouldn't reflect underlying realities and information.

E: There is something to that. But never fear. We've known for *twenty* years, for instance, that the stock market is efficient. But the army of investment analysts, brokers, consultants, advisers, newsletter peddlers, and tipsters has in the meantime *swelled,* not shrunk.

P: That's cognitive dissonance. If efficient-markets data are dissonant with your job, with weekend dabbling in the market, or self-respect, you throw the data overboard, not yourself.

E: There's more to it than that. Let me get a bit technical. Paul Samuelson and Benoit Mandelbrot proved the following theorem fifteen years ago: If information gathering is cheap, buying and selling is costless (apart from the price itself, of course), and everyone *interprets* information in the same way with regard to present and future prices, then stock market prices are *martingales*—[21]

P: Sounds like an exotic bird.

E: —or, in other words, a random walk. *Changes* in stock-market prices show no pattern. If there *was* a pattern, someone could profit by discerning it; the attempt to profit itself wipes out the pattern. Now, take a look at this neat diagram I happen to have handy. (See figure 9.2.) One of those charts is H. V. Roberts's simulated *random* levels for fifty-two weeks.[22] The other is his plot of *actual* stock-price levels during 1956. It is hard to tell them apart, isn't it?

P: Almost peas in a pod. I understand now why so many think martingales are, like nightingales, for the birds. One of the hardest of all ideas for man to accept is that the universe, or even a part of it, is aleatoric. Spill some ink, randomly, and you see all kinds of things in the blotter; some of my friends make their living from that. I'll bet a good analyst (investment, not psycho-) could tell a persuasive story about why Roberts's two charts are both systematic and not random.

E: Some of *my* friends make their living that way. Come to think of it, so do I, in a way.

P: One of the most revealing things about people is the extent

FIGURE 9.2
Will the Real Stock Price Chart Please Stand Up?

One of the two charts above is the actual level of the Dow-Jones Industrial Index, from January 6 through December 28, 1956. The other is simulated random levels for 52 weeks. Can you tell which is which?*

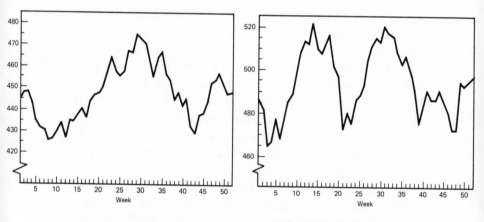

NOTE: H. V. Roberts, "Stock Market Patterns and Financial Analysis," *Journal of Finance* 14 (1959): 1–10.

*The left-hand chart is the real one; the right-hand chart is simulated.

to which they think they control their own destiny *(internals)* or are pawns of chance *(externals)*. Like Pip, in *Great Expectations,* externals tend to feel dependent, uncertain, and exposed to hundreds of uncertain chances. Like his creator, Dickens, Pip would likely steer clear of the stock market.

E: What's your point?

P: Simply this. People bring a good deal more to financial markets besides money and information. They bring themselves. Let me study their personalities, and I'll bet I can make a good guess as to how they will invest their money as individuals, or even as a group. *Markets* may be efficient, but people aren't. Besides, how do the random walkers explain sudden booms and busts? Where do bulls and bears come in?

E: There are objective reasons for bear or bull markets.

P: Remember what William James wrote in *The Will to Believe*? "Often enough, our faith beforehand in an uncertified result is the only thing that makes the result come true." If enough people believe in an uncertified result—for example, an impending price rise, with no solid information to back it up—it will happen. If nobody believes in a certified result, it won't. What *really* counts is how people *perceive* things. Even Samuelson and Mandelbrot presume people *interpret* information in the same way. Ever see that picture in the introductory psychology texts? Look at it once, it's an old hag; look at it again, it's a beautiful girl. Or ask two people what it is; one says it's a young girl, another, an old woman. They're both right. Maybe markets are like that picture.

E: Perhaps. But I doubt that perceptions can deviate much from cold, hard reality. As George Goodman once said, "if you don't know who you are, the stock market is an expensive place to find out."[23] If you act on expectations that are not fully rational —based on proper use of all available facts—you are going to take a bath.

P: Here's another paradox. The more rational people are, the less rational they become. The more efficient markets are, the more you need a psychologist to understand them.

E: I don't understand.

P: B. F. Skinner once performed an experiment with pigeons that belongs in the Hall of Fame.[24] He gave them food at brief, *random* intervals. They developed "superstitions." Whatever behavior the pigeon was performing before it got food—for instance, bobbing its head up and down—the food reinforced. So it bobbed its head some more. Chances are, it got food again while bobbing. That made bobbing even more logical and frequent. Soon, you have a cage full of birds hopping around, bobbing their heads, blinking their eyes, and so on. They *think* they have the world figured out. They *know* what elicits food. There is no way you could persuade them that the food delivery is random, patternless, and unsystematic. Even when you stop giving them food, they keep up the behavior they think brings birdseed. Some animals trained to earn a reward in this way will perform an action ten thousand times *unrewarded*.

E: It's like the college football player who threw up before a big game, played outstandingly, and made himself throw up before every ensuing game.

P: There are plenty of examples. The stock market is an ideal setting for superstition. Even with random-walk prices, people do profit from time to time. Like pigeons, they persist in doing whatever they think made them that profit. This creates its own reality. Whoever figures it out can do very well. That's why I said a moment ago: rational expectations create irrational behavior. Randomly changing prices breed superstitious behavior, which is part of my discipline, not yours. We call this, *operant conditioning*. I'll bet a whole lot of it goes on every day on Wall Street. I'll bet if you could pipe it into a balloon, you could bounce it against the eighty-foot ceiling of the New York Stock Exchange trading floor.

E: We have at least one thing in common, psychologists and economists.

P: What is that?

E: If we're so smart, why aren't we rich?

What Do People Bring to Investing Besides Money?

The Market as a Game

To study stock market behavior, Julian Simon, Randall Filer, and I conducted the following experiment.[25] The original idea was Simon's.

A week prior to the experiment eighty-seven undergraduates, enrolled in a corporate finance course, were each given a simulated thirty-six-week price history of seven fictitious stocks. No other information about the stocks was provided. For each of the seven stocks, week-to-week price *changes* were random, in order to reflect the *efficient-market* principle that prices, like dice or roulette wheels, have no memories. However each stock was given its own risk fingerprint—large or small variance of price changes (a measure of deviation from the mean), to reflect large or small degrees of risk. Participants were not, of course, told the price changes were random walks.

Each subject was asked to invest ten thousand dollars for maximum profit. A 1-percent commission was charged on stock purchases and sales. Holding cash was permitted; 5-percent interest per annum was credited. After each person announced his or her portfolio for a given "week," the price of each stock at the end of that week was revealed. Six "weeks" of the game were completed.

We reasoned that portfolio behavior should be related to at least two psychological traits. Julian Rotter's *locus-of-control* questionnaire measured the degree to which people felt they controlled their own destiny or were manipulated by others or by chance.[26] Hundreds of studies have shown it to reveal a fundamental attitude related to a great many types of behavior. People with internal control (that is, masters of their own fates), we felt, would follow riskier, more active investment policies and would be less likely to detect the random nature of the stock prices they faced. (In Rotter's questionnaire subjects chose one of a pair of statements they thought was closest to the truth. A sample pair: (a) Many of the unhappy things in people's lives are partly due to bad luck: (b) People's misfortunes result from the mistakes they make.)

Nathan Kogan's *chance-bets* questionnaire elicited a direct measure of risk-aversion by asking subjects to choose one of a pair of bets.[27] For example:

For each pair, choose the bet you prefer:

☐ 1/9 chance to win $120 8/9 chance to lose $15	O R	☐ ½ chance to win $60 ½ chance to lose $60

Bets with a wide spread of odds (for instance, 1/9 and 8/9) indicated affinity for risk. This affinity, we felt, should find expression in investment behavior. Note that for the above choice pair, and for all Kogan's chance bets, the expected value of each bet is zero: $1/9 \times \$120 + 8/9 \times -\$15 = 0$.

Among our findings:

- People with higher risk-aversion (as measured by the chance-bets questionnaire) chose less risky portfolios.
- People who believed in their own ability to control events and outcomes (as measured by the locus-of-control questions) picked riskier portfolios.
- Women invested much more conservatively than men. Relatively more women followed a buy-and-hold strategy compared with men. Perhaps for this reason women on the average made a net profit, as opposed to net loss for men.
- Demand for a stock was inversely related to its last price change. In other words, if the stock went down in week 38, people assumed it was likely to go up in week 39 and tended to buy it. This is the stock-market version of gambler's fallacy, mentioned in chapter 8 and is, apparently, a deeply rooted fallacy.

"There are no impartial facts," wrote David Krech, Richard Crutchfield, and Egerton Ballachey, authors of a leading social psychology textbook. "Data do not have a logic of their own that results in the same cognitions for all people."[28] Experts may prove beyond the slightest doubt—as indeed I believe they have—that stock prices are martingales. But people will continue to *see* those prices through the peculiar spectacles of their own personalities. They will act according to those perceptions, not according to what I or other economists expound.

Two Heads Are Riskier Than One

The marketplace for ideas is in normal times staid and placid. Scholars generally peddle old, well-worn, familiar theories with a corner snipped off here or a small patch put on there. Once in a while, like South Sea or Mississippi Company shares or gold or silver, a new thought or finding captures the imagination of the whole community, and everyone chases off after it.

In 1961 J. A. F. Stoner completed an innocuously titled master's thesis, "A Comparison of Individual and Group Decisions Involving Risk."[29] Stoner found that a person's willingness to take risks *rises* after taking part in a group discussion of the decision. Normally groups operate to make people conform. If individual members of the group are risk averse, why shouldn't group pressure toward conformity further *magnify* this risk-aversion instead of diminish it?

Following up on Stoner's study of management trainees, a string of replications showed the *risky-shift* phenomenon exists across age and occupational groups (grade-school children, undergraduates, mature adults, executives, and supervisors) and across international borders (American, English, Israeli, Canadian, French, and German subjects).

The bull market for risky-shift studies lasted almost two decades. The implications for financial markets are sweeping. To the extent that investment decisions are group phenomena—either through exchange of information, informal conversations in the broker's office, or "buy" recommendations by a team of experts—

those decisions will reflect greater risk than individuals acting alone would have chosen. At first the most promising explanation of the phenomenon was the simplest: Failure is an orphan, success has many parents. If responsibility for failing can be spread over many people, a group is more likely to risk it than an individual, who cannot alone deny fatherhood. Though a number of studies failed to support this explanation, Dion suggests that it may in fact explain risky shift, provided people experience actual, rather than hypothetical, consequences from their choices.[30]

According to the *leadership* theory, high risk takers dominate and persuade in group discussions, and they eventually lead the group to a riskier choice than individuals acting alone would choose. The data provide little support for this idea. Causal arrows may in fact run the other way; the risky shift itself may lead group members to attribute, post hoc, greater influence to those who took a pro-risk stand. Another theory posits that group debate *familiarizes* members with risk. If the unknown is unacceptable, and the familiar is fine, by debate and discussion groups improve comprehension of risk and hence diminish aversion to it. Attempts to create a risky shift by familiarization have not, however, worked out. Finally, the *cultural value* theory says that risk taking is a socially approved value. As part of a group, individuals will urge greater risk than they privately prefer, to be consistent with what they believe society wishes. Of the four theories, this one appears the strongest.

Some observers, though, have suggested that Americans are bedeviled, in investing, not by a risky-shift cultural value but by a *cautious shift.* Business schools teach *short-run,* not long-run, profit-maximization techniques, Lester Thurow argues. Inflation shortens time horizons for planning. Industry rewards management on the basis of *current,* not future, profits. "It is easier to invest based on current profits rather than trying to figure out who will be successful in ten years. The investor does not have to live with ten years of risk and uncertainty." In the age of daring entrepreneurship, managers were socialized to incur risk; now, "[they] are known only for . . . risk aversion."[31]

The implications for financial markets are exceedingly interesting. The same group-think force that apparently once acted to spur risk taking, when risk was socially approved, may now be at work in America to amplify and exaggerate caution, where caution has replaced daring in the pantry of our culture. The consequences for innovation and productivity are severe. Here again, the symptoms are economic, but the underlying causes can be found in the processes of group psychology and social values.

Conclusion: Human Destiny as Mean-Variance

"Wall Street Lays an Egg" was how Sime Silverman announced the stock market crash of 1929 in *Variety*. The economics and psychology of group risk, saving, and investing—illuminating when only money and self-respect are being lost—can also be pressed into service to question when and why the human race itself will lay an enormous egg.

"As the world has become safer on the average," Kunreuther and Slovic assert, "it has become potentially more dangerous at the extreme."[32] Science and technology have dramatically raised average life expectancy, but they have also introduced the possibility, however remote, of catastrophic loss on a scale that dwarfs even the 25 million deaths that bubonic plague caused in just six years.

The "then" portfolio of human destiny (see figure 9.3) once had a high mean and a small variance. The "now" portfolio has a lower mean; but it also has a long, foreboding right-hand tail. The irreversible nature of technology makes it impossible to wish the tail away. Since, for now, this is the only planet we have, and the only human race, it cannot be diversified away either. To shrink the tail, we are learning, is enormously costly.

FIGURE 9.3.

Mean-Variance of Destiny: A World Safer on Average, Riskier at the Extreme

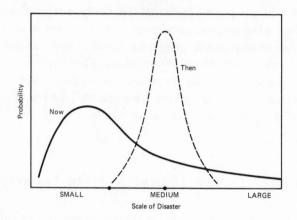

As individuals, we meet many types of risk over the course of our life cycle. We deal with them by ignoring them, embracing them, spreading them, or mean-variancing them downward. As members of society and trustees of posterity, the stakes are higher, and the issues more complex. Should we, the *Wall Street Journal* asks rhetorically, devote resources to "shave the last few percentage points off the risks we happen to care most about at the moment," thus depriving future generations of "increased resources that would help them deal better with the risks facing them further on down the road . . . of which we may as yet have not an inkling?"[33]

I don't know the right answer. If there *is* one, I think I know where it will be located: deep in layers where the strata of psychology—the science of behavior—and economics—the logic of choice —overlap.

PART V

People, on the Whole

10

HOW TAXING IS THE IRS? THE PUBLIC AND THE PUBLIC SECTOR

"MOST AMERICANS today are simply fed up with government at all levels."[1] The speaker was Richard Nixon, the year, 1972. President Nixon knew something. The angst and anomie Americans felt toward government was evident to him. Their dissatisfaction was to grow substantially over the coming decade. And along with it, government grew. In the past ten years public spending in the United States outpaced inflation by some 30 percent.[2]

What does economics have to say about the appropriate size and nature of the public sector? The conventional economics of collective action—anachronistically called *public finance,* from an era when governments paid for wars and railroads by selling bonds—has as little psychological content as the economics of the private sector. Yet economics, by its own assumptions and ground rules, needs psychology even more for analyzing the public sector than it does for analyzing the private sector.

When private goods and services change hands in free markets, it is assumed that both buyer and seller gain, and that the price at which the deal was struck reflects the satisfaction, or utility, each party derives from it. Where markets exist, economics believes people reveal their preferences by market behavior. In the preceding nine chapters, I have tried to show why we still need to explore the jungles of human likes and dislikes with psychology as our guide, even when markets exist to mirror those preferences.

For goods that are public—or collective—in nature, economists themselves abandon revealed preference. Certain goods and services, such as defense, extend an umbrella of benefits so wide that private markets for them are either inconceivable or exceptionally inefficient.

In strife-torn Lebanon, for example, there are said to be forty-three private militias. Most of them sprang up after 1976, when the Lebanese Army disintegrated during civil war. When a collective good, defense, is supplied privately in this manner, the result is chaos. It is hard to imagine the Hunts or Rockefellers constructing their own private MX missile system. If they did, at their expense, a great many of us would hitch a free ride. For those free riders, no *market* determination could be made of the total worth of the missiles' protection. Some other, nonmarket, method is required.

Some collective goods, such as education, are supplied both publicly and privately. Individuals derive private benefits from schooling—discussed, under the rubric of human capital, in chapter 4—but there may be public benefits as well, flowing from the contribution of educated persons to our collective well-being. Collective provision and consumption of defense, education, health care, transportation, police, and so on, are part of the democratic, electoral process, in which elected representatives vote on spending programs and the means to pay for them. Voter preferences are expressed through a glass darkly. The glass is the ritual that transpires the first Tuesday of each November, leading to state legislatures, Congress, and the president.

The public sector, then, is fundamentally different from the production, sale, and consumption of private goods and services in free markets. Psychology has at least as much to say about the relationship between the public and the public sector as it does about people and private markets. This chapter focuses on two major issues in public-sector economics on which psychology has a direct bearing: the so-called free rider problem and the subterranean economy.

A Ticket to Ride

In much of this book, the unifying model has been the tragedy of the commons or *Prisoner's Dilemma,* where individual rationality collides with social sensibilities. The specific settings of the models were people's roles as workers, investors, spenders, and savers—all of them private-market activities. Psychology helped us understand how interrelated persons act and react.

The original application of Garrett Hardin's tragedy of the commons was, however, the grassy Common, a resource available to all and a public good without vested property rights. Long before Hardin's article, economists used commons-type models to inquire about how public goods could best be provided and paid for. In his summary article on public finance, Dennis C. Mueller spelled out the crux of the problem in familiar terms: "Each individual is better off if all contribute to the provision of the public good than if all do not, and each is still better off if he alone does not pay for the good."[3]

Take, for instance, a country composed of two persons or two groups. Each person has the option of contributing, or not contributing, a share of the cost of, for example, a road. This is a kind of game, with four possible outcomes; the first person can choose one of two possible moves, and for each of those, the second person can also choose one of two possible moves.

Suppose the game's four outcomes, in terms of each player's preferences, are as follows (for illustrative purposes, I revive Al and Burt, resting from their efforts in chapter 5):

1. Both Al and Burt pay a share: second best outcome for Al and Burt.
2. Al pays, Burt does not: worst outcome for Al, best for Burt.
3. Al does not pay, Burt does: best outcome for Al, worst for Burt.
4. Neither Al nor Burt pay: third best outcome for Al and Burt.

This game is another *Prisoner's Dilemma*. Both Al and Burt have the same best strategy: not to pay. If Burt pays, Al's best move is not to pay. Doing so brings Al his first best outcome. If Burt doesn't pay, Al's best move still is not to pay; that way, Al gets his third best outcome, rather than the worst. The same reasoning applies to Burt. If both Al and Burt stick to their best strategies, either the road doesn't get built, or if it is already built, it crumbles from lack of maintenance. Both Al and Burt would love to hitch a free ride on one another's munificence. But both cannot do this simultaneously, any more than two people can be at the peak height of a seesaw at the same time. If Al and Burt try, they both lose. The fear of being exploited leads to collective ruin.

The free-rider problem is especially severe in the public-sector context precisely because it is *not* a two-person game, but rather a two-hundred-million-person game. A well-known result in experimental studies, previously mentioned, is that getting a cooperative solution (in this case, having everyone pay his fair share) is progressively harder as the number of players increases.

Another rather pernicious variation of this game results when a slight change of assumptions is made. Suppose the public good in question is considered essential—for example, law and order—so that both A and B would rather be exploited by the other party than suffer from a lack of the good. Now the game is as follows:

1. Both Al and Burt pay a share: second best for Al and Burt (as before).
2. Al pays, Burt does not: third best outcome for Al, best for Burt.

3. Al does not pay, Burt does:	best outcome for Al, third best for Burt.
4. Neither Al nor Burt pay:	worst outcome for both Al and Burt.

Neither Al nor Burt has a single best strategy in this game. They play a game of bluff, or "chicken," as this game has been called. "Not a red cent," Al asserts. If Burt believes Al's determination is ironclad, he—Burt—will foot the bill. Better that than the worst outcome: no law and order. If Burt thinks Al is bluffing, Burt bluffs back. When Al and Burt are eyeball to eyeball, who will blink first? Perhaps neither. An attempt to hitch a free ride in "chicken" may be a ride to mutual disaster, like two cars speeding toward one another on a highway with each driver determined not to flinch first.[4]

American public opinion about the size of government has been widely interpreted as pressing for less government spending and fewer taxes. But the psychology of that sentiment appears rather more complex. It appears to lie closer to seeking a free ride than to wanting fewer programs. Spending cuts are viewed with favor, provided the ax falls on someone else or on someone else's program. Budget cuts have free riders too.

A Vest-Pocket History of American Government

In this century the size of government has grown, in general, by a kind of ratchet effect. The public sector ballooned during wars. Then taxes and spending programs that wartime brought were only partly dismantled in peacetime. Prior to the First World War, U.S. government expenditures made up only one out of every twelve GNP dollars. By 1922, that figure had grown by half. From 1930 to 1970 public spending rose from one-tenth of the GNP to almost one-third. War provided the initial impetus through defense expenditures, and then from 1950 to 1970, civilian programs took over.

The major engines generating revenues for those programs were the personal and corporate income tax.

America's first tax on income was imposed in 1894. (This is apart from emergency Civil War taxes, which raised 20 percent of all internal revenue.) The rate of tax was a precipitous 2 percent on incomes above $4,000 (in today's dollars, around $40,000). The Supreme Court quickly declared the tax unconstitutional, on grounds that it was a direct tax not apportioned among the states. That resulted in the Sixteenth Amendment to the Constitution, ratified in 1913, which gives Congress the power to tax income (undefined) from whatever source, "without apportionment among the several states, and without regard to any census or enumeration."

Personal income-tax rates are progressive (they rise with income). Tax tables have marginal rates (the tax bite on the last dollar of income) that rise from 14 to 70 percent, although actual rates climb much less steeply. Once seen as a partial solution to economic inequality, the progressive income tax is now viewed as a part of the inflationary bind. Inflation shoves more and more Americans into higher nominal income brackets without appreciable improvement in their real purchasing power. Because of this effect, known as *tax-bracket creep,* income-tax collections rise about 16 percent for every 10 percent jump in money income. This was not the purpose of progressive tax rates, but it has made government a leading gainer from inflation. Wiping out tax-bracket creep would be easy—every year or two just adjust tax brackets downward for each consumer price index rise. The 1981 Tax Cut Act will do just that, beginning in 1984.

Who Gains? Who Loses?

Who really gains and who loses, on balance, from the impact of the public sector's spending and taxing powers? There are, of course, two sides to every government budget—spending and taxes. What we need to know, in studying the redistributive effect of government on people's incomes, is the *joint* impact of both taxes and public spending on each individual's income. But that requires estimates of the value that people attach to the public goods, such as defense, that government provides. Public goods by definition do not *have* a market value measurable by the price individuals pay for them since people do not, as individuals, directly pay for defense. Some indirect approach must be found.

By stringing together some heroic assumptions, I once tried to estimate what members of each income class got from the government, after deducting the taxes they paid.[5] The basic idea was that although the rich pay proportionately more in tax than the poor, they may sacrifice less than the poor, because a dollar means much less to a prince than to a pauper. Just how *much* less was, of course, crucial to my estimates, and it was represented by a parameter measured in several different ways. According to these calculations, it is the American middle class—families with average incomes—who pay more in taxes than they get in benefits from government. (See figure 10.1.) The government budget redistributes income from them to two groups—the poor and the rich.

The rich have always managed to find legal ways to avoid tax with the help of expensive, expert advice. The poor pay very little tax anyway. Once the middle-income families, from whom the great bulk of taxes are collected, develop the feeling they are helping shift income toward those wealthier than they, it is a very short step to extensive nonreporting of income. And the perceptions of middle America seem more in line with figure 10.1 than with other computations showing that the U.S. budget is consistently and heavily pro-poor. These perceptions about taxation increasingly appear closely connected with the phenomenon of unreported income and the underground economy.

FIGURE 10.1

Net Fiscal Incidence (Benefits Less Taxes), by Income Group, United States, 1968

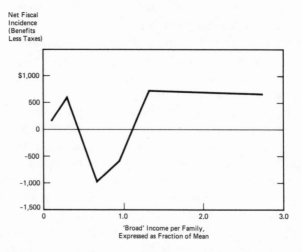

NOTE: Reprinted from S. Maital, "Apportionment of Public Goods Benefits to Individuals," *Public Finance* 3 (1975): 405. With permission of the publisher, Sage Publications, Beverly Hills.

Crime and Punishment

I don't know whether economists are especially fond of, or good at, bridge. But at least one expert advises us to apply his three-question version of economics' two-question logic before undertaking any bid or play:[6]

- How much can this win?
- How much can it lose?
- What are its chances of success?

The same principle that ensures success in fulfilling contracts in the game of bridge, with the most tricks, embodies the trick of making

246

people fulfill contracts, or abide by the law, in the game of life. "If we make the risk of punishment sufficient to outweigh the prospect of gain," says the calculus of pain and pleasure, "the potential law breaker will, as a rational man, choose to stay within the limits of the law."[7]

Let us apply this theory to tax evasion. What are the chances of getting caught and punished? What are the benefits of getting away with it? The Internal Revenue Service obligingly publishes the probability of your tax return being audited. Assume, as an upper limit, that an audit reveals all fraud, if it exists. The chances of getting caught for 1978 for various levels of adjusted gross income (the IRS's concept of gross earnings) are as follows:[8]

Below $10,000 (standard deduction):	less than 1 in 100
Below $10,000 (itemized deductions):	less than 3 in 100
Between $10,000 and $50,000:	less than 3 in 100
Over $50,000:	about 1 in 10

For ordinary garden-variety tax evasion, fines imposed are some multiple of the sum evaded. (Serious evasion may entail a jail sentence, though this is quite rare.) In addition, there is considerable social stigma resulting from possible publicity. This is why, it has been suggested, the IRS so often picks visible, public figures for highly publicized tax cases—to maximize the deterrent effect. (A few people are even jailed: about five hundred a year.[9]) Few, if any, fines are as high as thirty times, or even ten times, the sum evaded. This means that by cold, calculating two-question logic, the expected value of evading taxes is a positive gain. Suppose you evade $10,000 in taxes every year for ten years for an income over $50,000. On the average, you will get caught about once. (Of course, once you do get caught, the IRS will tend to watch you more closely in the future.) Unless the fine you pay is ten times $10,000 —not very likely—you come out ahead. (The IRS itself claims it could raise $2 in revenue for every $1 it spends on auditing, but deliberately moderates itself to take into account taxpayer costs.)[10]

Let me emphasize I am *not* arguing tax evasion is worthwhile. Precisely the opposite. The vast majority of Americans pay all their taxes voluntarily. They do so because they believe it is right to do so, because the law requires it, and because abiding by the law is right.

The point is, collection of income taxes—the basic means of support of the public sector—has worked incredibly smoothly over the years not because the pain-pleasure calculus made evasion unprofitable, but because most people willingly chose to pay true taxes and ignore possible economic gains from evasion. It is a voluntary system based on voluntary adherence to a set of rules. *Why* people adhere to those rules is more a matter for psychology than economics. So is this question: Why are people today apparently less and less willing to adhere to the rules of income tax?

One explanation for widespread tax compliance, despite what might seem like attractive odds against compliance, is that *perceived* penalties and odds of detection are greater than actual ones. In the eighth chapter, I cited evidence showing that people tend to see small probabilities as much larger than they really are. Perhaps one in ten, or one in one hundred, looms much larger to taxpayers than it really is. Also, perhaps taxpayers *believe* audits are run more frequently than they are, in fact. Together, misperception and overestimation can turn positive expected values into negative ones.

I also in chapter 8 suggested that people will take risks to avoid certain loss, but they prefer certain gains to risky bets. This applies to tax evasion too. For those whose point of reference is *income after deduction of full, honest taxes,* the risky chance of *gaining* income by evasion is more likely to be declined than for those whose point of reference is *before-tax* income. The latter will compare the *sure* loss from paying full taxes to the *uncertain* loss from evading (and possibly being apprehended, or possibly, escaping notice), and they are more likely to choose evasion. The more people believe that tax money is rightly theirs, the more evasion, therefore, will take place, by this *reference-point* effect.

How Taxing Is the IRS?

Americans now see tax evasion as less offensive, morally, than they once did. In taxation, as in language, usage and practice modify convention. As the practice of evasion spreads, the convention on which tax collection is based changes. Later, I will give attitudinal evidence supporting the claim that fewer Americans think tax evasion is wrong, and fewer Americans think the tax system is just and fair.

Together with a psychologist and a graduate student, I once ran an experiment to see which method was more effective in deterring tax evasion: raising the size of penalties or increasing the frequency of audits.[11] A group of undergraduates was given simulated monthly salaries and asked to report income and pay taxes. As expected, evasion rose substantially when tax rates climbed from 25 percent to 50 percent. Other things being equal, the higher the tax rate, the more it pays not to declare income—a finding that pins much evasion in recent years on tax-bracket creep and inflation. Our main finding was that large fines are more effective in deterring evasion than are higher probabilities of getting caught. This is consistent with the kind of subjective probability bias reported in chapter 8.

Hiking fines is essentially costless, while more frequent audits can be expensive. An economic approach to tax evasion, therefore, suggests stiffer penalties. A psychological approach, though, suggests finding ways to alter the perception of the tax system as inequitable, or to restore the feeling that evasion is morally reprehensible.

Attitude and Reality

How do Americans *perceive* government—how it spends, taxes, and deals with major economic problems such as inflation and unemployment? If indeed the economic relation between one American and another, and in particular between Americans and their government, is characterized by a nonzero-sum game such as

Prisoner's Dilemma, the psychological attitudes of the players toward one another are of crucial importance. Those attitudes determine whether the players adopt prosocial, cooperative stances or antisocial, proindividual behaviors.

With regard to government, which serves both as another player in the game of bidding for resources, and as the referee that sets the rules of the game, people feel mistrust, a lack of faith in the government's efficacy in dealing with pressing problems, and skepticism about how fairly the tax burden is shared. They are sure that a substantial part of public spending is wasted.

An August 1980 national survey, done by Gallup, revealed that for defense, health, education and training, and social security and energy, those who felt government should be spending *more* money than it is now outnumbered those who felt less should be spent. The ratio was between three- and four-to-one.[12] Only for welfare—the perennial weak sister of the welfare state, along with foreign aid, in public opinion polls—were these ratios reversed. The favored programs made up a very large part of total public spending (depending, though, on how social security expenditures are treated) in 1980. At the same time, a majority of respondents with opinions felt that:

- in the past decade, the additional services provided by government weren't worth the additional money spent to provide them.
- 20 percent or more of government spending is wasted.
- government spending slows growth and causes inflation.
- they pay *more* than their fair share of taxes.

George Katona traces the origins of mistrust in government to the late 1960s, "when the spread of violence, racial conflict and urban decay generated societal discontent."[13] Katona reports that an index of trust in government, constructed by the Center for Political Studies at the University of Michigan from five survey questions unrelated to economics, plummeted from 50 percent in 1958 to 25 percent in 1968, 3 percent in 1972, and −30 percent late in 1973. With mistrust has come pessimism about the government's ability to deal with inflation and unemployment. With regard to these two targets, only one person in five felt in September 1971 that the government was doing a "poor job." By February 1974 it was nearly one in two. Since December 1978 between 60 and 85 percent of Americans believe the government will do a fair or poor job during the coming year or two. In the summer of 1980 two Americans in three felt the U.S. economy was in "a real crisis."[14]

I spoke in chapters 5 and 7 of a theory of inflation where various demands for slices of the "social loaf" add up to more than the loaf itself. Among the various demanders is, of course, the government. Some economists have claimed that since governments have powers well beyond those of firms, and at least equal to those of families, to ensure they get as large a slice as they wish—by printing money, for example—governments cause both inflation and slow growth. "Where output is near to its capacity limits," W. Eltis reasons, "investment plus net exports are crushed between the irreducible shares of government and workers' consumption."[15] This appears to be a view widely held by many people who, rightly or wrongly, repeatedly lay the blame for inflation at the feet of government rather than with business or labor. In public perceptions, high taxes cause inflation, and both high taxes and inflation are problems that can be blamed on the government.

Taxes and the Just Man

The actual structure of taxes in America is made up of three tiers, according to the level of government. Federal revenues are derived mainly from income tax: 80 percent or more. State revenues come predominantly from sales taxes, while local taxes come from levies on property. Once, in the early 1970s, property taxes were considered the chief villains in Americans' eyes. A 1972 survey reported by William Watts and Lloyd Free showed 45 percent of Americans felt the property tax was "least fair," while only 19 percent chose the federal income tax.[16] Anti-property tax feeling was spread quite evenly across age, income, and socioeconomic groups; the main objection was the uncertain and arbitrary assessment methods.

Which taxes are perceived as fairest? In the last ten years a major change in perceived tax fairness has occurred. Income tax is now seen as the *worst* tax by 36 percent of respondents, with property tax seen as worst by only one-quarter.[17] Inflation and tax-bracket creep must be held responsible for much of this change. As Richard Rose has pointed out, even if you think property tax is unfair, you can't very well evade it by hiding your house. But if you think income tax is unfair, there is a lot you can do to act on your perception. The result: more evasion.

When Americans responded to a Gallup Poll about what form they would like a tax cut to take, 42 percent picked a cut in income taxes, and another 36 percent picked a half-and-half tax cut (half in lower incomes taxes, half in lower sales taxes).[18] Respondents favored a personal income tax cut by three- or four-to-one margins over lower social security taxes or lower taxes on savings and investment income.

This perceived unfairness in the tax system has led to the emergence of an underground economy. Whatever the true extent of the underground economy, a controversy I shall discuss later, Americans now *believe* it is extensive. That belief in itself is sufficient to generate a snowballing social illness of crumbling tax morality, infinitely harder to cure than to cause.

Asked about the pervasiveness of tax evasion ("people not paying the taxes the law says they are supposed to pay"), two-thirds of respondents said they thought many people, or at least some, do this. An even greater fraction, five in six, thought some people, or many, practice tax *avoidance* ("finding *legal* ways to take advantage of the tax laws to pay less tax than they fairly should").

The IRS itself sponsored a survey on tax morality, done by a private research firm, CSR Inc., in 1979. The survey was based on interviews with nearly five thousand persons in fifty communities. Their conclusion: Americans are cheating more and feel less guilty about it. According to the survey, one person in five admitted to understating income; one in ten overstated deductions, and one in six claimed a dependent illegally.[19] More than half said they thought nearly everyone would cheat if he felt he could get away with it.

A major reason for evasion, the report concluded, was simply that Americans "don't think cheating the government is a particularly serious crime." In releasing the report, on April 15, 1980, (tax return day, the last day for filing a tax return without penalty) Congressman Benjamin Rosenthal said "the study strongly suggests that Americans are exhibiting a growing willingness to engage in tax evasion schemes because they are increasingly cynical about the even-handedness of our tax laws." The current, largely voluntary self-assessment system, he warned, is threatened by "this growing public perception that the tax burden is inequitably distributed."[20]

"When there is an income tax," Plato wrote in Book I of *The Republic,* "the just man will pay more, and the unjust less, on the same amount of income."[21] Here is more evidence that people no longer associate justice with income tax.

- When the IRS asked a sample of Americans how much their consciences would bother them over various types of evasion, large fractions said they wouldn't worry much about failing to declare the value of a bartered service (62 percent), gambling earnings (53 percent), padded business-travel expenses (49 percent), or simply understated income (42 percent).
- A survey conducted by Y. Song and T. E. Yarbrough showed that in terms of seriousness, respondents ranked tax evasion as only slightly more serious than stealing a bicycle.[22]
- A study by Spicer and Lundstedt revealed that "the more tax evaders a taxpayer knows, the more likely he is to evade taxes himself." In the epidemiology of cheating, there is, in other words, spread of contagion—and no vaccine in sight.[23]

Taken together, all these attitudes form a game situation in which trying to avoid exploitation by the other side—other people and government—is both acceptable, sensible, and perhaps even necessary. Collectively, taxpayers' revolts and the *Proposition 13* phenomena gave some expression to these feelings, but they seem to have died out as quickly as they flared up. The major expression of anomie appears to lie in the realm of tax honesty. More and more, the subterranean economy—transactions that go unreported for tax purposes—appears to be on the rise.

Off the Top and Off the Books

" 'It was as true,' said Mr. Barkis [to David Copperfield], 'as turnips is' "—and then went on with emphasis, " 'It was as true . . . as taxes is. And nothing's truer than them.' "[24] How true are taxes? Of the 90 million tax returns that flood in to the Internal Revenue Service each year, how many cheat a lot or a little? How widespread is evasion?

Tax evasion is one of those economic phenomena that almost by definition cannot be directly observed. Estimating its extent, therefore, requires indirect methods—searching for footprints, like the physicists' bubble chamber—that are often controversial.

Peter Gutmann, a professor of economics and finance at the City University of New York's Baruch College, provided some of the first estimates.[25] He put the "underground" economy at about 10 percent of the GNP. Here is how he reached that figure.

First, he picked 1937–41 as a "normal base period." In 1938 a married couple with $4,000 income (around $22,000, at today's prices), paid federal income tax at the rate of 4 percent. A $2,500 deduction meant the couple paid only $50 or so in taxes. Assume, then, evasion was zero at this time. Gutmann calculated the ratio of cash-to-demand deposits then in effect. Had evasion stayed at zero, Gutmann reasoned, this ratio should have remained steady. But in fact, between pre–World War II and 1976, it rose substantially. Gutmann computed the amount of "excess" cash in 1976—beyond what the 1938–41 cash-to-deposits ratio would have required to support 1976's GNP—and inferred from that an underground GNP of a whopping 176 billion dollars. (See the box.)

An IRS task force was set up to refute Gutmann's surprising estimates. Using methods quite different from Gutmann's, task force leader Berdj Kenadjian affirmed that in 1976, "about 6½ to 8½ percent of income from legal sources . . . were not reported to the IRS."[26] Adjusted for comparability, Gutmann claims the IRS's upper estimate closely matches his, although the IRS vehemently denies it.

The Simple Arithmetic of Unreported Income

1. Assume no evasion took place in 1937–41. Then, for every demand-deposit dollar, there was 22¢ in cash. Suppose this is still the right ratio of "legal"-cash-to-demand deposits for 1976.

2. In 1976 demand deposits amounted to about 230 billion dollars. This means the amount of cash needed to support legal transactions was 22/100 times 230 billion dollars, or about 50 billion dollars.

3. The actual amount of cash in circulation in 1976 was more like 80 billion dollars. This left an "excess" of cash of some 30 billion dollars.

4. Assume all this "excess" cash reflects unrecorded transactions. Demand deposits plus "legal" cash totaled 280 billion dollars in 1976; in that year, GNP was about 1.7 billion dollars. This means that every dollar of "legal" cash and demand deposits supported $6 in GNP: $1,700 ÷ 280 ≈ 6.

5. Therefore, each dollar of the "excess" cash apparently supported $6 in unreported, underground GNP. In total there were 30 billion excess dollars. There must have been, therefore, 180 billion dollars in unreported GNP that year (30 billion dollars times 6).

A study by tax expert Vito Tanzi, of the International Monetary Fund, improves Guttman's methods by trying to account for "extra" cash by such factors as higher tax rates, higher interest rates, and higher incomes in addition to evasion.[27] Tanzi estimates that higher tax rates since 1937–41 caused an underground economy of between 3.4 and 5 percent of GNP, substantially less than Gutmann's 10 percent but still exceedingly large.

The most extraordinary and controversial estimate is that of Edgar L. Feige, an economics professor at the University of Wisconsin.[28] He bases his estimate on the quantity theory of money, which says that the quantity of money *(M)* multiplied by the frequency each dollar changes hands (*V*, velocity) equals the value of all goods exchanged (*PT*, or Price times Transactions).

Like Gutmann, Feige assumes that in 1939 there was no subterranean economy. For that year he calculates that the ratio of PT to GNP was around ten to one (that is, there were $100 in transactions for each $10 of GNP). Suppose this ratio is taken as a norm. Now Feige calculates PT for 1976 and 1978. He multiplies these estimates by 10 to infer actual Gross National Product for those years. The difference between these estimates of GNP, and actual GNP, Feige imputes to the underground economy. They are enormous. For 1978 they range from one-quarter to one-third of actual GNP. If 500 billion dollars of irregular GNP could be brought up from underground, Feige notes, tax rates could be cut *and* the deficit wiped out.

To sum up: If what is moral is what you feel good after, and what is immoral is what you feel bad after, as Hemingway once wrote,[29] then fewer and fewer Americans feel bad on April 15, even though more and more may have something to feel bad about.

Not everyone pays less than he should. Some people pay *more*. In 1979, as donations, 662 people gave money to the U.S. Treasury, often by paying more tax than they owed. They are called "National Debt Donors" by the Treasury, and money from them is deposited and held in a special account. The motives of National Debt Donors are often not unlike those of evaders: feelings of injustice and inequity and the wish to protest it by, perhaps, jousting with and defeating the Treasury computer.

Tax evasion falls solidly in the free-rider box. The more people seek free rides and evade taxes, the more those who *do* pay have to fork over, and the greater the incentive to evade—another of those closed-loop systems Americans seem to be increasingly caught up in.

Playing by the Rules

Economic theory portrays the economy as a collection of millions of people, each of whom applies fastidious two-question logic hundreds of times daily in supermarkets, gas stations, Wall Street, and banks. But a truer picture probably would show two other human penchants in firm control: habit and conformity.

Habit rules the unreflecting herd, Wordsworth observed. Most behavior matches the groove of some past behavior that worked out not too badly. Habit's ally, conformity—or compliance—also dominates. Every modern economy has a vast network of written and unwritten rules and regulations. These rules form the institutional setting within which decision making takes place. For the most part, we comply willingly with these rules. Otherwise, the wheels of the economy would grind to a deafening halt in no time. What makes people willing to comply with rules—a topic psychologists research—is as important for understanding economic behavior as, for example, how people weigh the chances of success and the risks of failure in noncompliance.

Three social psychologists, John Thibaut, Nehemia Friedland, and Laurens Walker, constructed a complex game played by groups of six undergraduates. Four players assumed the role of four "corporations." Two players, controlled by the experimenter, were the "government" and the "buyer." In the game, corporations negotiated commercial transactions with the buyer, then computed and paid income tax to the government. Government could inspect one of every ten tax payments and impose penalties if called for. Government revenue was disposed of by two different rules. One rule called for tax revenue above a certain minimum to be redistributed back to the four corporations. Another rule let the government demand a much higher minimum income, without redistributing its tax money back to the taxpayers. Experiments were run using each of the two rules, in turn.

Tax checks were invariably run after each corporation completed its fifth transaction (and tax return). Players knew only that up to the fifth transaction they could be audited, and after the fifth transaction they would not be.

Figure 10.2 graphs the result. When taxpayers knew their tax money would in part find its way back to them, they paid a larger

FIGURE 10.2

The Effect of Surveillance and Correspondence on Tax Compliance

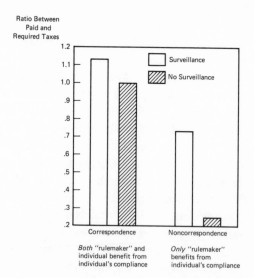

NOTE: Reprinted by permission of publisher from John Thibaut, Nehemia Friedland, Laurens Walker, "Compliance with Rules: Some Social Determinants," *Journal of Personality and Social Psychology* 30 (1974): 798. Copyright 1974 by the American Psychological Association.

fraction of their required taxes. When taxpayers knew they stood a chance of auditing (surveillance), again they paid more tax than when they knew they would go unchecked. Together, *noncorrespondence* (no perceived benefit to the taxpayer from compliance) and *nonsurveillance* resulted in actual tax payments of only a fraction of their required level.

"Critically important in determining the degree of compliance," the authors conclude, "is the policy governing the allocation of resources within the group (that is, tax revenue). Equitable sharing heightens the tendency to comply."[30] Moreover, they add, "equitable sharing requires little surveillance to ensure compliance; inequitable sharing depends strongly on surveillance to produce compliance."

Another experiment conducted among University of Colorado undergraduates, reported in the *National Tax Journal,* had participants receive simulated monthly salary checks and declare income and pay tax.[31] Random audits were run, and penalties for evasion were imposed. Everyone was told (correctly) that his own tax rate was 40 percent. One-third of the group was told (falsely) that *other* people's tax rates averaged 65 percent; another one-third was told *other* people's rates averaged only 15 percent; and the last one-third was told the truth, that its own rates were the same as everyone else's. Overall, the group evaded about one dollar in four of tax. But those who felt they were paying lower rates than everyone else evaded only 12 percent of their tax, while those who felt they were paying more than everyone else evaded nearly one-third of their tax. In the laboratory, and perhaps in life, compliance walks hand in hand with the perception of fairness and equity. Destroy the latter, and, penalties or no penalties, compliance plunges.

The tax burden in the United States may or may not be fairly distributed. But the fact that people *perceive* it to be unfair implies that either evasion will spread, or the means to detect and punish it will have to be greatly stiffened and expanded. Or, alternately, perceptions will have to be altered significantly.

Conclusion

Well before he wrote his famous book on economics, Adam Smith was a philosopher concerned with morality and ethics. In *The Theory of Moral Sentiments,* published when he was thirty-six years old, Smith compares society to a chess board. "The pieces upon the chess-board have no other principle of motion besides that which the hand impresses upon them," he wrote. "But . . . in the great chess-board of human society, every single piece has a principle of motion of its own, altogether different from that which the legislature might choose to impress upon it."[32]

"If those two principles coincide and act in the same direction," Smith continued, "the game of human society will go on easily and harmoniously, and is very likely to be happy and successful. If they are opposite or different, the game will go on miserably, and the society must be at all times in the highest degree of disorder."[33]

This chapter has offered evidence of increasing incompatibility among the "principles of motion" of individual members of society and between them and their elected legislatures. This conflict is no less real for being psychological in nature and for involving dimensions of trust, credibility, justice, efficacy, and mutual sympathy.

Economic relationships among people, and between people and their government, are, I have argued, characterized by "games of human society" containing sharp conflict. Underlying that conflict is the psychology of how we see ourselves in relation to others. What we see, know, and feel is the source of economic and social problems. Governments may at times exacerbate those problems, but big or small, governments do not principally *cause* them. Both the problem and its solution rest in the same place—with people, on the whole.

11

CONCLUSION: TOWARD A SYNTHESIS OF MINDS AND MARKETS

LIGHT AND FRUIT—these were the twin goals Arthur Pigou proclaimed for the pursuit of knowledge in general and economics in particular. The light was to illuminate human society and sharpen our vision of it. The fruit was to nurture wisdom needed to improve that society and its surroundings.[1]

Pigou's metaphor leads off his great book *The Economics of Welfare* (1920), published four years before Marshall's death. As Marshall's star pupil, Pigou inherited both Marshall's Chair in Political Economy at Cambridge University and his view of economic science. "In the sciences of human society," Pigou wrote, "it is the promise of fruit and not of light that chiefly merits our regard." His book broke new ground in the study of policy measures to maximize welfare (meaning "well-being" in Pigou's era, not payments to the poor and needy). Policy seeks to bridge the gap between what *is* and what *ought to be*. Despite Pigou's partiality to applied economics, he knew well that in science and society, as in nature, light—knowing what *is*—is indispensable for fruit. Lucidity of sight about who we are and what we are, is a vital condition for conducting our affairs, as individuals and as a nation, with intelligence and foresight. Without it, we will not prevail, or even endure or survive.

In this age the scarcest of all resources is not the air we breathe, the water we drink, the energy we burn, or the metals we smelt. It is, rather, the clarity with which we see ourselves in relation to those resources, and especially in relation to one another. In 1939, looking at a world about to erupt in war, Keynes said that what we needed then above all was lucid thought.[2] Four decades later, that is truer than ever before.

I began this book by noting how economics has lately had its conceptions of the world turned upside-down, literally. It is well-known that images as they appear on the retina of the eye are also upside-down. The brain rights them. A famous experiment had subjects wear special glasses that stood the world on its head. The brain, it emerged, quickly learned to put things right side up again. Science shares that peculiar talent of the brain. As dissonant evidence mounts and assails cherished propositions of a discipline, virtuoso acrobatics of that discipline's believers put things right again. In economic science I sometimes think we stand *ourselves* on our heads, rather than our models, in a vain attempt to see more clearly.

Such contortions are a clear signal that economics is on the threshold of what Thomas Kuhn labeled *a change of paradigm*— a complete revision in the fundamental framework of analysis. Evidence contradictory to the conventional wisdom of economics continues to accumulate. But science, like Nature, abhors a vacuum. No science will agree to junk its tried and true axioms, even when they become trying and untrue, until a new and more powerful set of axioms is available. The price of adhering to crumbling theories is high—what Voltaire called "the oeconomic style, or an expedient falsification of facts."[3]

What will economics' new paradigm look like when it arrives? Economists themselves have some thoughts on the subject. James

Cicarelli, an economics professor at the State University of New York at Oswego is conducting interesting research on "The Future of Economics."[4] His respondents, all of them economists, are asked to list areas in which breakthroughs in economics are most likely. They then go on to describe what they think those breakthroughs will be. At the top of the list: "Explicit merger of economic theory with aspects of political science, psychology, sociology, sociobiology and law resulting in models in which various political and social institutions are treated as identifiable determinants of economic behavior." A majority of respondents agreed with this description and felt it would occur in six to ten years.

In this book I have tried to map out areas where a useful merger could occur between the science of mind and the science of markets. While all the other related disciplines mentioned in Cicarelli's study have a great deal to offer, I believe the major contribution to economics' next breakthrough will come from psychology.

This concluding chapter discusses some general areas where economics and psychology are united, rather than divided, by a common denominator and where a real merger needs nothing more than a unified terminology. Other areas where economics and psychology lie light years apart and where radical reconstruction of economics' models and methods is in order are also examined. One day I hope current notions of Economic Man and pure economics —"the commercial doings of a community of angels," Pigou called it—will be replaced and displaced by "the actual world of men and women as they are found in experience to be," again Pigou's words.[5] Pigou did not see this happen in his time. I believe we shall see it in ours.

The Problem with Mathematics

In the first chapter I suggested that some of economics' failures stem from choosing, a century ago, the celestial mechanics of

Walras instead of the biological system of Marshall as a means of expression and analysis. Linguists like Noam Chomsky tell us that language not only reflects the nature of a culture, it also *shapes* that culture, in important ways. So has mathematics, the language of modern economics, shaped the discipline it communicates. Those parts of reality easily expressible in mathematical terms come to the forefront—generally, technology or relationships between things—while other parts of reality much less amenable to symbols and equations—relationships among people, the nature of people —are swept aside.

Marshall had a number of sensible things to say about the use of mathematics in economics. "The chief use of pure mathematics in economic questions," Marshall wrote, "seems to be in helping a person to write down quickly, shortly and exactly, some of his thoughts for his own use. . . . it seems doubtful whether any one spends his time well in reading lengthy translations of economic doctrines into mathematics, that have not been made by himself."[6] Increasingly, the vanguard of economic theory speaks in mathematical tongues. The labor of translation, for those of us who trail behind, is reversed—mathematics into economic doctrine, rather than economic doctrine into mathematics.

The answer is not to make economics less mathematical, as some economists have demanded (particularly those, Paul Samuelson noted wryly, whose mathematical skills are poor). Even Marshall speaks of mathematicians who "use their favorite weapons in clearing a way for themselves to the centre of some of those difficult problems of economic theory, of which only the outer fringe has yet been touched."[7]

Rather, a change in the *type* of mathematics is called for. At present, economics relies heavily on mathematical techniques that principally show how to optimize (bring some function to its maximum or minimum value). There are many difficulties with this. Use of *maximization mathematics* is based on the assumption that the people that mathematics describes *also* act to maximize functions. "In simple slow-moving situations, the assumption of maximization relieves us of any need to construct a detailed picture of economic man or his processes of adaption," Herbert Simon wrote in 1959. "As the complexity of environment increases, we need to know more and more about the mechanisms and processes that economic man uses to relate himself to that environment and its goals."[8] Furthermore, such mathematics requires knowledge of the function to be maximized. To depict people's aspirations, economics uses a highly unsatisfactory *"black box" utility function* whose inner workings are left vague and unspecified. Tibor Scitovsky's *Joyless Economy* opened and renovated this black box.[9] He argued that our well-being depends on three different components—novelty, comfort, and pleasure, or what we consumed yesterday, the cumulative amount consumed, and the rate of change in what we consume. The Scitovskian utility function yields both fruit and light, verbally, in the hands of its creator. Mathematically, I have found it almost intractable. Here reality obliterates the neat, compact results of unrealistic functions.

The major drawback of maximization mathematics is, I believe, that it forces us to *assume* a specific set of social institutions. But such institutions stem from human behavior. Ideally we should like mathematics to search for and describe the kinds of institutions likely to emerge from a given behavior set rather than assume those institutions from the outset.

The appropriate mathematics for a new behavioral economics is the theory of games. Game theory focuses on how people interact and on how they influence one another. It need not assume maximizing behavior. Above all, social institutions emerge from game-theory mathematics as part of the solution. In the initial years after its inception in 1944, game theory failed to fulfill its early promise. Lately, however, economics appears increasingly receptive to the use of game theory, a tendency that Cicarelli's survey seems to confirm.

In this book one particular type of game was used to characterize a variety of economic problems; it is a game in which the human heart is in conflict with itself, because players aspire to gain as

individuals and cooperate as group members, yet they shun mar-
tyrdom arising from "solo" altruism. This particular model, *Prisoner's Dilemma* or tragedy of the commons, is only one out of
many types of games. In fact, the simplest of all game-theory
models, the game with two players, each of whom has two possible
strategies, can result in no fewer than seventy-eight conceptually
different kinds of games; *Prisoner's Dilemma* is only one of these.[10]
Game theory is a powerful, elegant mathematical tool vastly useful
for "clearing our way to the center of some difficult problems." It
not only reveals the inner workings of social conflict, but it points
to social institutions that can solve them. I hope the current bull
market in game theory will continue.

Common Ground in Expected Value

Ironically, after assailing economics' current use of mathematics,
I find common ground between economics and psychology precisely in that most abstract of all disciplines. Economics and psychology merge and overlap in a region of human behavior related
to the mathematical concept of expected value, defined and discussed earlier in chapter 8, which dealt with probabilities.

I defined in chapter 8 the expected value of an event as the
probability it will happen, multiplied by its value if it does. The
expected value of a ticket eligible for a million-dollar prize when
there are 1 million tickets is one dollar—one-millionth of 1 million.
With that, mathematics ends. Psychology begins when we ask why
some people would pay five dollars for such a ticket and others,
only a quarter.

The concept of expected value lies at the core of a large and
important field of inquiry known as *the economics of risk and
uncertainty*. With more and more decisions revolving around a
choice of alternatives whose outcomes are uncertain, this field will
doubtless grow in importance.

Toward a Synthesis of Minds and Markets

The same concept pops up repeatedly in psychology. The leading psychological theories of decision making under uncertainty, though seemingly different or even contradictory, are at their core variations of the expected-value formula. Norman Feather listed some of these theories' inventors and the various labels they pasted on them.[11]

Theorist	Term for "Expected Value"	Term for "Probability"	Term for "Prize"
Kurt Lewin	Force (weighted valences)	subjective probability	valence
E. C. Tolman	performance vector	expectation	need-push, valence
Julian Rotter	behavior potential	expectancy	reinforcement value
W. Edwards	subjective expected value	subjective probability	utility
J. W. Atkinson	resultant tendency	expectancy	motive times incentive value

All the aforementioned psychologists would no doubt insist there are important, fundamental differences between *their* approach to decision making under certainty and those of others, and rightly so. But the fact that they all share a common mathematical denominator—expected value—is undeniable.

Psychology tends to divide itself along the fault line of a strict analytic-deterministic approach, which sees people as driven helplessly by inner forces, and a strict stimulus-response behaviorist approach, which sees people as passively shoved around by stimuli from their environment. Fortunately, economics need not pick either extreme. The middle ground is defined and captured by social-learning theory, an especially appropriate theory for application to economics.[12] The pioneer of social-learning theory, Julian Rotter, showed how behavior, personal factors, and environmental factors all operate as interlocking determinants of one another. Social-learning theory admits that behavior is shaped by our surroundings; however, those surroundings are partly of our own making. Behavior may be shaped by reinforcement, but human beings are the agents who make those reinforcements available, or scarce, for one another. Above all, behavior that is learned can also be taught. This leaves room for both hope and action. If economics must embrace some particular approach in psychology rather than continually and eclectically pick and choose from many approaches, I believe social-learning theory holds the widest appeal and bears the closest similarity to economics' current view of man.

The core principle of social-learning theory is the following:

> The occurrence of a behavior of a person is determined not only by the nature or importance of goals or reinforcements but also by the person's anticipation or expectancy that these goals will occur.[13]

The *value of reinforcement* for social-learning theorists is what economists call the *value,* or *utility,* of the prize. The *anticipation,* or *expectancy,* for social-learning theorists is what economists call *probability.* Multiplying reinforcement value by expectancy is conceptually the same as multiplying probability by utility of the prize. The framework is the same; how it is used and interpreted differs.

Economics and psychology, therefore, can at least *begin* on the same square of the checkerboard of behavioral sciences, even if they end up far apart. But in other areas even their starting points are light years apart. In those areas I believe economics must reform itself to merge minds and markets.

Error, Perception, Observation

A new behavioral economics must first embrace the idea that human beings err. A considerable part of psychology is devoted to elucidating the systematic errors people make. A major part of economics is built on the idea that the very term *theory of errors* is a contradiction in terms. As George Stigler has argued, the concept of waste, for instance, is not a useful economic concept because "waste is error, . . . and it will not become a useful concept until we have a theory of error." The implication is that a theory of error, involving the assumption of "nonmaximizing behavior," is, as Stigler says, "a mighty methodological leap into the unknown."[14] But perhaps the leap is not so great, nor the unknown so terrible. Psychologists know a great deal about errors and have many theories about them. Their results are a public good free to all and positively welcome free riders from other sciences. Using those results might save us from claims like the following, recently published in economics' leading professional journal:

> Note further that if heroin were used even though the subsequent adverse consequences were accurately anticipated, the utility of the user would be greater than it would be if he were prevented from using heroin.[15]

Even in the economic theory of drug addiction—an area where Irving Fisher pleaded for more research (see chapter 3)—the economic theory of choice will not permit error. Just to make sure this is understood, the authors state in a footnote that when they describe addictive effects as "harmful," they refer only to the sign of one of the mathematical derivatives in their equations, and do not mean "that it is unwise for addicts to consume such commodities."[16]

One of the frequent ways people err relates to the potential differences between reality and the way it is *perceived*. Whatever the quality of their vision, everybody sees reality through spectacles whose lenses consist of psychological factors such as emotion and past experience. Earlier, I argued that it is the perceived money supply, rather than the statistical one, that is crucial to the economy. How we perceive the credibility of government, the anticipated behavior of others, and a wide range of other variables, and not the actuality of those variables, is what in the end determines behavior. Economics must realign its theories and premises to take into account perception and the frequent and systematic diversion of perception from reality.

This leads me to a third major area (in addition to errors and perceptions) where economics must undergo change. The only known way to determine people's perceptions is by studying them. Experiments, questionnaires, surveys, and in particular small-group studies are research tools much less acceptable in economics than in other social sciences. Though such studies do exist in economics, many of them resulting in important and widely cited findings, it remains true that most economic research comprises either theoretical model building or empirical testing using existing, highly aggregated data. A doctoral thesis in economics based on data originated and generated by the candidate is as rare as a doctoral thesis in psychology that is *not* based on such data. Sooner or later, we must accept the idea that a 200-million-person economy cannot be understood, let alone guided, until we fully understand the economic psychology of the individuals who make up that 200-million figure. And that understanding will be denied us so long as we abnegate the direct study and observation of individual behavior.

Economic journals now appear willing to provide scarce pages for accounts of experiments with pigeons and rats.[17] These experiments tend to confirm for *animals* basic premises of microeconomic behavior of humans. It would be comforting to find the same openness to experiments with human subjects.

These reflections bring to mind the story of a long-married couple driving their Cadillac down the turnpike, the husband at the wheel. The wife complains to the husband that once, when they were first married, they sat very close together. The husband responds wistfully that *he* hasn't moved.

It is the same with economics, which began its life as political economy, with politics, sociology, and psychology firmly present. Gradually it drifted away from the other social and behavioral sciences in its quest for scientific and mathematical rigor. What other disciplines are saying, softly, is: *We* haven't moved. Economics should, and, I believe, will reestablish its former relationships with these other disciplines. Doing so will not be easy. It will require abandonment of some of the most fundamental assumptions economics now holds dear.

Keynes once noted that the basic axiom of Euclidean geometry is that parallel lines never meet. When Euclidean geometers encounter parallel straight lines that *do* in fact meet, he observed that they rebuke the lines rather than the geometry.[18] It is interesting that the two pioneers of non-Euclidean geometries, Hugo Riemann and Nicholas Lobachevsky, each dumped Euclid's *parallel lines never meet* assumption, and proceeded to try to build new geometries while fully expecting to collide with an absurdity or contradiction that reaffirmed Euclid. But instead of colliding with an absurdity, as expected, they each presented the world with powerful new geometrical systems.

Economics should embrace three new ideas: the possibility that human agents err, the centrality of human perceptions, and the necessity for direct observations of individuals and small groups. If it does so, these new "axioms" will lead to a new and more powerful science of choice. They will eliminate some current absurdities in economics rather than lead to new ones. And they may, I would hope, inject fresh insights into the two-century-old debate between free markets and planning—a debate whose weary combatants have heard each other's arguments so often that responses can be made in code or by number.

The Invisible Hand, One Last Time

The great fault line within psychology lies between Freud and Skinner. In economics, it lies between Smith and Marx—between free enterprise and government intervention.

In principle the plea to integrate the concepts and techniques of psychology with mainstream economics need not join up with either Adam Smith or Karl Marx. A distinction is commonly drawn between positive and normative economics. Positive economics deals with what is—Pigou's *light*. It focuses on testable, falsifiable (capable of being proven false) propositions. Normative economics centers around what ought to be—Pigou's *fruit*. Smith and Marx joust in normative tournaments. Behavioral economics asks anew, what *is*.

The tree of science has at rare times borne fruit in utter darkness. I am reminded of this each time I look at the calendar. Invented in 46 B.C., the Julian calendar was, after fifteen centuries of service, a full two weeks out of kilter. A new calendar, named after Pope Gregory, was drawn up in 1582. Fifty years earlier, Nicolaus Koppernigk (Copernicus) had, literally, seen the light—the sun as the earth spins around it. But the calendar makers kept faith with the pope and rejected Copernicus's theory and computations. They firmly believed the sun revolved around the earth, and they based their data on this. The result: our Gregorian calendar, which is off by only one day in every three millennia.

Contemporary economics and the policies it trumpets commit less propitious errors. A new set of positive propositions inevitably leads to different normative ones. And no book on contemporary economics can avoid addressing the central normative issue of markets versus meddling. Let me briefly outline the stand behavioral economics might suggest.

The most famous "Exhibit A" for free markets, seen by millions of television viewers, is Milton Friedman's lead pencil. The price system and the free market, Professor Friedman explains eloquently, bring cedar from northern California, graphite from Ceylon, rapeseed oil from Indonesia, and brass from elsewhere to Wilkes-Barre, Pennsylvania, where the pencils are manufactured in just the right quantity and quality for our needs. "No one sitting in a central office gave orders," Professor Friedman notes. "No military policy enforced the orders that were not given."[19]

Thomas Schelling gives us "Exhibit B"—the pat of butter

wrapped in aluminum foil on the airline traveler's tray that, by the miracles of the price system, gets to the right place, a Boeing 747, at the right time, noon, at 30,000 feet altitude, with no central planning.[20]

Underlying Friedman's pencil and Schelling's part of butter is the idea of voluntary exchange. When people buy and sell freely in markets and each applies two-question logic, no transaction takes place unless it benefits both the buyer and seller, it is argued. Schelling refers to so-called waves of selling and buying on the stock market and points out that "there is no known way to sell a share of stock—even a share you do not possess—except to somebody who buys it. And no way to buy except from somebody who sells."[21]

In Professor Friedman's words, "If an exchange between two parties is voluntary, it will not take place unless both believe they will benefit from it. Most economic fallacies derive from the neglect of this simple insight, from the tendency to assume that there is a fixed pie, that one party can gain only at the expense of another."[22]

If all transactions benefit both buyer and seller, then freedom to enact those transactions must produce at least as efficient a result as a perfectly controlled, regulated system. And surely in reality, there exists no perfect centralized system. The conclusion that logically follows from this is the essential, basic theorem in economics, Adam Smith's invisible hand principle: A collection of individuals operating in unfettered markets, each seeking only his own well-being, will generate the largest possible social loaf. The trouble with this argument is that the type of transaction Professor Friedman describes—voluntary exchanges between two parties, with no one else involved—is the exception in economic life rather than the rule.

It is true that all economic relationships sooner or later find expression in transactions—usually those in which goods and services are exchanged for money. Some of those transactions are initially unilateral in nature, such as decisions taken by people about how much of their income to spend or to save, how to hold their wealth, and so on. These decisions are taken by each person in consultation with himself and perhaps advisers, based on what he believes is in his own interest. Other transactions are on the surface bilateral—for example, the purchase of an automobile from an eager salesman—but may in fact involve many others. Suppose that purchase arises from the desire to buy ahead of expected price rises. Using the model described earlier, if everyone tried that, dwindling stocks of cars would soon stiffen the terms salesmen offered and the prices would rise.

The invisible hand does not operate on unilateral transactions. What people choose to save or spend may be far from the social optimum, for example. Nor does the invisible hand work well on bilateral transactions affecting third, fourth, or nth parties. The buyer and seller may both be happy, but what about the others who feel the effects of the transaction in the air they breathe, the water they drink, the streets they walk on, or the roads they drive on? In the bilateral transaction, who speaks out for their interests?

In economic life, I have tried to show that again and again, in contexts ranging from schooling to labor, spending, saving, and risk taking, one economic agent, acting legitimately in his own self-interest, causes harm to others, and ultimately, to himself as well. Evading taxes necessitates higher tax rates for those who pay their true shares. People who accelerate their spending in anticipation of higher future prices help cause more inflation. Slacking off at work increases the burden on others or lowers the output available for everyone. In every case the amount of "harm" caused to any one person is very small. But a great many other people may be affected, directly and indirectly. And a very small number (average harm to a person) multiplied by a proportionately large one (total number of people affected) can amount to a substantial aggregate amount of damage. What, then, is the appropriate role for government?

Big Government, Small Government, or None of the Above

Once psychology is used to help understand our underlying social and economic problems, it is clear that neither nineteenth-century capitalism nor twentieth-century socialism or planning is the answer. Neither system alone, I believe, is adequate to deal with conflicts that will threaten our well-being in the twenty-first century.

Chapter and verse for those who seek to limit the role of government in economic affairs generally come from either Adam Smith —often-cited passages confine the role of government to national defense—or Thomas Jefferson. In his first inaugural address, at the turn of the nineteenth-century, Jefferson delimited "wise and frugal government, which shall restrain men from injuring one another, which shall leave them otherwise free to regulate their own pursuits of industry and improvement."[23] This theme was later echoed by John Stuart Mill's famous essay *On Liberty,* published as America ended its bloody Civil War over states' rights. "The only purpose for which power can be rightfully exercised over any member of a civilized community, against his will, is to prevent harm to others."[24]

"The only part of the conduct of anyone, for which he is amenable," Mill continued, "is that which concerns others. In the part which merely concerns himself, his independence is, of right, absolute. Over himself, over his own body and mind, the individual is sovereign."[25]

On their own terms, I would argue that Jefferson and Mill were outright socialists. My text comes from another inaugural address —Roosevelt's second Inaugural (the first such address, incidentally, to be given on January 20 instead of on March 4 as was previously the practice).

"We have always known that heedless self-interest was bad morals," Roosevelt said. "We now know that it is bad economics."[26] In 1937 history had given new force to the idea of "bad economics." Self-interest coupled with tightly woven interdependence spells trouble.

I quoted in chapter 2 an early social psychologist, James Baldwin: "We are all members of one another."[27] Just how true this is was shown in mathematics by a political scientist and in life by a psychologist.

Small World

Ithiel de Sola Pool once calculated the odds that any two Americans drawn at random know each other. Surveys showed that in the course of one hundred days, an average person comes in contact with five hundred other people. If every person knows five hundred other people, there is only one chance in two hundred thousand that any two Americans drawn at random will know one another. But the probability of their having a mutual acquaintance rises sharply. And the chances are better than 50/50 that any two people can be linked up with two intermediate acquaintances.

Psychologist Stanley Milgram set out to test the *"small world"* theory. A group of people from all walks of life in Wichita, Kansas, was chosen. Each person was given a folder with the name of a target person in Cambridge, Massachusetts, a set of rules for reaching that person—intermediate contacts could be only people known on a first-name basis—and a roster for listing the name of each person in the chain. In Milgram's words:

> Four days after the folders were sent to a group of starting persons in Kansas, an instructor at the Episcopal Theological Seminary (in Cambridge) approached our target person on the street. "Alice," he said, thrusting a brown folder toward her, "this is for you." We found to our surprise that the document had started with a wheat farmer in

Kansas. He had passed it on to an Episcopalian minister in his home town, who sent it to the Minister who taught in Cambridge, who gave it to the target person. Altogether the number of intermediate links between starting person and target person amounted to *two!*[28]

In the experiment, chains varied in length from two to ten intermediate acquaintances. The median was only five. It is truly a small world.

Jefferson as a Socialist

To paraphrase Thomas Jefferson and John Stuart Mill, the part of our conduct for which we are amenable is that which concerns others. By my argument, therefore, that covers almost every conceivable human action. If, as Mill said, power can rightfully be exercised over members of the community to protect others, then that power can be used to regulate virtually every facet of our economic life. I do not believe, however, that such regulation is in itself the sole answer to our problems.

Sir John Hicks wrote in 1941, "Man in society . . . is sometimes able to achieve his individual ends, not by increasing the efficiency of production, but at the expense of his neighbors."[29] Such behavior can perhaps be reduced or even halted temporarily by imposition of heavy penalties. But psychologists tell us that sticks—negative reinforcement or punishment for disapproved behavior—are generally less effective than carrots—positive reinforcement of desired behavior.

Garrett Hardin quoted Alfred North Whitehead, who defined tragedy as "the solemnity of the remorseless working of things."[30] The tragedy of self-interest coupled with interdependence is the remorseless inevitability of the trap it leads us into. It cannot be legislated away. Is the problem one of lack of awareness? Do people not *realize* that many of their actions, while individually rational, benefit them at the expense of others? I believe that on the whole, people *are* aware of this. Chapter 7 provided some evidence of this.

We must realize, as Hardin urges, that for the crucial economic problems we face, there are no *technical* solutions. A technical solution is defined by Hardin as one that requires a change "only in the techniques of the natural sciences, demanding little or nothing in the way of change in human values or ideas of morality."[31] A technical solution for inflation would involve budget cuts, changes in taxes, tinkering with interest rates and the money supply, and other conventional steps. A human solution involves altering how people perceive, and act toward, one another.

Altruism Is Legitimate

The first step toward fundamentally resolving our economic problems must be to alter a particular part of social consciousness: the assumption that, as Hardin puts it, "decisions reached individually will, in fact, be the best decisions for an entire society."[32] Adam Smith said that "what is prudence in the conduct of every private family can scarce be folly in that of a great kingdom."[33] Yet as a professor of logic Adam Smith surely taught the perils of the fallacy of composition: claiming what is true of component parts is also true of the whole. In our era, and perhaps to a lesser extent in Adam Smith's, what is prudence in the conduct of every private family may be greater than folly for the kingdom as a whole, and ultimately, for the family itself. Widespread understanding of that fact of twentieth-century life is essential.

The second step, once awareness is heightened, is to provide some alternative for unbridled egoism and to legitimize altruism. A construction manager once asked a *Wall Street Journal* reporter rhetorically, "Are the people in this country willing to sacrifice to stop inflation?" His answer: "Absolutely not. It's asinine to think that any one of us is going to voluntarily give up anything. We're going to have to be forced."[34]

A sales manager told the same reporter, candidly: "I'm like most Americans—greedy and very selfish. I won't give up anything. I think most of us are that way—until it's put to us that we absolutely have to."[35] The paradox of sacrifices is that if enough people are willing to make them, the sacrifice itself, and the need to compel it, vanish. What this implies, then, is the need for a fundamental change in both psychology and morals. Generally, values and ethics are topics science puts well beyond the Pale. But they can no longer be skirted.

Adam Smith as a Psychologist

Our search for solutions has now come full circle, back to the wise and frugal Scot. In *Wealth of Nations* (1776) Adam Smith's ideal economic system was simple. Book Five, on "the revenue of the sovereign," calls for a minimal role for government, confined mainly to national defense.

But as a philosopher and a psychologist, roles he filled long before he tackled economics, Adam Smith took a quite different view of society. His *Theory of Moral Sentiments* (1759) bases all moral feelings—without which, no society could survive, even if every second person was a policeman—on a fundamental human quality: mutual sympathy. It is possible, even likely, that Adam Smith's social prescription in the spirit of 1759—respect, love, and sympathy—is more relevant, feasible, and fitting than his more widely touted spirit of 1776—self-interest.

The late Fred Hirsch, in his book *Social Limits to Growth,* argued that twentieth-century man is led to believe he is *obligated* to act in his own self-interest, in the interests of efficiency, and in aid of the invisible hand.[36] In the beginning free markets and the price system that they embody were designed to serve the needs of man. Does man now exist to serve free markets?

We are free to choose. Only in a truly free community is that choice circumscribed by its effect on other people. It is here, where science and morality blend, that psychology and economics should together begin their quest.

Conclusion

Psychology *has* in the past found use in economics. It has served as economics' alibi for failure. Let psychology now become a springboard for economics' future successes.

NOTES

Chapter One

1. For a lucid analysis of "wrong-way" propositions in economics, see W. A. Lewis, "Rising Prices: 1899–1913 and 1950–1979," *Scandinavian Journal of Economics* 82 (1980): 425–436.
2. "Sustained monetary restraint, by encouraging greater confidence in the price outlook, will in time help bring interest rates lower." Paul A. Volcker, Chairman, Federal Reserve Board, in the *New York Times,* 22 July, 1981, p. D1.
3. Auguste Comte, quoted by A. C. Pigou, *The Economics of Welfare* (London: Macmillan, 1920), p. 5.
4. The account of Nathan Rothschild's coup is drawn in part from John Reeves, *The Rothschilds: The Financial Rulers of Nations* (New York: Gordon Press, 1975), p. 170. Reeves embellishes the legend by describing how Nathan Rothschild was actually present at Waterloo and rushed back to London to make his profit. Virginia Coles, in *The Rothschilds: A Family of Fortune* (New York: Alfred A. Knopf, 1973), p. 50 debunks the whole tale, pointing out that Rothschild had already made huge sums lending to Wellington long before Waterloo. She traces the origins of his post-Waterloo coup to the inventions of a French journalist, who used them to try to blackmail James Rothschild in Paris.
5. A. C. Pigou, *The Economics of Welfare,* p. 202n.
6. U.S. Bureau of the Census, *Statistical Abstract of the United States: 1979* (Washington, D.C.: U.S. Bureau of the Census, 1979), p. 625.
7. *Webster's Third New International Dictionary* (Springfield, Mass.: Merriam, 1976) and the *Oxford English Dictionary* (Oxford: Oxford University Press, 1933).
8. Albert Einstein, "Physics and Reality," *Franklin Institute Journal* 221 (1936).
9. Alfred Marshall, *Principles of Economics*, 8th ed. (London: Macmillan, [1890] 1962), p. 38.
10. George Hendry, "Letter to the Editor," in the *New York Times,* 25 March, 1980.
11. U.S. Bureau of the Census, *Statistical Abstract,* pp. 487–489.
12. The minimum-cost diet is from Victor E. Smith, *Electronic Computation of Human Diets* (East Lansing, Mich.: Michigan State University Business Studies, 1963). His menu was originally calculated for relative prices prevailing in 1955. By substituting items whose relative prices fell during 1955–1979 for items whose relative prices rose, households could reduce even further the twenty-three dollar minimum-cost budget.
13. Engel's data on Saxony is from Marshall, *Principles,* p. 97n.

Notes

14. William J. Baumol, personal communication.
15. Paul Samuelson, "The Pure Theory of Public Expenditures," *Review of Economics and Statistics* 36 (1954): 387–389; and "Diagrammatic Exposition of a Theory of Public Expenditure," *Review of Economics and Statistics* 37 (1955): 350–356.
16. Bertrand Russell, "Recent Work on the Principles of Mathematics," *International Monthly* 4 (1901): 184.
17. Gary Becker, "A Theory of Marriage: Part I," *Journal of Political Economy* 81 (1973): 813–846; Gary Becker, "A Theory of Marriage: Part II," *Journal of Political Economy* 82 (1974): S11–S26; and Gary Becker, E. M. Landes, and R. T. Michael, "An Economic Analysis of Marital Instability," *Journal of Political Economy* 85 (1977): 1141–1187.
18. Paul Samuelson, *Foundations of Economic Analysis* (New York: Atheneum, 1965), pp. 91–92.
19. Marshall, *Principles,* p. 1.
20. Leon Walras, *Elements of Pure Economics* [1871] (London: Allen & Unwin, 1954).
21. Milton Friedman, "The Marshallian Demand Curve," *Journal of Political Economy* 57 (1949): 489.
22. In *Bartlett's Familiar Quotations,* 14th ed. (Boston: Little, Brown, 1968), from *Punch* 29 (1855).
23. William Baumol, personal communication.
24. Richard Lipsey and Peter Steiner, *Economics,* 5th ed. (New York: Harper & Row, 1972), p. 54.
25. Tibor Scitovsky, *The Joyless Economy* (New York: Oxford University Press, 1976), p. 28.
26. Frank Knight, *The Economic Organization,* multilith (Chicago: University of Chicago Press, 1933).
27. Rudyard Kipling, "The Elephant's Child," in *Just So Stories,* [1902] (New York: Doubleday, 1972).
28. Walter Guzzardi, "The New Down-to-Earth Economics," *Fortune* (Dec. 31, 1978): 72–79.
29. Harvey Leibenstein, "The Missing Link: Micro-Micro Theory?" *Journal of Economic Literature* 17 (1979): 477–502.
30. Marshall, *Principles,* p. 3.
31. Oscar Wilde, *The Works of Oscar Wilde* (London: Spring Books, 1965), p. 31.
32. Norman Cousins, "The Fallacy of Cost-Benefit Ratio," *Saturday Review* (April 14, 1979): 8.
33. *Business Week* (March 17, 1980): 52.
34. U.S. Bureau of the Census, *Statistical Abstract,* p. 71.
35. William Stanley Jevons, *Theory of Political Economy,* [1874], 3rd ed. (London: Macmillan, 1884), p. 265.
36. Lionel Robbins, *Essay on the Nature and Significance of Economic Science,* [1933], 2nd ed. (London: St. Martins, 1935).
37. Quoted by Erik Erikson in "Life Cycle," *International Encyclopedia of the Social Sciences,* vol. 9 (New York and London: Macmillan/Free Press, 1968), p. 290.

Notes

Chapter Two

1. H. A. Simon, *Models of Man* (New York: John Wiley & Sons, 1957), p. xxiii.
2. Robert Solow, "A Contribution to the Theory of Growth," *Quarterly Journal of Economics* 70 (1956): 65.
3. Simon, *Models of Man*, p. xxiii.
4. Alfred Marshall, *Principles of Economics*, 8th ed. (London: Macmillan, 1962), p. 643.
5. Orville Brim, "Socialization Through the Life Cycle," in Orville Brim and Stanton Wheeler, eds., *Socialization After Childhood: Two Essays* (New York: John Wiley & Sons, 1966), p. 5.
6. James Duesenberry, cited in S. Maital, "The Nature of Man in Conventional Microeconomic Theory," working paper, Woodrow Wilson School of Public and International Affairs, Princeton University, 1978.
7. A. Bandura, "Psychotherapy Based on Modelling Practices," in A. E. Bergin and S. L. Garfield, eds., *Handbook of Psychotherapy and Behavior Change* (New York: John Wiley & Sons, 1971), pp. 653–709.
8. James W. Baldwin, "Social and Ethical Interpretations in Mental Development: A Study," in *Social Psychology*, 3rd ed. (London: Macmillan, 1902), p. 30; quoted by R. B. Cairns, J. A. Green, and D. J. MacCombie, "The Dynamics of Social Development," in *Early Experiences and Early Behavior: Implications for Social Development* (New York: Academic Press, 1980).
9. James Duesenberry, *Income, Saving and the Theory of Consumer Behavior* (Cambridge, Mass: Harvard University Press, 1949).
10. W. Arthur Lewis, *Theory of Economic Growth* (London: Allen & Unwin, 1955), p. 14.
11. Sigmund Freud, *Leonardo da Vinci, A Study in Psychosexuality* [1916] (New York, Random House, 1966).
12. *Wall Street Journal*, 7 March 1980, p. 32.
13. *Family Weekly*, 20 March 1978.
14. Texas Council on Economic Education, "Helping Teachers to Teach Economics," *Exxon Motoring News*, 17 (1978).
15. *Yediot Aharonot*, 15 June 1980, p. 19.
16. Marilyn Kourilsky, "The Kinder-Economy: A Case Study of Kindergarten Pupils' Acquisition of Economic Concepts," *Elementary School Journal* 77 (1977): 182–191.
17. Thomas Schelling, *Micromotives and Macrobehavior* (New York: Norton, 1978), pp. 21–22.
18. Adam Smith, "Of Restraints Upon Importation," in *The Wealth of Nations*, Book IV (New York: Random House, Modern Library, 1937), p. 423.
19. *Bartlett's Familiar Quotations*, 14th ed. (Boston: Little, Brown, 1968).
20. Adam Smith, *The Wealth of Nations* [1776] (New York: Random House, Modern Library, 1937).
21. See chapter 11, footnote 28.
22. Garrett Hardin, "The Tragedy of the Commons," *Science* 162 (1968): 1243–1248.
23. Marshall, *Principles*, pp. 599–600.

Notes

24. Karl Marx, *Capital,* vol. 2 (New York: Random House, 1936), chap. 15.
25. "Child Labor," in *Encyclopedia Americana,* vol. 6 (Montreal: Americana of Canada, 1953).
26. G. H. Elder, Jr., *Children of the Great Depression* (Chicago: University of Chicago Press, 1974), p. 291, cited by Uri Bronfenbrenner in *The Ecology of Human Development: Experiments by Nature and Design* (Cambridge, Mass: Harvard University Press, 1979).
27. American Council on Life Insurance, *Current Social Issues* (Washington, D.C.: American Council on Life Insurance, April, 1979).
28. Ibid.
29. J. M. Keynes, "Economic Possibilities for our Grandchildren," *Essays in Persuasion* (London: Macmillan, 1933).
30. George P. Knight and Spencer Kagan, "Development of Prosocial and Competitive Behaviors in Anglo-American and Mexican-American Children," *Child Development* 48 (1977): 1385–1394; S. Kagan and M. C. Madsen, "Experimental Analysis of Cooperation and Competition of Anglo-American and Mexican Children," *Developmental Psychology* 6 (1972): 49–59.
31. M. C. Madsen, "Cooperative and Competitive Motivation of Children in Three Mexican Sub-cultures," *Psychological Reports* 20 (1967): 1307–1320.
32. D. Rosenhan, "Some Origins of Concern for Others," in P. Mussen, J. Langer, and M. Covington, eds., *Trends and Issues in Developmental Psychology* (New York: Holt, Rinehart & Winston, 1969).
33. M. R. Yarrow, P. M. Scott, and C. Z. Waxler, "Learning Concern for Others," *Developmental Psychology* 8 (1973): 240–260.
34. Uri Bronfenbrenner, *The Ecology of Human Development,* p. 53.
35. Joseph Adelson, "Adolescence and the Generation Gap," *Psychology Today* (Feb. 1979): 33–37; Joseph Adelson, "The Mystique of Adolescence," *Psychiatry* 27 (1964): 1–8.
36. James S. Coleman, et al., "Needed: New Routes to Adulthood," in *Youth: Transition to Adulthood* (Chicago: University of Chicago Press, 1974).
37. Oscar Lewis, *La Vida* (London: Panther, 1968), p. 53.
38. David Elkind, "Growing Up Faster," *Psychology Today* 12 (1979): 38–45.
39. Carl Danziger and Matthew Greenwald, "Alternatives," cited in *Trend Analysis Program Report,* no. 8 (Washington, D.C.: American Council of Life Insurance, n.d.).
40. Bettye M. Caldwell, "Aggression and Hostility in Young Children," *Young Children* 32 (1977): 4–13.
41. Marshall, *Principles,* p. 597.
42. Marshall, *Principles,* p. 171*n*.
43. Henry P. David and Wendy H. Baldwin, "Childbearing and Child Development: Demographic and Psychosocial Trends," *American Psychologist* 34 (1979): 866–871.
44. "The Baby Boom Muddies the Picture," *Wall Street Journal,* 27 March 1980, p. 26.
45. Quoted in "The Baby Boom," p. 26.
46. U.S. Bureau of the Census, *Statistical Abstract of the United States: 1979* (Washington, D.C.: U.S. Bureau of the Census, 1979), pp. 8–9.

Notes

Chapter Three

1. Roy Harrod, *Life of Keynes* (London: Macmillan, 1951), p. 8.
2. See Don Patinkin, "Interest," *International Encyclopedia of the Social Sciences*, vol. 7 (New York: Macmillan/Free Press, 1968), p. 471.
3. Irving Fisher, *The Rate of Interest* (London: Macmillan, 1907).
4. *New York Times,* 19 February 1980, p. A1.
5. *Economic Report of the President, 1980* (Washington, D.C.: U.S. Government Printing Office, 1980).
6. *Trenton Times,* 6 April 1980, p. C1.
7. Sigmund Freud, "Formulations on the Two Principles of Mental Functioning," *The Complete Psychological Works of Sigmund Freud,* vol. 13 (London: Hogarth Press, 1946).
8. Irving Fisher, "The 'Impatience' Theory of Interest," *Scientia* vol. 9 (18) (1911): 380–401.
9. U.S. Bureau of the Census, *Statistical Abstract of the United States: 1979* (Washington, D.C.: U.S. Bureau of the Census, 1979), p. 73.
10. Milton Friedman, "Windfalls, the 'Horizon' and Related Concepts in the Permanent Income Hypothesis," in Carl Christ et al., eds., *Measurement in Economics: Studies in Mathematical Economics and Econometrics* (Stanford, Calif.: Stanford University Press, 1963).
11. M. Kurz, R. G. Spiegelman, and R. W. West, "The Experimental Horizon and the Rate of Time Preference for the Seattle and Denver Income Maintenance Experiments," *Memorandum 21* (Stanford, Calif.: Stanford Research Institute, November 1973).
12. W. Mischel, "Process in Delay of Gratification," in L. Berkowitz, ed., *Advances in Experimental Social Psychology,* vol. 7 (New York: Academic Press, 1974).
13. W. Mischel, "Preference for Delayed Reinforcement: An Experimental Study of a Cultural Observation," *Journal of Abnormal and Social Psychology* 56 (1958): 57–61.
14. W. Mischel and R. Metzner, "Preference for Delayed Reward As a Function of Age, Intelligence and Length of Delay Interval," *Journal of Abnormal and Social Psychology* 64 (1962): 425–431.
15. Jean Piaget, *The Child's Conception of Time* (New York: Ballantine, 1971).
16. Mischel and Metzner, "Preference for Delayed Reward," pp. 429–430.
17. K. H. David and S. Bochner, "Immediate Versus Delayed Reward Among Arnhemland Aborigines," *Journal of Social Psychology* 73 (1967): 157–159.
18. W. Mischel and E. B. Ebbeson, "Attention in Delay of Gratification," *Journal of Personality and Social Psychology* 16 (1970): 329–337; W. Mischel, E. B. Ebbeson, and A. R. Zeiss, "Cognitive and Attentional Mechanisms in Delay of Gratification," *Journal of Personality and Social Psychology* 21 (1972): 204–218; W. Mischel and B. Moore, "Effects of Attention to Symbolically Presented Rewards on Self-Control," *Journal of Personality and Social Psychology* 28 (1973): 172–179.
19. W. Mischel, "Father Absence and Delay of Gratification," *Journal of Abnormal and Social Psychology* 63 (1961): 116–124; W. Mischel, "Delay of Gratifi-

cation, Need for Achievement and Acquiescence in Another Culture," *Journal of Abnormal and Social Psychology* 63 (1961): 543–522.

20. Sharone Maital, "An Analysis of Delay of Gratification as a Two-Part Process," (master's dissertation, Tel Aviv University, 1976).

21. W. Mischel, "Process in Delay of Gratification," p. 261.

22. Christopher Jencks et al., *Inequality* (New York: Harper & Row, Colophon, 1973), p. 226.

23. James Morgan et al., *Five Thousand American Families*, vols. 1, 2, and 3, (Ann Arbor: Institute for Social Research, University of Michigan, 1974, 1975).

24. Oscar Lewis, *The Children of Sanchez* (New York: Random House, 1964), p. xxvii.

25. Ibid.

26. E. Liebow, *Talley's Corner* (Boston: Little, Brown, 1968).

27. A. R. Mahrer, "The Role of Expectancy in Delayed Reinforcement," *Journal of Experimental Psychology* 52 (1956): 101–105.

28. J. K. Galbraith, *The Nature of Mass Poverty* (Cambridge, Mass.: Harvard University Press, 1978).

29. Allison Davis, *Psychology of the Child in the Middle Class* (Pittsburgh, Pa.: University of Pittsburgh Press, 1960).

30. Allison Davis and John Dollard, *Children of Bondage* (Washington, D.C.: American Council on Education, 1940); S. Kagan and M. Madsen, "Cooperation and Competition of Mexican, Mexican-American, and Anglo-American Children of Two Ages Under Four Instructional Sets," *Developmental Psychology* 5 (1971): 32–39.

31. Allison Davis, *Social Class Influences Upon Learning* (Cambridge, Mass.: Harvard University Press, 1962).

32. A. C. Pigou, *The Economics of Welfare* (London: Macmillan, 1920), pp. 112–113.

33. A. Bandura and W. Mischel, "Modification of Self-Imposed Delay of Reward Through Live and Symbolic Models," *Journal of Personality and Social Psychology* 2 (1965): 698–705.

34. Edward C. Banfield, *The Unheavenly City* (Boston: Little, Brown, 1968), pp. 229, 231.

35. One such case is the *Peter Doe* case; the Supreme Court accepted the claim for minimum quality of education, but it rejected the suit because it would "open the floodgates."

36. Anthony Davids and Jack Sidman, "A Pilot Study—Impulsivity, Time Orientation and Delayed Gratification in Future Scientists and in Underachieving High School Students," *Exceptional Children* 29 (1969): 170–174.

37. U.S. Bureau of the Census, *Statistical Abstract,* pp. 461–467.

38. Julian Simon and Rita J. Simon, "Class, Status and Savings of Negroes," *The American Sociologist* (August 1968): 218–219.

39. Oscar Handlin, *Race and Nationality in American Life* (Boston: Little, Brown, 1948).

40. Irving Norton Fisher, *My Father, Irving Fisher* (New York: Comet Press, 1956), p. 77.

41. Milton Friedman, quoted in *Forbes* (April 28, 1980): 36; James Tobin, "An Essay on Principles of Debt Management," in Commission on Money and Credit, *Fiscal and Debt Management Policies* (Englewood Cliffs, N.J.: Prentice Hall, 1963), pp. 143–218.

Notes

42. Alfred Marshall, *Principles of Economics,* 8th ed. (London: Macmillan, 1962), p. 638.
43. W. S. Jevons, *The Theory of Political Economy* [1874], 3rd ed. (London: Macmillan, 1884), p. 72; Pigou, *The Economics of Welfare*, p. 25; Roy Harrod, *Towards a Dynamic Economics* (London: Macmillan, 1948), p. 40; Maurice Dobb, *An Essay on Economic Growth and Planning* (London: Routledge, Kegan Paul, 1960), p. 40; Frank Ramsay, "A Mathematical Theory of Saving," *Economic Journal* 38 (1928): 543–559.
44. United Nations Industrial Development Organization, *Guidelines for Project Evaluation* (New York: United Nations, 1972); J. K. Schmedtje, "On Estimating the Cost of Capital," Report No. EC-138, World Bank (Washington, D. C., 1965).
45. *Trenton Times,* 6 April, 1980, p. C1.
46. Fisher, *My Father, Irving Fisher*.
47. Marshall, *Principles,* p. 484.

Chapter Four

1. U. S. Bureau of the Census, *Statistical Abstract of the United States: 1979* (Washington, D. C.: U. S. Bureau of the Census, 1979), p. 132.
2. Edwin Markham, "The Man with the Hoe," in Louis Untermeyer, ed., *A Treasury of Great Poems* (New York: Simon & Schuster, 1955), p. 992.
3. Theodore Schultz, "Capital: Human," in *International Encyclopedia of the Social Sciences,* vol. 2 (New York and London: Macmillan/Free Press, 1968), pp. 278–287.
4. Irving Fisher, *The Rate of Interest* (London: Macmillan, 1907), p. 225.
5. Alfred Marshall, Appendix D, "Definitions of Capital," in *Principles of Economics,* 8th ed. (London: Macmillan, 1962).
6. Ibid.
7. T. W. Schultz, "Investment in Human Capital," *American Economic Review* 51 (1961): 1–17; and Gary Becker, *Human Capital* (New York: Columbia University Press, 1964).
8. Marshall, *Principles,* p. 115.
9. Becker, *Human Capital,* p. 146; and Dorothy Projector, "Average Family Holdings of Specific Types of Net Wealth (Dec. 31, 1962)," in "Consumer Assets," *International Encyclopedia of the Social Sciences,* vol. 3 (New York and London: Macmillan/Free Press, 1968), p. 345.
10. H. S. Houthakker, "Education and Income," *Review of Economics & Statistics,* table 2 (Feb. 1959): 26.
11. W. Lee Hansen, "Total and Private Rates of Return to Investment in Schooling," *Journal of Political Economy* 81 (1963).
12. Randall Keith Filer, "The Influence of Affective Human Capital on the Wage Equation," in Ronald G. Ehrenberg, ed., *Research in Labor Economics*, vol. 3 (Greenwich, Conn.: J.A.I. Press, 1981); Randall Keith Filer, "The Influence of Affective Human Capital of the Wage Equation," working paper, Brandeis University, Department of Economics, 1979.

13. Ibid., p. 34.
14. Ibid., p. 46.
15. Gene Dalton and Paul H. Thompson, "Accelerating Obsolescence of Older Engineers," *Harvard Business Review* 49 (1971): 57–67.
16. James L. Medoff, "The Earnings Function: A Glimpse Inside the Black Box," mimeo (Cambridge, Mass.: Harvard University, 1977); James L. Medoff and Katharine G. Abraham, "Experience, Performance and Earnings," mimeo (Cambridge, Mass.: Harvard University, 1978); and James L. Medoff and Katharine G. Abraham, "Can Productivity Capital Differentials Really Explain the Earnings Differentials Associated with Demographic Characteristics? The Case of Experience," Discussion Paper no. 705 (Cambridge, Mass.: Harvard University, 1979).
17. Medoff and Abraham, "Experience, Performance and Earnings," p. 20.
18. Medoff and Abraham, "Productivity Capital Differentials," p. 48.
19. Daniel Yankelovich, "Who Gets Ahead in America," *Psychology Today* (July 1979); and Christopher Jencks, interviewed by Christopher T. Cory, "Making It: Can the Odds be Evened," *Psychology Today* (July 1979).
20. *The Book of Popular Science,* vol. 9 (New York: Grolier, 1953), p. 3671.
21. See J. R. Mercer, *Labeling the Mentally Retarded* (Berkeley, Calif.: University of California Press, 1973); J. R. Mercer and J. F. Lewis, "System of Multicultural Pluralistic Assessment: Conceptual and Technical Manual," Unpublished manuscript; J. Goodman, "The Diagnostic Fallacy: A Critique of Jane Mercer's Concept of Mental Retardation," *Journal of School Psychology* 15 (1977): 197–206; Jane Mercer, "In Defense of Racially and Culturally Nondiscriminatory Assessment," *School Psychology Digest* 8 (1) (1979): 89–115; and Harvey F. Clarizio, "SOMPA: A Symposium Continued: Commentaries," *School Psychology Digest* 8 (2) (1979): 207–209.
22. "A Psychologist Takes a Closer Look at the Recent Landmark Larry P. Opinion," *American Psychological Association Monitor* 10 (1979).
23. "PL-94-142: Answers to the Questions You're Asking," *Instructor* 87 (1978): 63–65, 72–73.
24. George A. Akerlof, "The Market for 'Lemons': Quality, Uncertainty and the Market Mechanism," *Quarterly Journal of Economics* 84 (1970): 488–500.
25. J. E. Hunter and F. L. Schmidt, "Fitting People to Jobs: The Impact of Personnel Selection on National Productivity," in E. A. Fleishman, *Human Performance and Productivity,* cited in Michael Rothschild, "Social Effects of Ability Testing," mimeo, University of Wisconsin, June 1979.
26. Rothschild, "Ability Testing."
27. Ibid.
28. Lee J. Cronbach, "Five Decades of Public Controversy Over Mental Testing," *American Psychologist* 30 (1975): 1–13.
29. Ibid., p. 13.

Notes

Chapter Five

1. Quoted by David Gordon, "Capital-Labor Conflict and the Productivity Slowdown," *American Economic Review* 71 (June 1981): 30.
2. Richard Lipsey and Peter Steiner, *Economics*, 3rd ed. (New York: Harper & Row, 1972), p. 532.
3. E. H. Phelps-Brown, "Seven Centuries of Building Wages," *Economica* (Aug. 1955): 195–206.
4. M. Abramovitz and P. David, "Economic Growth in America: Historical Parables and Realities," Reprint No. 105 (Stanford, Calif.: Stanford University, Center for Research in Economic Growth, 1973).
5. John Kendrick, "Productivity Trends in the United States," in Shlomo Maital and Noah M. Meltz, eds., *Lagging Productivity Growth: Causes and Remedies* (Cambridge, Mass.: Ballinger, 1980), pp. 9–30.
6. Albert Rees, "On Interpreting Productivity Change," in Maital and Meltz, *Lagging Productivity Growth,* pp. 1–6.
7. Quoted by Rees in "Interpreting Productivity Change."
8. Amitai Etzioni, "The Inflation Habit: A Case of Stunted Growth," *Psychology Today* 12 (1979), pp. 14–15.
9. Randall Filer, "The Downturn in Productivity Growth: A New Look at Its Nature and Causes," in Maital and Meltz, *Lagging Productivity Growth,* pp. 109–123.
10. U.S. Bureau of the Census, *Statistical Abstract of the United States: 1979* (Washington, D.C.: U.S. Bureau of the Census, 1979), pp. 798–799.
11. Harvey Leibenstein, *Beyond Economic Man* (Cambridge, Mass.: Harvard University Press, 1976); also, Harvey Leibenstein, "X-Efficiency: From Concept to Theory," *Challenge* 22 (1979).
12. Harvey Leibenstein, interviewed by Edward Meadows, "A Difference of Opinion," *Fortune* (June 1978).
13. George J. Stigler, "The Xistence of X-efficiency," *American Economic Review* 66 (1976): 213–216; Leibenstein's reply: "X-Inefficiency Xists—Reply to an Xorcist," *American Economic Review* 68 (1978): 203–211.
14. Leibenstein, "Difference of Opinion."
15. John P. Shelton, "Allocative Efficiency vs. X-Efficiency: Comment," *American Economic Review* 57 (1967): 1252–1258.
16. Walter Primeux, Jr., "An Assessment of X-Efficiency Gained Through Competition," *Review of Economics and Statistics* 59 (1977): 105–07.
17. Quoted by Leibenstein in "X-Efficiency."
18. Ibid.
19. Central Bureau of Statistics, *Statistical Yearbook* (Jerusalem, Israel: Bank of Israel, 1978).
20. Quoted by Leibenstein in "X-Efficiency."
21. Mieko Nishimizu, "U.S. and Japanese Economic Growth, 1952–1974: An International Comparison," *Economic Journal* 88 (1978); also, M. Nishimizu, "Total Factor Production Analysis: A Disaggregated Study of the Post–War Japanese Economy with Explicit Consideration of Intermediate Inputs and Comparison with the United States," (Ph.D. dissertation, Johns Hopkins University, 1975).

Notes

22. "U.S. Firms, Worried by Productivity Lag, Copy Japan in Seeking Employees' Advice," *Wall Street Journal,* 21 Feb. 1980, p. 48.
23. See Maital and Meltz, *Lagging Productivity Growth.*
24. Adam Smith, *Wealth of Nations,* [1776], (New York: Random House, Modern Library, 1937), p. 3.
25. Ibid., p. 4.
26. Ibid., p. 5.
27. "Automobile," in *Encyclopedia Americana,* vol. 2 (Montreal: Americana of Canada, 1953).
28. Michael Argyle, *The Social Psychology of Work* (New York: Penguin, 1972), p. 33; and "Industrial Engineering," in *Encyclopedia Americana,* vol. 15 (Montreal: Americana of Canada, 1953).
29. Upton Sinclair, *The Jungle,* [1906] (New York: New American Library, 1973).
30. Argyle, *Social Psychology of Work,* p. 34; citing G. Friedman, *The Anatomy of Work* (London: Heinemann, 1961).
31. Matt. 9:17.
32. Winston Churchill, *The Malakand Field Force,* [1898], cited in *Bartlett's Familiar Quotations* (Boston: Little, Brown, 1968).
33. For an account of *Prisoner's Dilemma,* see Howard Luce and H. Raiffa, *Games and Decisions* (New York: John Wiley & Sons, 1957), pp. 94–106.
34. Phillip Bonacich, Gerald H. Shure, James P. Kahan, and Robert J. Meeker, "Cooperation and Group Size in the N-Person Prisoner's Dilemma," *Journal of Conflict Resolution* 20 (1976): 687–706.
35. Sven Lindskold, Douglas C. McElwain, and Marc Wagner, "Cooperation and the Use of Coercion by Groups and Individuals," *Journal of Conflict Resolution* 21 (1977): 531–550.
36. *Webster's New World Dictionary of the American Language,* College ed. (Cleveland and New York: World, 1962).
37. Bibb Latané, Kipling Williams, and Stephen Harkins, "Many Hands Make Light the Work: The Causes and Consequences of Social Loafing," *Journal of Personality and Social Psychology* 37 (1979): 822–832.
38. Robert Sutermeister, *People and Productivity* (New York: McGraw-Hill, 1963), pp. 55–56, citing Peter Drucker.
39. Bibb Latané, Kipling Williams, and Stephen Harkins, "Social Loafing," *Psychology Today* 13 (1979): 382.
40. Ibid.
41. Ibid.
42. *Consumer Opinion Survey,* Survey Research Center, U.S. Chamber of Commerce (Chamber-Gallup Survey), April 1981.
43. Ambrose Bierce, *The Devil's Dictionary,* [1906], (New York: Hill and Wang, 1957).

Notes

Chapter Six

1. This chapter draws on a paper written jointly with Jay Schmiedeskamp, Vice-President, Gallup Organization, on "Inflation Expectations and the Changing Nature of Consumer Borrowing and Credit," presented to the annual meeting of the American Economic Association, Denver, Colorado, Sept. 3–5, 1980.
2. 1 Tim. 6:10; and George B. Shaw, *Man and Superman,* [1903] (New York: Penguin, 1950).
3. Gallup Poll survey, August 1979.
4. U.S. Bureau of the Census, *Statistical Abstract of the United States: 1979* (Washington, D.C.: U.S. Bureau of the Census, 1979), pp. 537–538.
5. American Council on Life Insurance, *Current Social Issues* (Washington, D.C.: American Council on Life Insurance, April, 1979).
6. Lester Thurow, "The Optimum Lifetime Distribution of Consumption Expenditures," *American Economic Review* 59 (1969): 324–330.
7. Charles Dickens, *David Copperfield* (New York: New American Library, 1962), p. 182.
8. U.S. Bureau of the Census, *Statistical Abstract,* pp. 536, 792–94.
9. Gallup Poll Survey, August 1979.
10. Leon Festinger, *A Theory of Cognitive Dissonance* (New York: Harper & Row, 1957).
11. Leon Festinger and J. M. Carlsmith, "Cognitive Consequences of Forced Compliance," *Journal of Abnormal and Social Psychology* 58 (1959): 203–210. See also John H. Sherwood, James W. Barrown, and H. Gordon Fitch, "Cognitive Dissonance: Theory and Research," in Richard V. Wagner and John J. Sherwood, eds., *The Study of Attitude Change* (Belmont, Calif.: Brookes/Cole Publishing Co., 1969).
12. *Wall Street Journal,* 3 January 1980, p. 32; and *New York Times,* 7 March 1980, p. D1.
13. Edward Bellamy, *Looking Backward: 2000–1887,* cited in David Wallechinsky and Irving Wallace, *The People's Almanac* (New York: Doubleday, 1975).
14. Wallechinsky and Wallace, *The People's Almanac.*
15. My source was a Federal Reserve Bank official.
16. Alfred Marshall, *Principles of Economics,* 8th ed. (London: Macmillan, 1962), p. 17.
17. George Katona, *Psychological Economics* (New York: Elsevier, 1975), pp. 146–148.
18. "Here Comes the Credit Crunch," *Business Week,* 31 March 1980, p. 36.
19. "The Fed's Saturday Surprise," *Wall Street Journal,* 9 October 1979.
20. Marshall, *Principles,* p. 36.

Chapter Seven

1. Parts of this chapter draw on S. Maital and Y. Benjamini, "Inflation As Prisoner's Dilemma," *Journal of Post-Keynesian Economics* 2 (1980): 459–481.
2. U.S. Bureau of the Census, *Statistical Abstract of the United States: 1979* (Washington, D.C.: U.S. Bureau of the Census, 1979); and *Historical Statistics of the United States: Colonial Times to 1970* (Washington, D.C.: U.S. Government Printing Office, 1976).
3. Thomas Sargent, Federal Reserve Bank of Minneapolis.
4. Abba Lerner, "Employment Theory and Employment Policy," *American Economic Review* 57 (1967): 5.
5. George Katona, *Psychological Economics* (New York: Elsevier, 1975), p. 133.
6. Hilde Behrend, "Research into Inflation and Conceptions of Earnings," *Journal of Occupational Psychology* 50 (1977): 169–176.
7. American Council on Life Insurance, *Current Social Issues* (Washington, D.C.: American Council on Life Insurance, April, 1979); Gallup Economic Service, June 1979.
8. Alfred Marshall, *Principles of Economics,* 8th ed. (London: Macmillan, 1962), pp. 51–52.
9. Central Bureau of Statistics, *Statistical Yearbook* (Jerusalem, Israel: Bank of Israel, 1980). Nineteen-eighty-one also saw triple-digit inflation.
10. Arnon Gafni, Governor of the Bank of Israel, "Principles for a General Agreement for Stabilizing the Economy, Sept. 1980–March 1981," memo (Hebrew), Bank of Israel, Jerusalem, Sept. 2, 1980.
11. Lester Thurow, *The Zero-Sum Society* (New York: Basic Books, 1980).
12. U.S. Bureau of the Census, *Statistical Abstract,* 1979, p. 474.
13. Ogden Nash, *Hymn to the Thing that Makes the Wolf Go,* [1934], cited in *Bartlett's Familiar Quotations* (Boston: Little, Brown, 1968).
14. Milton Friedman, "Nobel Lecture: Inflation and Unemployment," *Journal of Political Economy* (June 1977): 467.
15. "New York," in *Encyclopedia Americana,* vol. 20 (Montreal: Americana of Canada, 1953).
16. J. M. Keynes, "War and the Financial System, *Economic Journal* (August 1914).
17. Roy Harrod, *Life of Keynes* (London: Macmillan, 1951), p. 489.
18. J. M. Keynes, *How to Pay for the War* (London: Macmillan, 1940), pp. 5–6.
19. Ibid., p. 61.
20. Ibid., p. 6.
21. Ibid., p. 70.
22. Ibid., p. 5.
23. J. M. Keynes, *Collected Works,* vol. IV (London: Macmillan, 1974), quoted by Paul Davidson, "Post–Keynesian Economics," *The Public Interest,* special ed. (1980): 15.
24. Eugene Smolensky, Selwyn Becker, and Harvey Molotch, "The Prisoner's Dilemma and Ghetto Expansion," *Land Economics* 64 (1968): 428.

Notes

25. Maital and Benjamini, "Inflation as Prisoner's Dilemma."
26. Hilde Behrend, "Attitudes to Price Increases and Pay Claims," Monograph #4 (London: National Economic Development Office, 1974).
27. Milton Friedman and Rose Friedman, *Free to Choose* (New York: Avon, 1981), p. 243.
28. *Wall Street Journal,* 22 March 1979.
29. Katona, *Psychological Economics*.
30. J. R. Hicks, *Value and Capital* (New York: Oxford University Press, 1939).
31. Shlomo Maital and Sharone L. Maital, "Individual-Rational and Group-Rational Inflation Expectations," *Journal of Economic Behavior and Organization* 2 (1981): 179–186.
32. William Fellner, ed., *Contemporary Economic Problems* (Washington, D.C.: American Enterprise Institute, 1978).
33. Oliver Wendell Holmes, *The Autocrat of the Breakfast Table,* [1858], (New York: Hill and Wang, 1957).
34. Mancur Olson, *The Logic of Collective Action: Public Goods and the Theory of Groups* (Cambridge Mass.: Harvard University Press, 1965).
35. Garrett Hardin, "The Tragedy of the Commons," *Science* 162 (1968): 1243–1248.
36. CBS/*New York Times* poll results, courtesy of Professor Michael Kagay, Woodrow Wilson School of Public and International Affairs, Princeton University, Princeton, N.J.
37. J. L. Kearl, Clayne L. Pope, Gordon C. Whiting, and Larry T. Wimmer, "A Confusion of Economists?" *American Economic Review* 69 (1979): 28–37.
38. The account of Truman-era controls is based on conversations with Robert Donovan and parts of his forthcoming second volume of Truman's biography.
39. See R. F. Lanzillotti, M. Hamilton, and R. B. Roberts, *Phase II in Review: The Price Commission Experience* (Washington, D.C.: The Brookings Institution, 1975); M. Kosters, *Controls & Inflation: The Economic Stabilization Program in Retrospect* (Washington, D.C.: American Enterprise Institute, 1975); Alan Blinder and William Newton, "The 1971–74 Controls Program and the Price Level," National Bureau of Economic Research working paper # 279 (Cambridge, Mass.: National Bureau of Economic Research, 1979); Frank Reid, "Control and Decontrol of Wages in the U.S.: An Empirical Analysis," working paper, (Department of Political Economy, University of Toronto, September 1978).
40. Katona, *Psychological Economics,* pp. 345–346.
41. William J. Baumol, *Welfare Economics and the Theory of the State* (London: Longmans, 1952), p. 141.
42. Richard Nixon, "Economic Report of the President" (Washington, D.C.: U.S. Government Printing Office, 1970).

Chapter Eight

1. Benjamin Franklin to M. Leroy (1789), quoted in *Bartlett's Familier Quotations* (Boston: Little, Brown, 1968), p. 423.
2. John von Neumann and Oskar Morgenstern, *The Theory of Games* (Princeton, N.J.: Princeton University Press, 1944), p. 28.
3. See Daniel Kahneman and Amos Tversky, "Prospect Theory: An Analysis of Decision Under Risk," *Econometrica* 47 (1979): 263–291.
4. Quoted in Philipp Frank, *Einstein, His Life and Times* (New York: Alfred A. Knopf, 1953).
5. Amos Tversky, "Intransitivity of Preferences," *Psychological Review* 76 (1969): 31–48.
6. David Grether and Charles Plott, "Preference Reversal Phenomenon," *American Economic Review* 69 (1979): 623–638.
7. Kahneman and Tversky, "Prospect Theory."
8. Ibid.
9. Cynthia Lee Phillips, "Tversky-Kahneman Probability Biases: An Empirical Test Among Risk-Experienced Subjects with Special Reference to Income Tax Evasion," (A.B. thesis, Princeton University, 1980).
10. Bernoulli's formula is discussed by Albert Marshall in his *Principles of Economics,* 8th ed. (London: Macmillan, 1962), p. 693, n. VIII.
11. L. L. Thurstone, "The Indifference Function," *Journal of Social Psychology* 2 (1931):139–167.
12. Marshall, *Principles,* p. 16.
13. Milton Friedman and Leonard Savage, "The Utility Analysis of Choices Involving Risk," *Journal of Political Economy* 61 (1948): 279–304.
14. General George Smith Patton, letter to his son, 6 June 1944.
15. Samuel Johnson, *The Idler,* 1758–1760, no. 57, quoted in *Bartlett's Familier Quotations* (Boston: Little, Brown, 1968), p. 428.
16. Kenneth S. Arrow, *Essays in the Theory of Risk-Bearing* (Amsterdam: North-Holland Publishing Co., 1970).
17. Data on gambling and insurance are from U.S. Bureau of the Census, *Statistical Abstract of the United States: 1979* (Washington, D.C.: U.S. Bureau of the Census, 1979), pp. 245, 545–548; on lotteries: M. J. Bailey, M. Olson, and P. Wonnacott, "The Marginal Utility of Income Does Not Increase: Borrowing, Lending and Friedman-Savage Gambles," *American Economic Review* 70 (1980): 372–379.
18. Benjamin Eden, "The Role of Insurance and Gambling in Allocating Risk Over Time," *Journal of Economic Theory* 16 (1977): 228–246.
19. Kahneman and Tversky, "Prospect Theory."
20. Ibid.
21. Ibid.
22. Cited in "Gambling," in *International Encyclopedia of the Social Sciences,* vol. 6 (New York and London: Macmillan and Free Press, 1968).
23. B. M. Ross and N. Levy, "Patterned Predictions of Chance Events by Children and Adults," *Psychological Reports* 4 (1958): 87–124.
24. *Wall Street Journal,* 13 March 1979, p. 22.
25. Marshall, *Principles,* p. 509*n*.

Notes

Chapter Nine

1. The chapter title is by Julian Simon, from a similarly titled paper that I wrote jointly with him and Randall Filer.
2. Thomas R. Henry, *The Strangest Things in the World* (Washington, D.C.: Public Affairs Press, 1958); "Lemming," in *Encyclopedia Americana*, vol. 17 (Montreal: Americana of Canada, 1953); *Book of Popular Science*, vol. 5 (New York: Grolier, 1953).
3. J. K. Galbraith, *The Great Crash (1929)*, (Boston: Houghton, Mifflin, 1955).
4. Quoted in Steven Plaut, "After Silver and Gold: Some Sober Thoughts on Speculative Bubbles," *Economic Commentary*, Federal Reserve Bank of Cleveland, May 5, 1980.
5. Ibid.
6. Ibid.
7. C. P. Kindelberger, *Manias, Panics and Crashes* (New York: Basic Books, 1978); Lester V. Chandler, *America's Greatest Depression: 1929–1941* (New York: Harper & Row, 1970).
8. Plaut, "After Silver and Gold."
9. "Crises," in *Encyclopedia Americana*, vol. 8 (Montreal: Americana of Canada, 1953).
10. Quoted in Albert J. Hettinger, "Director's Comment," in Milton Friedman and Anna Schwartz, *The Great Contraction, 1929–33* (Princeton, N.J.: Princeton University Press, 1965), p. 127.
11. Ibid., p. 130.
12. George Katona, *Psychological Economics* (New York: Elsevier, 1975), chap. 15.
13. C. D. Hamburger, R. T. Holmes, and R. S. Mukai, "Experimental Study of the Cognitive Dissonance Effect on Saving and Spending," *Proceedings,* 76th Annual Convention, American Psychological Association (Washington, D.C., 1968), pp. 665–666.
14. Katona, *Psychological Economics,* p. 148.
15. U.S. Bureau of the Census, *Statistical Abstract of the United States: 1979* (Washington, D.C.: U.S. Bureau of the Census, 1979), pp. 469–472.
16. Martin Feldstein, "Toward a Reform of Social Security," *The Public Interest* 40 (1975): 75–95; Feldstein, "Social Security, Induced Retirement, and Aggregate Capital Accumulation," *Journal of Political Economy* 82 (1974): 905–926.
17. George Katona, *Private Pensions & Individual Saving* (Ann Arbor, Mich.: Institute for Social Research, 1965); Phillip Cagan, "The Effect of Pension Plans on Aggregate Saving," National Bureau of Economic Research occasional paper #95 (New York: Columbia University Press, 1965).
18. Joseph Friedman, "Patterns of Private Wealth Accumulation and Liquidation: Evidence from the Retirement History Study," working paper (May 1980).
19. For a lucid treatment of portfolio theory see William J. Baumol, *Portfolio Theory: The Selection of Asset Combinations* (Morristown, N.J.: General Learning Press, 1970).

20. Charles Dickens, *American Notes* (Boston: Estes & Lauriat, 1892), p. 117.
21. Paul Samuelson, "Proof that Properly Anticipated Prices Fluctuate Randomly," *Industrial Management Review* 6 (1965): 41–49; Benoit Mandelbrot, "Forecasts of Future Prices, Unbiased Markets, and Martingale Models," *Journal of Business: Security Prices: A Supplement* 39 (1966): 242–255.
22. H. V. Roberts, "Stock Market 'Patterns' and Financial Analysis: Methodological Suggestions," *The Journal of Finance* 14 (1959): 1–10.
23. George Goodman [Adam Smith], *The Money Game* (New York: Random House, 1967), p. 41.
24. B. F. Skinner, "Superstition in the Pigeon," *Journal of Experimental Psychology* 38 (1948): 168–172; cited by Paul Slovic, "Psychological Study of Human Judgment: Implications for Investment Decision-Making," *Journal of Finance* (1972): 779–99.
25. Randall Filer, Shlomo Maital, and Julian Simon, "What Do People Bring to the Stock Market Besides Money?" working paper (Woodrow Wilson School of Public and International Affairs, Princeton University, 1980).
26. Julian B. Rotter, "Generalized Expectancies for Internal versus External Control of Reinforcement," *Psychological Monographs* 80 (609) (1966).
27. Nathan Kogan and Michael A. Wallach, *Risk Taking: A Study in Cognition and Personality* (New York: Holt, Rinehart & Winston, 1964).
28. David Krech, Richard Crutchfield, and Egerton Ballachey, *Individual in Society* (New York: McGraw-Hill, 1962), p. 24.
29. J. A. F. Stoner, "A Comparison of Individual and Group Decisions Involving Risk," (Master's thesis, School of Industrial Management, M.I.T., 1961); cited by Kenneth Dion et al., "Why Do Groups Make Riskier Decisions than Individuals,"in L. Berkovitz, ed., *Advances in Experimental Social Psychology*, vol. 5 (New York: Academic Press, 1970), pp. 306–378.
30. Dion et al., "Why Do Groups Make Riskier Decisions?"
31. Lester Thurow, "Productivity: Japan's Better Way," *New York Times,* 8 February 1981, p. 5 IE.
32. Howard Kunreuther and Paul Slovic, "Economics, Psychology and Protective Behavior," *American Economic Review, Papers & Proceedings* 68 (2) (1978): 64–69.
33. "Cutting the Risk," *Wall Street Journal,* 13 March 1979, p. 22.

Chapter Ten

1. Richard Nixon quoted in William Watts and Lloyd Free, *State of the Nation* (Washington, D.C.: Potomac Associates, 1973), p. 233.
2. U.S. Bureau of the Census, *Statistical Abstract of the United States: 1979* (Washington, D.C.: U.S. Bureau of the Census, 1979), pp. 254–57.
3. Dennis C. Mueller, "Public Choice: A Survey," *Journal of Economic Literature,* 14 (1976): 397–398.
4. See Irwin Lipnowski and Shlomo Maital, "Voluntary Provision of a Pure Public Good as the Game of 'Chicken'," discussion paper (Haifa, Israel: Technion, April 1981).

Notes

5. S. Maital, "Public Goods and Income Distribution: Some Further Results," *Econometrica* (May 1973), 561–568; S. Maital, "Apportionment of Public Goods Benefits to Individuals," *Public Finance* 3 (1975): 397–416.
6. S. J. Simon, *Why You Lose at Bridge* (London: Nicholson & Watson, 1945), p. 11.
7. John Thibaut, Nehemia Friedland, and Laurens Walker, "Compliance with Rules: Some Social Determinants," *Journal of Personality and Social Psychology* 30 (1974): 792.
8. Jane Bryant Quinn, *Trenton Times,* 16 March 1979, p. A13.
9. Former IRS Commissioner Jerome Kurtz, in an Associated Press report, *Trenton Times,* 16 April 1979, p. B7.
10. Personal communication to author by an economist at the American Enterprise Institute, 1979.
11. Nehemiah Friedland, Shlomo Maital, and Aryeh Rutenberg, "A Simulation Study of Income Tax Evasion," *Journal of Public Economics* 10 (1978): 107–116.
12. U.S. Chamber of Commerce & Gallup Organization, *Consumer Attitudes Toward Government Taxation & Spending* (Washington, D.C.: U.S. Chamber of Commerce, 1981), p. 49.
13. George Katona, *Psychological Economics* (New York: Elsevier, 1975), p. 352.
14. Gallup Economic Service, June 1978, and Daniel Yankelovitch and Larry Kagan, "Assertive America," *Foreign Affairs* 59 (1981): 696–713.
15. W. Eltis, "How Rapid Public Sector Growth Can Undermine the Growth of the National Product," in W. Beckerman, ed., *Slow Growth in Britain: Causes and Consequences* (London: Oxford University Press, 1978), p. 129.
16. Watts and Free, *State of the Nation.*
17. Jack C. Horn, "Tax Evasion Gets Less Taxing," *Psychology Today* (March 1981): 25–26, citing Opinion Research Corp. and Richard Rose.
18. U.S. Chamber of Commerce, *Consumer Attitudes,* p. 49.
19. "Tax Cheaters Feeling Less Guilty," Associated Press in *Courier News,* 16 April 1980, p. A1.
20. Ibid.; see also Horn, "Tax Evasion," p. 25.
21. Plato, *The Republic,* Book I, (New York: Walter J. Black, 1942), p. 243.
22. Y. Song and T. E. Yarbrough, "Tax Ethics and Taxpayer Attitudes," *Public Administration Review* 38 (1978): 442–457;
23. M. W. Spicer and S. B. Lundstedt, "Understanding Tax Evasion," *Public Finance* 31 (1976): 295–305.
24. Charles Dickens, *David Copperfield* (New York: New American Library, 1962), p. 313.
25. Peter M. Gutmann, "The Subterranean Economy," *Financial Analysts Journal* (November–December 1977): 26–27, 34.
26. Berdj Kenadjian, "The Direct Approach to Measuring the Underground Economy: IRS Estimates of Unreported Incomes," Internal Revenue Service 1980; Internal Revenue Service, *Estimates of Income Unreported on Individual Income Tax Returns,* August 31, 1979.
27. Vito Tanzi, "Underground Economy and Tax Evasion in the United States: Estimates and Implications," *Banco Nazionale del Lavoro Quarterly Review* (in press).
28. Edgar L. Feige, "How Big Is the Irregular Economy?" *Challenge* (November–December, 1979): 5–13.

29. Ernest Hemingway, *Death in the Afternoon* (New York: Charles Scribner's Sons, 1932).
30. Thibaut, Friedland, and Walker, "Compliance with Rules."
31. M. W. Spicer and S. B. Lundstedt, "Fiscal Inequity and Tax Evasion: An Experimental Approach," 33 *National Tax Journal* (1980).
32. Adam Smith, *Theory of Moral Sentiments* [1759] (Oxford: Oxford University Press, 1976).
33. Ibid.

Chapter Eleven

1. A. C. Pigou, *The Economics of Welfare* (London: Macmillan, 1920), p. 1.
2. J. M. Keynes, *How to Pay for the War* (London: Macmillan, 1940), p. 1.
3. J. A. Hobhouse, "Economy," in the *Oxford English Dictionary* (Oxford: Oxford University Press, 1933).
4. Personal correspondence.
5. Pigou, *Economics of Welfare*, pp. 6–7.
6. Alfred Marshall, *Principles of Economics,* 8th ed. (London: Macmillan, 1962), p. ix.
7. Ibid.
8. Herbert A. Simon, "Theories of Decision-Making in Economics and Behavioral Science," *American Economic Review* 49 (1959): 253–283.
9. Tibor Scitovsky, *The Joyless Economy* (London: Oxford University Press, 1976).
10. Anatol Rapoport and M. Guyer, "A Taxonomy of 2 × 2 Games," *General Systems* 11 (1966): 203–14.
11. N. Feather, "Subjective Probability and Decision Under Uncertainty," *Psychological Review* 66 (1959): 150–164.
12. Julian B. Rotter, June E. Chance, and E. Jerry Phares, *Applications of a Social Learning Theory* (New York: Holt, Rinehart & Winston, 1972).
13. Ibid., p. 11.
14. George J. Stigler, "The Xistence of X-Efficiency," *American Economic Review* 66 (1976): 213–216.
15. George J. Stigler and Gary Becker, "De Gustibus Non Est Disputandum," *American Economic Review* 67 (1977): 76–90.
16. Ibid.
17. R. C. Battalio, John H. Kagel, and Howard Rachlin, "Commodity-Choice Behavior with Pigeons as Subjects," *Journal of Political Economy* 89 (1981): 67–91; and J. H. Kagel, R. C. Battalio, H. Rachlin, and L. Green, "Demand Curves for Animal Consumers," *Quarterly Journal of Economics* 89 (1981): 1–16.
18. J. M. Keynes, *General Theory of Employment, Interest & Money* (London: Macmillan, 1936), p. 11.
19. Milton Friedman and Rose Friedman, *Free to Choose* (New York: Avon, 1981), pp. 3–5.

Notes

20. Thomas Schelling, *Micromotives and Macrobehavior* (New York: Norton, 1978), p. 22.
21. Ibid., p. 51.
22. Friedman and Friedman, *Free to Choose*, p. 5.
23. Thomas Jefferson, first Inaugural, quoted in Friedman and Friedman, *Free to Choose*, p. xviii.
24. John Stuart Mill, *On Liberty*, cited in Friedman and Friedman, *Free to Choose*, p. xvi.
25. Ibid.
26. *Bartlett's Familiar Quotations* (Boston: Little, Brown, 1968).
27. James W. Baldwin, "Social and Ethical Interpretations in Mental Development: A Study," in *Social Psychology*, 3rd ed. (London: Macmillan, 1902), p. 3.
28. Stanley Milgram, "The Small-World Problem," *Psychology Today* 1 (1967): 61–67.
29. J. R. Hicks, "The Rehabilitation of Consumers' Surplus," *Review of Economic Studies* 8 (1940–41): 111.
30. Garrett Hardin, "The Tragedy of the Commons," *Science* 162 (1968): 1243–1248.
31. Ibid.
32. Ibid.
33. Cited by J. M. Keynes in *General Theory of Employment, Interest & Money* (London: Macmillan, 1936), p. 361.
34. *Wall Street Journal*, 11 October 1979.
35. Ibid.
36. Fred Hirsch, *Social Limits to Growth* (Cambridge, Mass.: Harvard University Press, Twentieth Century Fund, 1976).

INDEX

Index

Index

Index

Index